WHITE COLLAR CRIME

WHITE COLLAR CRIME
Criminal justice and criminology

HAZEL CROALL

Open University Press
Buckingham · Philadelphia

Open University Press
Celtic Court
22 Ballmoor
Buckingham
MK18 1XW

and
1900 Frost Road, Suite 101
Bristol, PA 19007, USA

First Published 1992

A catalogue record of this book is available from the British Library.

Library of Congress Cataloging-in-Publication Data

Croall, Hazel, 1947–
White collar crime: criminal justice and criminology/Hazel Croall.
p. cm.
Includes bibliographical references (p.) and index.
ISBN 0-335-09657-3 (hb) ISBN 0-335-09656-5 (pbk.)
1. White collar crimes. 2. White collar crimes—Great Britain.
3. White collar crimes—United States.
HV6768.C76 1992
364.1′68--dc20 91-44926
CIP

Typeset by Gilbert Composing Services, Leighton Buzzard
Printed in Great Britain by St Edmundsbury Press, Bury St Edmunds, Suffolk

CONTENTS

I

WHITE COLLAR CRIME

1

INTRODUCTION

The phrase white collar crime is often associated with scandals in the financial and business world and the sophisticated frauds of senior executives. It also incorporates what is popularly known as corporate crime, which includes the many activities of powerful corporations which exploit relatively powerless consumers, workers and citizens. The last few years have seen several notorious examples of white collar crime, as the collapse of the Bank of Credit and Commerce International amid allegations of fraud, bribery and corruption replaced the Guinness takeover as the white collar crime of the century. A spate of major accidents like the sinking of the Herald of Free Enterprise, the Clapham and Purley rail crashes and the poisoning of consumers by contaminated water in Camelford have also led to increasing demands for the trial and punishment of those whose inattention to safety and health regulations endangers the lives of workers, passengers and consumers. Criminologists have often argued that these kinds of crimes are more widespread, more serious, and more damaging to society than many other common crimes like robbery, burglary or theft.

Despite this, white collar crime is not generally regarded as part of the 'crime problem'. The public tend to be far more afraid of being mugged, raped or robbed by a stranger on the street than they are of being killed on a commuter train, poisoned at a wedding party or seduced by a host of misleading advertisements, cheap bargain offers or bogus investment schemes. While the publication of the Annual Criminal Statistics automatically leads to public examination of the crime problem, discussions rarely mention fraud, public health or safety offences. This illustrates that the notion of crime itself is socially constructed and that white collar crimes are not readily defined as crime. Indeed, the concept of white collar crime has assumed political and ideological connotations as drawing attention to the offences of otherwise respectable business executives and labelling businesses who pollute rivers, adulterate food, threaten the safety of their workers and market unsafe goods as 'criminal' is often criticized as an essentially political exercise. The subject of white collar crime therefore raises many fundamental questions about the nature of crime and its treatment.

White collar crime 'news'

This ambivalent reaction to white collar crime is well reflected in its treatment by the mass media, often accused of perpetuating the social construction of crime by neglecting white collar crime and focusing on the more sensational activities of primarily lower class criminals. Such 'ideological one-sidedness' in the view of one commentator has meant that:

> the majority of people are . . . continually exposed to a portrait of crime in which the background consists of murder, rape, robbery and theft and the foreground is full of characters mainly drawn from poor, disorganized lower class neighbourhoods. No wonder that corporate crime is not viewed by many people, including most criminologists (!), as a pressing, serious social problem. (Box 1983: 17)

However, at the same time, 'scandals sell newspapers' (Levi 1987a: 12). The extensive coverage given to the 'Guinness four', and the collapse of the Bank of Credit and Commerce International, hailed as the 'largest bank fraud in world history' (*Financial Times* 30/7/91) demonstrates that white collar crime can be newsworthy. Indeed, Levi (1991b) argues that cases like these cast doubt on the common view that white collar crime is neglected by the media – commenting that 'the media love degradation tales among the rich and famous'.

A brief exploration of what makes crime newsworthy can partly explain these divergent views. In general, both 'bureaucratic' and 'ideational' factors affect how events are translated into news stories (Cohen and Young 1973). To the professional journalist, a successful news story is one which is immediate, dramatic, and capable of being personalized, simplified and titillated (Chibnall 1977). While rape, murder or robbery contain many of these elements, many white collar crimes do not. Fraud trials, for example, tend to last for many weeks and evidence often involves the interpretation of financial accounts and legal technicalities. This makes them expensive to report fully (Levi 1987a), and means that they are not immediate, not readily simplified and far from dramatic. Companies, not individual actors, are often the culprits, making personalization let alone titillation difficult. In addition, as Evans and Lundmann (1987: 241) point out, 'newspaper journalists are not accustomed to viewing corporations as capable of criminality'.

Some white collar crimes on the other hand involve well-known personalities, have a dramatic impact and are therefore more likely to attract publicity. This is especially noticeable where prominent personalities or institutions are involved. The prosecutions of both Lester Piggott and Ken Dodd for tax offences attracted much publicity and front page treatment (Cook 1989a; Levi and Pithouse 1989). Allegations of shady operations which involve well-known companies are also likely to receive considerable coverage as the recent Guinness trials demonstrate (Levi 1991a). Stories about these cases focus on the personalities of the main participants who become household names, and complex issues are simplified. Dramatic accidents and disasters are also newsworthy. These are not automatically associated with 'crime', although following major accidents like the Zeebrugge disaster and the Clapham rail crash, the media attempt to point the finger at the 'guilty party' and calls for criminal prosecution are increasingly common. Subsequent inquiries and trials are also extensively covered. Accidents tend to be more newsworthy when members of the public are killed or injured whereas routine accidents in which individual workers are killed or injured rarely attract much publicity (Hutter and Lloyd Bostock 1990).

Therefore, while much white collar crime lacks the immediate media appeal of rape, robbery or violence it is not all neglected. However, the media tend to focus on scandals and frauds involving millions of pounds, well-known personalities and on major accidents and disasters at the expense of more mundane and trivial cases. This is not unique to white collar crime, as the tendency to concentrate on murder, sex and violence gives a similarly fase picture of conventional crime. The more statistically prevalent but less dramatic problems of theft, shoplifting, burglary and car theft are also relatively neglected. None the less, the concentration on fallen idols and the rich and famous tends to perpetuate the association of white collar crime with rich and wealthy offenders, who are rarely portrayed in the same way as murderers or rapists. The concentration on dramatic incidents, personalities and violence also means that many white collar offences, which lack these elements, are relatively neglected. On the other hand, as recent press coverage shows, there is arguably more attention being paid to white collar crime than hitherto – indeed, the last few years have been described as a 'fraud scandal era' (Levi 1989b: 89). Yet white collar crime is not a new problem.

The unacceptable face of business?

Business, trade and commerce have always been associated with various forms of fraud, cheating and corruption. Geis and Edelhertz (1973: 990), for example, suggest that Christ's driving of the money-lenders from the temple represents an early 'response of moral outrage against business cheating and indecency'. They also report that in early Greece a prominent family substituted concrete with marble veneer in the building of a solid marble temple (Geis and Edelhertz 1973). Many kinds of fraudulent trade practices were prevalent throughout the middle ages, with some attracting draconian punishments by today's standards – in 1428 for example, traders using unjust balances could be excommunicated (O'Keefe 1966). Frauds involving false weights and measures have been reported since the dawn of trading, and dealers in precious metals regularly used false scales, necessitating the passage of the Pewter and Brass Act of 1503 (O'Keefe 1966). Consumers and traders have been protected from the sale of underweight or adulterated foods for many centuries and, under the Assizes of Bread and Ale, offenders could be fined 20 shillings, pilloried, put in the stocks or banished from the town (O'Keefe 1966; Harvey 1982). The following examples illustrate the continuity of many everyday frauds on consumers. In 1735, the following case was reported:

> Richardson, amerced £20 for selling coal in sacks that want near 3 inches in length and near 2 inches in breadth of the standard or assize by law directed. (cited in Harvey 1975: 991)

And in 1761,

> upon the return of the fleshtasters, Mr Harrison, butcher, for exposing to sale fleshmeat not fit for Christians to eat, and refusing to remove the same, amerced 5 shillings. (cited in Harvey 1975: 991)

Socio-economic development tends to be accompanied by changing crime patterns (McIntosh 1974). Early trading took place literally in the market place, where buyers and sellers lived in the same small community. Sellers of goods were typically producers and depended on a good reputation to make a living. Buyers could generally judge the quality of goods for themselves and trusted producers as they knew them personally. Therefore, commercial exchanges were based on knowledge and trust (Borrie and Diamond 1977). However, as commerce expanded, production was separated from selling and commercial transactions more typically involved several parties. Each stage in the chain of production, distribution and sale provides opportunities for theft and fraud. Deceptive sales practices can also adversely affect competition. The sale of substandard goods, falsely presented as high quality, threatens the livelihood of honest traders particularly where consumers cannot tell the difference. During the nineteenth century both traders and consumers were the victims of many fraudulent sales pitches which misrepresented the origins and quality of metals and goods (O'Keefe 1968). The world of finance also provides many opportunities for fraud – insider dealing has been a problem since the seventeenth century (Naylor 1990) and the financial world has always suffered from recurrent scandals (Clarke 1986).

The development of capitalism, particularly in the United States, was characterized by many sharp practices including the activities of 'robber barons' who on occasion used violence against each other and organized labour in the struggle to secure monopolies (Sutherland 1949; Pearce 1976). The application of science and technology to industry, which spurred the industrial revolution, also brought death, illness and injury to workers, consumers and the general public. Transport, then as now, caused accidents and disasters (Wells 1988). Workers in early factories were exposed to appalling conditions, long hours and low wages, with often disastrous effects on their health and life expectancies (Carson 1974). Food adulteration, which was regarded as a normal trading practice, was fraudulent, threatened the public health and on occasion even led to death (Burnett 1966; Paulus 1974). In one case alone, known as the 'Bradford incident', 200 people were poisoned and fifteen died as a result of eating adulterated lozenges (Paulus 1974).

While many of these practices were prohibited and are now widely regarded as unacceptable, the twentieth century has seen old problems taking on new forms. In the United States, a group of writers known as 'muckrakers' exposed the appalling conditions in early twentieth century industries (Sutherland 1949; Geis and Edelhertz 1973) and the 1960s saw the growth of the consumerist movement which, through the work of people like Ralph Nader exposed the dangers of many modern products. In Britain, there was a growing recognition that the growth of the consumer society had brought with it many practices which adversely affected consumers. Consumers were increasingly spending enormous sums on goods like cars and washing machines whose technological nature they could not understand, opening the door to exploitation (Moloney Report 1962). Recent concerns over the quality of mass produced food have revealed what has been described as the 'legalized adulteration' of food by an assortment of 'chemical cocktails', and the considerable dangers of modern convenience foods (see Chapters 2 and 8). Pollution has been the source of recurrent concern and more stringent legal controls, and the recent spate of transport disasters has demonstrated the significance of safety regulations.

Changes in the financial world have also brought new opportunities for fraud, necessitating new regulatory arrangements. Hitherto, the regulation of the city depended on the 'gentlemen' (and they were men!) who controlled major financial institutions and who constituted the majority of shareholders. Transactions were characterized by privacy and confidentiality in a world where those from a restricted and exclusive social background could trust each other and where a gentleman's word was his bond. However, wider share ownership, the proliferation of organizations providing financial services and the impact of new technology opened up financial markets to 'outsiders', which created new opportunities for fraud and exposed the weaknesses of existing structures of regulation (Clarke

1986, 1990). In addition, the internationalization of commercial and financial transactions has been accompanied by large scale international financial frauds, and the spread by computers of sophisticated computer frauds. The development of the European Community has also created multiple opportunities for fraud, particularly in relation to agricultural subsidies (Nelken and Passas 1991).

White collar crime, therefore, appears to be an inevitable concomitant of business, trading and commerce. What is often hailed as technological progress brings with it new and more technologically sophisticated frauds, and may also have undesirable side effects which threaten the health and safety of workers, consumers and the general public. Many of these activities are not always immediately defined and recognized as crime, particularly those which are regarded as normal, acceptable and legitimate business practices. The line between acceptable and unacceptable, legal and illegal practices is consequently blurred and constantly shifting.

Defining white collar crime

Despite the prevalence of white collar crime, it was relatively ignored by early criminologists, and considerable controversy has always surrounded its definition and inclusion in the study of crime. The writer generally associated with placing the subject on the criminological agenda was Edwin Sutherland, who defined white collar crime as:

> approximately . . . a crime committed by a person of respectability and high social status in the course of his occupation. (Sutherland 1949: 9)

He thereby distinguished white collar crime from upper class crime which was not occupational, and from the offences of the underworld who were not respectable or of high social status. White collar crime was thus restricted to crime committed in the course of a legitimate occupation. Sutherland described and analysed many forms of white collar crime following this definition, including activities which were not, at the time, sanctioned by the criminal law, but which, being violations of civil or administrative law were punishable by law. This, along with his stress on the social status of offenders, attracted considerable criticism, leading to what have been described as 'futile terminological disputes' (Aubert 1977: 88).

Much of this criticism was directed at the inclusion of activities which were not legally 'crimes'. Sutherland justified this by arguing that many civil laws dealt with practices which were essentially similar to well established criminal offences. Thus, for example, false advertising was basically similar to common law fraud and 'other laws for the regulation of business are . . . rooted in moral sentiments' (Sutherland 1949: 32). However, critics argued that criminologists should restrict their attention to criminal law, otherwise they could define anything they disapproved of as crime and thus undermine their academic objectivity (see, for example, Tappan 1977). None the less, it has already been seen that there is a very blurred line between criminal and non-criminal activities, and some activities can be the subject of both civil and criminal proceedings. Indeed, the whole issue of how and in what circumstances unacceptable business activities are criminalized and how often the criminal law is used against them is in itself important. This justifies an inclusive definition which allows an analysis of law and its enforcement. As Aubert (1977: 93) argues:

> for purposes of theoretical analysis it is of prime importance to develop and apply concepts which preserve and emphasize the ambiguous nature of white collar crimes and not to solve the problem by classifying them as either crimes or not crimes. Their controversial nature is exactly what makes them so interesting from a sociological point of view.

Another problem posed by Sutherland's definition is whether the social status of offenders should be part of the definition of offences. Sutherland's reason for including this was to draw attention to the substantial criminality of business groups and to challenge the almost automatic equation of crime with lower class offenders. This had led, he argued, to the development of class based theories of crime which were unable to explain the criminality of senior corporate executives, let alone corporations themselves. He also wished to draw attention to class bias in the criminal justice system by pointing to the relative immunity of offenders from prosecution and to the more lenient sanctions which followed prosecutions.

None the less, the inclusion of social status and respectability in the definition has created many problems for research and analysis. Individual offence categories include offenders from all levels of the occupational hierarchy (see Chapter 3). Similar frauds can be perpetrated by the caretaker or managing director of a company (Levi 1987a), and the consumer can be ripped off by both small corner shops and large corporations. Do researchers in these categories of crime have to eliminate a large part of any sample because offenders are not of high status or respectability? How, in any case, are high status or respectability to be defined or measured? The identification of white collar crime with high status offenders has also tended to focus attention on the issue of class bias at the expense, many argue, of the offences themselves (see for example, Braithwaite 1985; Shapiro 1990).

Accordingly, there have been suggestions that the concept should be done away with altogether, re-defined, or 'liberated' (Shapiro 1990). Essentially, many argue, white collar crime is crime that is committed in the course of legitimate employment and involves the abuse of an occupational role (Braithwaite 1985; Hagan 1988; Shapiro 1990). Quinney (1977), for example, suggested that the term occupational crime, incorporating both blue collar and white collar crime should be used. This would focus attention on the opportunities for crime provided in the world of work and organizations. Class, status or respectability need not therefore be part of the definition of the concept, but are nonetheless significant for its analysis. For example, an analysis of what Shapiro (1990) describes as the social organization of trust draws attention to the differential distribution of trust throughout the occupational hierarchy, in which senior employees or professional staff, who are more likely to be trusted, have more opportunities to abuse that trust. In addition, they may be better placed to conceal their illegitimate activities and to prevent discovery and subsequent prosecution. Thus, she argues that offender characteristics such as class or organizational position should be consequential to the definition of white collar crime rather than forming a part of it. I propose to adopt her approach.

Varieties of white collar crime

However defined, white collar crime encompasses an enormous range of activities, well illustrated by research and writing in the area, which also reveals attempts at subcategorizations. A collection by Geis and Maier (1977) entitled *White Collar Crime* includes subsections on 'Corporate and Business White Collar Crime', 'Commercial and Professional White Collar Crime', and 'Political White Collar Crime'. A recent collection by Ermann and Lundman (1987) focuses on corporate and governmental deviance, and specific studies have focused on particular industries like the Pharmaceutical Industry (see, for example, Braithwaite 1984a). British work in the last decade has covered areas as diverse as pollution (Richardson *et al.* 1982; Hawkins 1984), commercial fraud (Levi 1987a), corruption (Doig 1984), crimes against consumers (Croall 1988, 1989), income tax evasion (McBarnet 1984; Cook 1989a), Health and Safety regulations (Pearce and Tombs 1990), and the growing area of fraud in the European Community (Tutt 1989; Nelken and Passas 1991; Leigh and Smith, forthcoming). A recent work entitled *Business Crime* includes separate Chapters on Employee Crime, Insurance Fraud, Taxation, Liquidations and Receiverships, Financial Institutions and Health and Safety at Work (Clarke 1990).

Despite this wide variety of offences, there have been few successful attempts to develop neat typologies or subcategorizations. Pearce (1976), for example, differentiates between offences which threaten the interests of capitalism and those which are primarily committed in the course of capitalist activity. The former he argues are dealt with more harshly than the latter. Thus:

> not all white collar crimes are equally immune to prosecution; If for example, embezzlement was left unprosecuted and there was a large

> increase in such activity, capitalism may well collapse . . . on the other hand, violations of anti trust laws do not pose a threat to the social structure of American capitalism, and can, therefore, be tolerated. (Pearce 1976: 81)

Broadly speaking, this parallels legal differences – fraud and embezzlement, both crimes often committed *against* corporations are indictable offences which are generally seen as more serious, and attract higher maximum penalties. On the other hand, much organizational or corporate crime is classified as non-indictable (therefore less serious) and carries lower maximum penalties. However, it is not always easy to determine whether any given activity operates in or against the interests of capitalism, or even to determine what these interests are. Capitalists themselves may disagree about the extent to which some offences, for example, insider dealing, pose a threat to their interests. Some activities which appear to pose little threat can none the less damage the credibility and reputation of capitalist institutions and can therefore be defined as threatening capitalist interests (see Chapter 8).

Many writers now accept a broad distinction between offences which are committed *against* organizations, and offences committed *by* organizations, thereby differentiating occupational crime from organizational or corporate crime (see, for example, Box 1983; Braithwaite 1985; Levi 1987b). This reflects a basic difference between the activities of individual or groups of individuals which result in personal gain at the expense of the organization, and activities which benefit the organization itself. While in both cases abuses of occupational roles are involved, they may well arise from different motivations and pose different kinds of problems to regulators. Occupational crime can thus be defined as:

> offences committed by individuals for themselves in the course of their occupations and the offences of employees against their employers. (Clinard and Quinney 1973, cited in Braithwaite 1985: 19)

Corporate crime on the other hand can be defined as:

> illegal corporate behaviour which is a form of collective rule breaking in order to achieve the organizational goals. (Clinard 1983: 17)

A similar and arguably preferable description of the latter category is the term organizational crime, which has the benefit of including within it offences of public as well as private organizations (Braithwaite 1985).

Many writers now focus almost exclusively on either occupational crime or on organizational and corporate crime. While sharing many common elements in that both originate in occupational positions, they differ in many respects. Organizational crime, in which no immediate personal benefit may be involved, may arise not from any malevolent intent, but from a desire to further the goals of the organization. With occupational crime, the benefit is more immediate and issues of intent are more clear cut. Occupational crime therefore conforms more closely to the stereotype and social construction of crime, organizational crime, less so. This may in turn lead to differences in the way in which offences are regulated and sanctioned. However, the essential characteristics of white collar crime, many of which derive from its location in occupational roles, are common to both. Following the analyses of Shapiro (1990), Clarke (1990) and others, these characteristics will now be outlined.

Characteristics of white collar crime

Low visibility

An essential feature of white collar offences is that they take place under the cover of normal occupational routines (Shapiro 1990), and involve the exploitation of occupational expertise or organizational systems. They can therefore be readily disguised as 'business offenders are legitimately present at the scene' (Clarke 1990: 21). All of this means that victims are often unaware that any offence has been committed at all. In addition, offences are generally 'private' rather than public, leaving little visible evidence of their commission. This relative invisibility means that offences are peculiarly resistant to detection, and even when detected, are often not reported to public authorities.

Complexity

While many white collar crimes can essentially be reduced to lying, cheating and stealing (Shapiro 1990), many are extremely complex. The expertise which is being abused, which forms the basis of the offender's occupational position, may be scientific, technological, financial or legal. Many are also highly organized, involve many employees, and may have been going on for several years. Organizational offences may involve a complex web of falsifications, cover ups, action and inaction. Many of the regulations and laws which are being flouted are themselves exceedingly complex, making it difficult to determine exactly what offences have been committed and who is responsible for them.

Diffusion of responsibility

This complexity is further compounded by the division of labour within occupations and organizations, in which functions are separated and responsibilities delegated. Consequently, it is often difficult to determine who is immediately responsible for any offence. This is particularly the case with organizational offences which may involve neglect or deliberate flouting of the many regulations covering health, safety, quality control, information or sales practices. Finding out whose actions have directly caused specific problems may be difficult enough, let alone determining who is morally or legally responsible. Individual employees may ignore regulations but their supervisors may be blamed for inadequately monitoring their performance. In turn, several levels of management may be blamed for inadequately monitoring those beneath them in the hierarchy and ultimately employers are responsible for instituting systems to ensure adequate compliance. At all levels of the chain of responsibility therefore individual employees can deny responsibility by claiming that they were only 'following orders' or that their orders were ignored.

This means that in practice it is often difficult to assign blame or to find the 'guilty party'. In addition, many organizational offences do not result from any criminal *intent*. Neither the employees whose inattention to safety may directly cause an accident, nor their supervisors and company directors who have neglected their responsibilities, can be accused of intending to kill, injure or defraud employees or consumers. This means that many organizational offences are less likely to be defined as 'criminal', a definition which normally involves notions of individual blame and intent.

The diffusion of victimization

Victimization is also diffused. Whereas in many conventional offences individual identifiable offenders harm individual identifiable victims, in many white collar offences there is no single identifiable victim. The victim may be an abstract entity such as the government or the company, or there may be many victims who suffer only a minimal loss. Sutherland (1949) for example pointed to the 'rippling effect' of white collar crimes, many of which involve only a small loss to individual victims but enormous gains to the perpetrators. This makes many white collar offences less readily definable as crime. The following example well illustrates this point:

> The public understands more easily what it means for an old lady to have five pounds snatched from her purse than to grasp the financial significance of 25 million customers paying one penny more for orange juice diluted beyond the level permitted by law. The public tend to focus more on the one penny than the quarter of a million illegal profit and conclude that the incident is insignificant. But it is not. (Box 1983: 31)

And, of course, the old lady is likely to be terrified by the experience of being robbed, whereas the customer is unlikely to be aware of any loss.

The seriousness and impact of white collar crime is further minimized as it does not appear to involve either physical violence or any 'public order violation' (Clarke 1990: 20). While Box (1983) points out that corporate crime can kill, and does have a physical impact, the diffusion of responsibility means that no-one appears to have intended these outcomes. Even where organizational offences have disastrous consequences there is no evidence of deliberate violence. Comparing 'accidents' which result from criminal neglect of safety regulations with a conventional picture of criminal violence, Wells points out that:

> our image of criminal violence is more likely to be of an interpersonal aggressive act between two or more strangers than of an industrial injury or disease or transport accident. (Wells 1988: 790)

Robbery, rape, sexual violence, mugging and other violent crimes which involve direct threats of violence are likely therefore to attract more 'fear of crime' and conform more closely to the 'social construction of crime' (Wells 1988).

Detection and prosecution

A major consequence of all these factors is that white collar crimes are particularly difficult to detect by victims, supervisors or law enforcers. Enforcers must possess the same scientific and technical knowledge as perpetrators and it may take many weeks, months or even years of careful investigation to unravel the more complex offences. Examination of company books, individual bank accounts or scientific testing to ascertain the quality and contents of goods is time consuming and costly. Effective enforcement therefore often has to be proactive and preventive, rather than reactive, responding to the minority of offences which are discovered. However, this is also costly, either for individual businesses or public agencies, and as will be seen, the high costs of detection leave many offences undiscovered.

Even when offences are detected, it may be difficult to *prove* that an offence has been committed and to establish who is responsible for it (see, for example, Braithwaite and Geis 1982). The complexity of many offences creates difficulties for establishing legal proof, and key witnesses may be reluctant to divulge information to investigators, particularly where it might incriminate themselves (Mann 1985). Companies may be able to obstruct investigations. Both companies and public enforcement agencies may therefore prefer to deal with offences using informal rather than formal procedures. Employees can be sacked, companies can be threatened with closure if they do not improve their safety records and back taxes can be collected – all of which may prevent further offending without resorting to costly prosecutions. Therefore in all categories of white collar crime, only a minority of offenders are prosecuted (see Chapter 5).

Lenient sanctions

Even when prosecuted, it is often argued that white collar offenders are not dealt with severely. Few offenders are sent to prison and the vast majority are fined amounts which are often described as 'derisory' (see Chapter 7). While this is often associated with the high status of offenders it is also related to the offences themselves (see Chapter 7). Offenders who can credibly claim that they didn't intend to cause any harm and in any case are not directly responsible may well be seen as not really criminal. The absence of violence and the diffusion of victimization also means that offenders are not likely to be seen as 'dangerous'. They are often first offenders because this is the first time they have been caught and they can also claim that they have already been punished by losing their reputation or livelihood.

Ambiguous laws

The nature of offences also creates many legal problems. Their complexity means that it is often difficult to capture the essence of offences in legislation and to specify precisely the situations in which an offence has been committed, leaving many loopholes to be exploited. For some offences, as soon as one illegal practice is prohibited, another practice is developed which evades the provisions of any particular statute. The law therefore has to keep pace with offenders whose very success depends on their ability to stay one step ahead of the law. For example, laws controlling tax evasion have to keep up with increasingly complex avoidance schemes (McBarnet 1984), laws attempting to regulate city fraud must take account of new technical and financial innovations (Clarke 1986), and laws which attempt to regulate health or safety standards must keep up with changes in industrial technology. In addition, the fine line between legal and criminal, acceptable and unacceptable behaviour means that law must keep up with changing standards of public tolerance (Hadden 1983). The diffusion of responsibility in organizations also means that it is difficult to determine who is *legally* and *criminally* responsible, leading to problems in deciding who should be prosecuted, and whether a company can be legally 'guilty' of an offence (see, for example, Schraeger and Short 1977; Hadden 1983; Wells 1988).

Ambiguous criminal status

The narrow borderline between legality, illegality and criminality makes the criminal status of many offences ambiguous. For many organizational offences, the underlying rationale for the use of criminal law is not that the activities in question are morally wrong but that they must be regulated in order to protect the public. In legal terms, they are *mala prohibita* rather than *mala in se*, wrong in themselves. Many are strict liability offences, where no proof of *mens rea*, or intent is required to secure a conviction. However, these are often seen as not 'really criminal' and defendants can readily claim that the offence in question is the result of an unfortunate mistake or a technical omission, thus distinguishing themselves from 'real criminals' (see Chapter 6).

Taking all these characteristics together, it can be seen that relatively few white collar offences are detected, prosecuted and publicly punished. Clearly, some of these characteristics are more typical of some forms of white collar crime than others. There is, for example, less ambiguity surrounding the criminal status of embezzlement or employee theft which involve clearer elements of intent and criminal responsibility. However, for many occupational offences, the borderline between what are acceptable 'perks' and outright theft is difficult to determine (Clarke 1990). Similarly while the diffusion of responsibility and victimization is taken to be a central feature of organizational crime, many occupational crimes involve many participants, some of whom may be less directly implicated than others, and they can also involve diffuse and impersonal victims. Nonetheless, organizational offences are less likely to conform to the social construction of crime.

These characteristics also broadly distinguish white collar crimes from others, although this distinction can be overdrawn. The determination of some conventional offences also involves drawing a fine line between the legitimate and the criminal, and there are other offences whose criminal status is problematic. The distinction, for example, between legitimate and illegitimate drug use is difficult to draw and the definition and criminal status of drug abuse is similarly controversial. Many other conventional crimes, particularly those generally described as crimes without victims often take place in private and are difficult to detect in the absence of a victim. There is also a close relationship between some forms of white collar crime and so called organized or business crime, where businesses are set up with the primary intention of illegal business activity. Such businesses, in order to survive, need a legitimate 'front', and use legitimate business for many purposes such as money laundering. It may therefore be difficult to distinguish between the so called underworld and the 'upperworld' (Van Duyne 1991; Van Duyne and Levi 1991.

Criminology and white collar crime

Despite the undoubted prevalence of white collar crime, there are relatively few analyses of it in mainstream criminological theories, texts and journals, especially in Britain (Levi 1987a), and it is relatively under-researched in comparison with many other forms of crime. None the less, its existence has assumed a peculiar significance within criminology. Official criminal statistics and public discussions of the 'crime problem' are routinely criticized for neglecting white collar crime, as are theories of crime which focus on lower class offenders. The apparently favourable treatment which offenders enjoy in the criminal justice process is contrasted with the punitive policing and sentencing of lower class street criminals. The significance of white collar crime has therefore tended to lie in its association with rich and powerful offenders.

The absence of research can be explained by a number of factors. The invisibility and complexity of offences make them difficult to research as well as to detect. Criminologists tend to be lawyers, sociologists or psychologists rather than scientists, accountants or economists and consequently they find many of the offences and regulations difficult to understand (Levi 1987a). The aspiring participant observer or interviewer also faces severe 'entry' problems as senior corporate executives, stockbrokers or insider dealers are not readily available for observation or in depth interviews, and in any case are unlikely to answer incriminating questions (Geis and Maier 1977). In addition, the scarcity of prosecutions means that it is difficult to amass large samples. As will be seen in Chapter 2, there is also a dearth of reliable information about offences. It may also be more difficult to obtain funds to support research. Most criminological research is Government funded and as has been seen, white collar crime is not generally viewed as such a pressing social problem as 'street crime'. As Levi comments (1987a: xxiii):

> criminological research and theorizing . . . tends to reflect definitions by 'the public' and by state agencies of what the principal social problems are.

In short, the would be researcher is likely to turn to a subject where offences are more visible, offenders more available, and funding more forthcoming. These difficulties may lead to a tendency to rely on the few cases involving 'fallen idols' and on media accounts, which may well be atypical.

As Sutherland himself pointed out, early attempts to devise theories of crime virtually ignored white collar crime. The vast majority of criminological theories, whether individual, cultural or sociological, focused almost entirely on lower class crime, accepting both official statistics and research which found that lower class individuals formed the majority of convicted criminals. Crime was therefore associated with individual pathologies or with poverty, educational and social deprivation. Sociological approaches such as anomie, subcultural theory and social disorganization similarly accepted that crime was a lower class problem and sought to explain it as a consequence of social inequality. Thus white collar crime was not incorporated into these mainstream theories, leading to the many criticisms that they uncritically accepted the association between criminality and low socio economic status (Hirschi and Gottfredson 1987).

It was, of course, this equation of crime with poverty and individual pathology which was the target of Sutherland's critique and which partly explains the stress he placed on the high status and respectability of the offenders. In addition, as Geis and Edelhertz (1973: 996) comment, Sutherland's thrust was mainly polemical, representing:

> an attempt to demonstrate the serious nature of white collar offenses and the culpability of the criminal justice system for failing to deal with them more harshly.

In turn, this polemicism became the focus of many attacks on Sutherland's work, as it was unacceptable to those who saw criminology as an objective, value free, scientific discipline whose subject matter was determined by the criminal law.

The so called 'break' from what was described as conventional or correctional criminology greatly enhanced the significance of white collar crime, as many of the issues raised by 'new' or 'radical' criminology (Taylor *et al.* 1973) were also raised by analyses of white collar crime. Intrinsic to the critique of 'bourgeois' criminology was an attack on the uncritical acceptance of official statistics and official definitions of crime. The apparent immunity of white collar criminals to prosecution and severe punishment raised issues of class bias in the criminal justice process, and the extent to which the law criminalized lower class crime at the expense of the crimes of the powerful (Pearce 1976). The process by which offences and offenders were detected and prosecuted therefore became major issues for research and analysis, as did the very definition of some activities and not others as 'criminal' or 'deviant'. As Carson (1971: 195) points out, a developing interest in the sociology of law made it possible for criminologists to develop an interest in white collar crime as:

> It is an area,... in which the student of white collar crime may legitimately engage without arraignment for the apparent heresy of extending his basic definitions to embrace behaviour as 'non crime' and with theoretical justification attempt to isolate the factors operative in keeping it outside the confines of the criminal law despite its marked similarities to 'real crime'.

Following this kind of argument, much research focused on the emergence of business regulatory laws and the process of law enforcement.

Thus, the concept of white collar crime raises many important questions for criminologists, involving both the definition of crime itself and the activities of law enforcers towards different groups of offenders. Much contemporary research has focused on aspects of legislation and regulation, an emphasis which may also be affected by the practical realities of research. None the less, this has arguably been at the expense of research and analysis of the offences themselves, and of issues of motivation and explanation (see, for example, Braithwaite 1985; Shapiro 1990). As will be seen in successive chapters, a growing body of research has questioned the equation of white collar crime with high status offenders, and challenged the view that their treatment in the criminal justice system is necessarily favourable or characterized by class bias. As will also be seen, while it is often argued that there is insufficient attention paid to the subject of white collar crime within criminology, the volume of literature to be reviewed is extensive and rapidly growing. This provides some basis for exploring critically the assumptions and generalizations which have previously characterized discussions of white collar crime and its significance to criminology.

Summary and discussion

White collar crime is therefore a subject which raises many significant issues. Yet its very definition is controversial and its criminal status ambiguous. Indeed, many writers prefer to avoid the use of the term white collar crime preferring less ideologically laden terms such as business, economic or commercial crime. It has been argued that it is desirable to adopt a broad, inclusive definition in which white collar crime is defined as the abuse of a legitimate occupational role which is regulated by law. Such a definition incorporates the distinctive areas of occupational and organizational or corporate crime. It also avoids the difficulties of including the social status of offenders within the definition of the offences, but at the same time does not rule out their significance for analysis. Despite various arguments that the description, white collar crime, is misleading and somewhat out of date, I intend to retain it on the grounds that by and large criminologists, lawyers, students and the public identify with such a description. As Braithwaite (1985: 3) argues,

> the concept is shared and understood by ordinary folk as more meaningful than occupational crime, corporate deviance, commercial offences, economic crime or any competing concept.

As he also points out, European countries use similar depictions – in France it is known as 'crime en col blanc', in Italy, as 'criminalita in colleti bianchi', and in Germany as 'weisse-kragen-kriminalitat'. To avoid tedious repetition terms such as business or commercial crime will be used particularly where researchers and writers whose work is being described use these terms.

However defined, the scope of white collar crime is vast and therefore the approach taken in this book must inevitably be selective, a selection determined mainly by the availability of relevant information and research. Successive chapters will centre on the main themes already indicated, which emerge from research and academic discussion. The focus of the book is primarily on British research and literature, although the international scope and significance of white collar crime is recognized and will be referred to where relevant. To do justice to even the European dimensions of white collar crime, especially in view of contemporary social, political and economic changes in both Western and Eastern Europe would undoubtedly require a larger volume.

2

EXPOSING WHITE COLLAR CRIME

While it is often argued that white collar crime is more prevalent and has a greater impact than conventional crime (see, for example, Box 1983; Braithwaite and Pettit 1990), it is enormously difficult to estimate or even 'guesstimate' its amount or cost. It has already been seen that few offences are detected or prosecuted, which means that official figures are likely to represent only a tiny proportion of the total volume of offences. Further problems are created by legal offence categories, many of which contain both white collar and conventional crimes. Official criminal statistics also give fewer details about white collar offences than they do for many others (Levi 1987a). Some statistics are compiled by relevant Government departments or enforcement agencies, but as will be seen, these are not always reliable or comprehensive. In addition, victim surveys, often used to make unofficial estimates of the prevalence of crime are inappropriate for those offences where so many victims are unaware of their victimization (Walklate 1989). This chapter will attempt to examine the potential extent and impact of white collar crime taking these difficulties into account. It will explore who the victims of offences are, why so many of them are unaware of and unlikely to report offences, and why so few offences are detected and prosecuted. This will be followed by a series of illustrations of some of the major categories of white collar crime, exploring their potential significance and highlighting the characteristics of offences identified in Chapter 1.

The victims of white collar crime

The effect of many offences on victims is so diffuse that they are on occasion portrayed as victimless. However, at the same time, it is regularly argued that most citizens are victims of many different kinds of white collar crime, and that it involves both economic loss and physical harm (Box 1983; Walklate 1989). None the less, this impact remains hidden. Some of the reasons for this will be explored below.

Who are the victims?

The most obvious victims of occupational crime are organizations and employers but other groups also suffer. Consumers, for example, can suffer both directly and indirectly. Many kinds of occupational crime conform to a classic pattern in which individual consumers are charged a small amount extra for goods, which, when added together amounts to a substantial illegal profit for employees. In other cases consumers are given less than they have paid for, or are charged for services they do not need. Consumers can also be indirectly affected by having to pay higher prices to compensate organizations for the effects of 'shrinkage' from employee theft. The Government, and by extension the taxpayer, are also victims of employee crime, not only through the crimes or corruption of public servants, but through the millions of pounds lost annually through tax evasion.

Corporate crime victimizes employees, consumers, investors and the public in general (Schrager and Short 1977; Box 1983). Employees can be injured and killed as a result of inattention to safety regulations or subjected to long-term health risks from working in unhealthy environments or with hazardous or carcinogenic substances (Miller 1985; Box 1987). They can also be penalized by non-compliance with wages legislation (Box 1983, 1987). Consumers are ripped off by a host of misleading and fraudulent sales practices which deceive them about the quality, amounts or value of goods and services. They can be injured or killed by unsafe products or 'foreign bodies' in food, poisoned by food, and have their health threatened by a surfeit of additives or chemicals in food and water. Passengers can be killed or injured as a result of inattention to safety. The public health in general is threatened by the pollution of beaches, rivers and waterways or illegal emissions of toxic substances. Pollution can also cause specific outbreaks of disease, let alone causing the death of fish, birds and other animals. Corporations and financial institutions can themselves be the victims of the offences of other corporations and organizations, as can the Government (Box 1983; Levi 1987a). Competitors may resort to espionage, arson, hostile take-overs or bribery and corruption (Box 1983), and the credibility of financial institutions may be damaged by revelations of insider dealing and other questionable share transactions.

Therefore, all citizens, whether as consumers, workers, investors, passengers, residents, employers or business executives can be victimized from many forms of white collar crime. While often portrayed as the arch villains, businesses themselves suffer considerable losses from the crimes of their employees and other businesses but the nature of this victimization is such that these losses, while considerable, are often not evident, not counted, not attributed to crime and not reported.

Why do victims not report offences?

The inability of victims to detect offences is of course the major reason why so much white collar crime is unreported. As seen in Chapter 1, this is a consequence of the location of offences in occupational and organizational roles. Employers hire staff to perform tasks which they themselves cannot perform, cannot directly supervise and in many cases lack the relevant expertise to evaluate (Shapiro 1990). Consumers employ the services of builders, car mechanics, plumbers, lawyers, accountants or doctors because they lack the skill and knowledge to perform the desired service themselves, and in many cases do not even know what kind of service they require. Similar considerations apply to corporate or organizational crimes, where the role of law is often to protect the public from harm or deception which they cannot protect themselves from. Few consumers, for example, have either the knowledge or means to check the safety of goods or the quality of food for themselves, nor can they be expected to detect pollution in water supplies. The public therefore trust the providers of goods and services and the regulatory machinery, to which they as tax payers contribute, to ensure that they are not harmed.

Even when victims are aware of some loss or damage, they may not define their problem as a 'criminal' one. They may be annoyed or irritated and even feel that something should be done, but their response may not involve reporting the matter as a crime. In the first place, they may simply be unaware that legally, an offence has been committed. Many consumers, for example, are aware that they have some rights, know that goods should be sold in standard weights, that ingredients of food should be labelled on the packet and that bargain prices should reflect a real discount. However, they may not know the precise details of the relevant regulations or that these regulations are enforceable by the criminal law.

Even when they are sufficiently aggrieved to take action, they do not always contact the relevant enforcement authority. The irate consumer, for example, has a number of different options. Many simply decide never to go to the same shop or buy the same goods again and may even advise their friends to do the same (Cranston 1979). Others complain directly to the shop or manufacturer concerned hoping to gain some sort of compensation. Yet others go to Citizens' Advice Bureaux, seek private legal advice or even write to newspapers, *That's Life*, or their MP. Probably very few go directly to the local Trading Standards or Consumer Protection department (Cranston 1979; Croall 1987). Victims of other offences have a similar number of options open to them which means that many offences are defined and dealt with as 'complaints', and settled privately.

Victims may feel partly or wholly responsible for their own victimization. Victims of fraud, for example, may accept a taken for granted notion of the legal principle of *caveat emptor*, let the buyer beware (Levi 1987a, 1991a) and feel that they themselves should make sure that they are not ripped off. Consumers may blame themselves for having been taken in by sharp selling practices. For example, when a bargain designer outfit shrinks in the wash many blame themselves for being stupid enough to think that it was really a high quality item, and do not define themselves as 'victims' of a highly organized counterfeit fraud. Investors whose investments don't pay off may feel that they have taken a bad risk and ought to have known better.

There are many other reasons why victims, even when they know that a crime has been committed, take no action. Victim surveys have found, for example, that many crimes are not reported because victims feel they are too trivial to bother about (Bottomley and Pease 1986). The diffuse nature of victimization associated with white collar crime makes it likely that for many victims, the time and potential cost of complaining may be seen as being out of proportion to the damage done. How many times, for example, do consumers simply throw mouldy food or rotten fruit into the bin – even if they know that they could report it to the local Consumer Protection Department? Many other offences appear equally as trivial and are equally as unlikely to be reported.

Other reasons for not reporting crime, such as the fear of reprisals or embarrassment (Bottomley and Pease 1986), are also relevant to white collar offences. Employees might be afraid of losing their jobs if they are seen as troublemakers or 'whistleblowers'. Employers may prefer to turn a blind eye to employee fiddles rather than risk losing staff or damaging industrial relations (Mars 1982). The tendency of victims to blame themselves for having foolishly parted with their money may mean that they are too embarrassed to report frauds. A major reason why companies do not report the offences of employees, particularly senior employees, is that they fear unwelcome publicity and loss of face (Levi 1987a, 1988). In addition, victims of fraud may have little confidence in the ability of official agencies to take effective action (Levi 1987a). All of these factors taken together mean that vast amounts of white collar crime are undetected, not defined as crime or not reported.

Detecting and prosecuting white collar crime

The onus for detection and prosecution therefore lies with organizations themselves and public enforcement agencies. However, it has already been seen that offences are particularly difficult to detect. Investigations may be time consuming, costly and technically complex. Public enforcement agencies tend to make routine inspections, testing products and checking arrangements to monitor compliance but many public agencies are short of funds and visits may have to be curtailed and functions prioritized (see Chapter 5). This can mean that some offences are more likely to be detected than others. Levi (1987a), for example, suggests that the Fraud Squad concentrates on cases which are simpler and more likely to produce 'results' at the expense of complex and especially international frauds. Many other agencies similarly have to target offences which are easier and less costly to investigate (see Chapter 5).

Even when detected, many offences are not prosecuted. Organizational victims, fearing adverse publicity, may feel that if offenders are dismissed they have been sufficiently punished and that future offences have been prevented. The many public enforcement agencies dealing with business regulatory offences tend to adopt what are generally described as compliance strategies, as a result of which businesses are persuaded to comply with regulations rather than being prosecuted, and prosecution is generally reserved for only the most serious offences or persistent offenders (see Chapter 5). Many public agencies also have powers to object to or withdraw licences, make out of court financial settlements or close businesses down. These are seen as a more effective way to prevent offences and protect the public. All of this means that many white collar offences are dealt with by 'private' rather than public injustice.

Estimates and guesstimates of white collar crime

Any attempts to estimate the amount or costs of offences are, therefore, inevitably speculative. Official data is sparse, hard to locate and difficult to interpret. The Official Criminal Statistics are more than usually unhelpful in relation to white collar crime. Less information for example, is given about the costs of fraud than is provided for other property crimes, which, argues Levi (1987a), in itself indicates the low priority accorded to fraud. Most organizational offences, often described as business regulatory crime, are counted as 'other indictable' or non-indictable offences. Information about these offences is very sparse, and, according to the 1977 annual *Criminal Statistics* the amount of information given about any particular offence reflects 'public concern'. Slightly more information can be located in the far less available *Supplementary Criminal Statistics*, but this is still rudimentary. Table 2.1 lists the numbers convicted for a selection of offence categories, taken from the Supplementary Statistics for 1988. Companies are listed as 'other' offenders.

Other data can be obtained from relevant Government departments, but is often rather basic and uninformative. Office of Fair Trading reports list total numbers of convictions and gross amounts of fines for offences under consumer protection legislation, and Inland Revenue and Customs and Excise departments provide some information about the costs of tax fraud (Levi 1987a). However, the DTI neither publishes nor collects data on the

Table 2.1 Persons found guilty of selected offences in crown and magistrates courts in England and Wales 1988[1],: by offence category and sex.

	Crown Court			*Magistrates Court*		
Offence	*M*	*F*	*O*	*M*	*F*	*O*[2]
Theft by employee	985	184	1	2743	776	–
Fraud by company director, etc.	49	4	–	41	7	1
False accounting	209	41	3	273	106	–
Other fraud	3955	833	3	11,026	3281	1
Bankruptcy offences	42	1	–	125	9	1
Revenue law	71	5	2	25	1	1
Trade Descriptions Act, etc.	88	3	14	776	35	449
Health and Safety at Work Act 1974	6	–	17	296	16	724
Adulteration of food	2	–	1	266	27	746
+ summary offences				55	3	130
Public health	10	1	5	650	58	394
+ summary offences				971	191	502
Sunday trading, etc.				181	15	231
Weights and Measures Acts				121	7	81

[1]Compiled from the Supplementary Criminal Statistics of 1988.
[2]M – male; F – female; O – 'other' (companies).

costs of fraud, (Levi 1987a) and in respect of insider dealing, Naylor (1990: 58) comments that the DTI has no idea about how much there is and 'worse, one gets the impression that . . . (it) . . . does not care to know'. Researchers therefore have to rely on a variety of sources for information – some Local Authority departments for example, publish prosecution statistics (Croall 1987), some enforcement agencies collect information, and others have used victim surveys (Levi 1988) or interviewed enforcement agents (Clarke 1989).

The costs of white collar crime are similarly impossible to estimate, although it can be pointed out that frauds often involve thousands if not millions of pounds compared with thefts which typically involve smaller amounts. Despite these difficulties, some have tried to estimate the amount and impact of selected white collar and corporate crimes, and to compare these estimates with ordinary crime. Often quoted is Conklin's (1977) attempt to estimate the comparative costs of selected white collar and conventional crimes. Using a variety of indices he estimated that in the USA, robbery, theft, larceny and auto-theft cost $3–4 billion, compared with the $40 billion attributable to various white collar offences including consumer fraud, illegal competition and deceptive practices. On the basis of this and similar estimates, many argue that the total volume of white collar crime is likely to exceed that of conventional crime (Braithwaite 1982; Box 1983). While this is very likely, statistical comparisons based on dubious estimates are likely to be confusing and possibly misleading. Thus no attempt will be made here to estimate the total cost or extent of white collar crime, or to compare it directly with ordinary crime. A brief outline of some of the major forms of white collar crime is given below.

Employee theft

'Theft by an employee' is a major category of occupational crime. Table 2.1 reveals that in 1988, taking together the figures for both Crown and Magistrates Courts, a total of 3728 men and 960 women were convicted of this offence, less than two per cent of the convictions for all thefts. In 1987, an average loss of £1099 was attributed to employee theft, substantially higher than the £512 average loss attributed to all kinds of theft, with only theft of a motor vehicle, costed on average at £1802, having a higher cost (*Criminal Statistics* 1987). Employee theft therefore involves comparatively larger sums than other thefts – in 1987, a total loss of £19,108 thousand was recorded for this category.

These figures of course represent only the small tip of a potentially large iceberg. It is generally argued that only a 'minute' proportion of employee theft is reported and only a small proportion prosecuted (Clarke 1990: 37). Companies rarely estimate the losses from employee theft, including it under the general heading of 'shrinkage'. Indeed, within many occupations and organizations a certain amount of fiddling or pilfering is widely tolerated and forms part of what some writers refer to as an informal 'total reward system', where the rewards of fiddles are part of a taken for granted effort–reward bargain (Mars 1982; Clarke 1990). Management may turn a blind eye to much fiddling, recognizing that if they interfere, the delicate balance of industrial relations could be upset. This means that in many situations companies may prefer not to call in the police, fearing that their intervention could be disruptive (Clarke 1990) and that embarrassing publicity could follow the prosecutions of employees.

As with many white collar offences there is a gap between social and legal definitions of what constitutes 'crime'. In most workplaces there are informal norms which determine at what point the 'theft' of stationery, telephone calls and other assorted items is defined as deviant or criminal. Indeed, as Mars (1982) points out employees can steal not just goods, but time from employers – as the expressions 'my own time' or 'their time' indicate. Equipment can also be 'borrowed' for employees' use, either for personal purposes or to assist them in various moonlighting schemes. These norms, common in many workplaces, are very different from legal classifications, which could define such commonplace activities as 'theft'.

While the definition and essence of theft may appear unambiguous, its application in the workplace can be extremely ambiguous, and the example of employee theft well illustrates the very fine line which divides acceptable and unacceptable activities. It also reveals that many employees are likely at some time to participate in activities which could be defined as employee theft!

Fraud

Fraud is a vast category of white collar crime which cross cuts formal legal classifications. Not all offences legally classified as fraud are properly white collar crime, and many other offence categories include essentially fraudulent activities. Taking those offences which are officially categorized as fraud, Table 2.1 reveals that in 1988, a mere 90 males, 11 females and one company were convicted of 'fraud by a company director, etc., and 482 men and 147 women were convicted of false accounting. Four companies plus 14,981 men and 4114 women were convicted of 'other frauds' a category which includes a diverse range of offences including obtaining property or pecuniary advantage by deception, 'purporting to act as a spiritualistic medium for reward', 'frauds by farmers in connection with agricultural charge', 'railway frauds', 'making off without payment' and 'other fraud' (*Criminal Statistics* 1987).

Many of these of course are not white collar crimes, as they are not committed in the course of the offender's occupation and it is virtually impossible to estimate what proportion are occupational offences. In a survey of organizational victims of fraud, Levi found that statistically the largest category of frauds against organizations was credit and cheque fraud, largely perpetrated by conventional criminals, which accounted for 23 per cent of reported fraud. However, these only accounted for a small proportion of the total cost of fraud, involving around £50 million annually (Levi 1988: 5). Many other frauds are perpetrated by individuals against family and friends (Levi and Pithouse 1989).

Discounting these offences, the scope and impact of what can be defined as white collar fraud is considerable. In Levi's study of organizational victims nearly 40 per cent of 56 large corporations surveyed reported at least one fraud costing over £50,000 (Levi 1988). Three-quarters of the total frauds reported involved employees and included embezzlement and expenses frauds, false invoicing, forgery of bank paying in stamps, and computer and investment frauds. In a sample of fraud victims in Cardiff and the Old Bailey, Levi and Pithouse (1989) found that the majority of victims were commercial organizations, such as banks, customers and clients, employers, suppliers of goods and services, insurance companies, finance companies, building societies and retail services. Losses by these kinds of institutions accounted for an estimated 60 per cent of the total cost of frauds

(Levi 1988). Frauds can also be perpetrated by one company against another, or on consumers and investors by the use of fraudulent sales techniques or investment schemes.

Estimates of the potential cost of fraud involve calculations running into millions and billions of pounds. Levi for example (1987a: 21–4) calculated that the total cost of fraud reported to fraud squads in 1985 amounted to £2113 million. This, he estimated, constitutes approximately twice the cost of theft, burglary and robbery in the same year. In addition, individual frauds involve larger sums than other property crimes. In 1985 for example, an average cost of £615 was attributed to burglary in a dwelling and £1256 to robbery (excluding attempts). However, the average amount at risk in frauds dealt with by the Metropolitan Police Company Fraud Branch in that year amounted to a staggering £1,944,000 (figures from Levi 1987a: 25). Currently, the Serious Frauds Office, who only become involved where sums of over 2 million pounds are involved, are investigating 56 cases with a total value of 1.6 billion pounds (*Sunday Times* 14/7/91). The impact of frauds on victims can also be more severe – while individual householders are insured against burglary, fraud insurance is less common (Levi 1987a, 1988).

Again of course it has to be borne in mind that these figures only represent detected and reported cases. Given the difficulties of detecting fraud and the reluctance of companies to report it, both the amount and cost of frauds are likely to be far greater. It is perhaps surprising therefore that despite increasing concern about fraud there are so few efforts to find more precise estimates of its associated costs. Concern has recently been voiced, for example, about insurance fraud, which the Chartered Institute of Loss Adjusters was warned could spiral as businesses face up to the recession and the growing number of bankruptcies and insolvencies. Businessmen, said a 'top city lawyer', could be 'driven through desperation to commit burglary and arson' (*Lloyds List* 6/9/90). Yet only a small number of frauds have been recorded by investigators, whose attitudes and methods have been described as not particularly denunciatory, and Insurance Companies make no systematic attempt to calculate the extent of their losses (Clarke 1989). None the less, some investigators estimated the amount of real fraud at around 1–5 per cent of total claims. Much insurance fraud is not strictly occupational or organizational as it involves individual claimants opportunistically exaggerating their losses, but struggling businesses may resort to setting fire to their premises in order to profit from their insurance.

All of this of course pales into insignificance in comparison with the massive frauds uncovered at the Bank of Credit and Commerce International, variously known as the 'Bank of Crooks and Criminals International' (*Sunday Times* 21/7/91), the 'Bank of Cocaine, Conmen and Impostors' (*Sunday Telegraph* 7/7)91) or more commonly, BCCI. Amidst a host of revelations of fraud, bribery, corruption and associations with drug cartels, international terrorism and organized crime, a massive fraud was revealed, estimated to involve anything between 5 and 15 billion pounds (*Sunday Times* 14/7/91). Essentially, the fraud itself was relatively straightforward, albeit on a worldwide scale and concealed by the existence of a 'bank within a bank'. The Bank lost heavily, in common with other more reputable banks, in stock market trading, using its clients' money. In addition it made many loans to customers, real or fictitious, who could not or did not pay – thereby 'robbing the poor to give to the rich' (*Sunday Times* 14/7/91), as small investors' money was financing loans to wealthy customers who were not asked for sufficient collateral. These losses were covered up by taking out fictitious loans and raising around 600 million dollars in unrecorded deposits. These 'assets' were then transferred to accounts showing losses (*The Economist* 27/7/91). This money was shifted around from account to account, often from country to country to create an apparent balance – thus hiding one fraud behind another one (*The Economist* 13/7/91). A majority of senior executives were implicated and are reported in the Price Waterhouse report to have 'simply followed instructions they should have questioned' (cited in *Independent* 3/8/91).

Of the many thousands of victims, many of whom were small businesses and individual investors in third world countries, British Local Authorities alone are estimated to have lost up to 100 million pounds (*Sunday Times* 14/7/91) and the net total for the thousands of Asian businesses involved is possibly higher. Considerable controversy has also surrounded the issue of why, when rumours of fraud, bribery and corruption had surrounded the bank for years and when convictions for money laundering had been upheld, no action was taken. According to one commentator BCCI was able to 'run rings round the regulators' (*Sunday Times* 14/7/91) and the Governor of the Bank of England is reported as commenting that the fraud was so sophisticated and well hidden that it was extremely hard to detect, a comment which casts doubt on the entire regulatory system (*Independent* 9/8/91).

A complex web of frauds and other inherently deceptive practices are found in the financial world, where many offences are so complex that they defy ready classification and description to those unfamiliar with corporate finance or law. None the less, the publicity accorded to the Guinness trials, let alone the public discussion following the non-prosecution of those involved in the Harrod's takeover (Levi 1991b) reveal a growing public concern with these affairs. Very little is known about the prevalence of these kinds of activities – for example, insider dealing as its very title indicates is notoriously difficult to uncover, and the DTI and the Stock Exchange rarely provide information (Naylor 1990). Only a small number of prosecutions have been made for insider dealing – Naylor, for example, reports that between 1980 and 1986 the Stock Exchange is 'rumoured' to have referred 100–110 cases to the DTI, out of which only five were prosecuted and four convicted. From

1986–1989 a further nine convictions were reported. None the less, it is acknowledged that it is far more widespread than complaints indicate – Naylor (1990), for example, cites an estimate by a member of the Insider Dealing group that successful prosecutions account for only one per cent of the total.

For these as for most other white collar crimes, the amounts of money and the nature of the losses involved are impossible to calculate. The recent prosecution of Geoffrey Collier revealed profits from the use of inside information of several hundred thousand pounds (Naylor 1990). Other city frauds can involve even larger losses. In the Dunsdale Securities case an estimated 8.2 million pounds of investors' money went missing, reputedly having been spent on fast cars, houses and high living (*Sunday Times* 14/7/91). Scandals involving enormous sums have also occurred in Lloyd's. In one celebrated case, the Chairman of Alexander Howden, three directors and Ian Postgate, a Lloyd's underwriter, transferred a total of 41 million dollars into their own offshore accounts. In another scandal, a former chairman and an underwriter stole 53.2 million dollars from syndicate members. None of the individuals in these cases were ever punished, as they had left the country, died or were too ill to stand trial. Only one was tried and subsequently cleared of charges of theft. Again the prevalence of such activities is unknown, however it has been argued that they are likely to represent the 'tip of a huge iceberg' (*Sunday Times* 14/7/91).

Many of these kinds of offences involve activities whose criminal status is highly controversial and ambiguous. In many circles, the use of inside information to make a profit or the manipulation of share prices, as happened in the celebrated Guinness case, is regarded as an acceptable part of the competitive world of business and finance, and many offences appear to be victimless. As one commentator points out:

> the public perception of stock market price ramping, insider dealing, warehousing and massaging of share prices has been of a 'victimless crime'. Integrity and ethics, to those labouring in city wine bars, were concepts which generally could be safely ignored. (*Guardian* 28/8/90)

Insider dealing, only recently criminalized, is the most obvious example of an activity which seems to involve little direct loss, and the complexities of hostile take-overs also tend to conceal the potential harm done. However, summarizing Judge Henry's conclusions in the Guinness trial, the commentator cited above demonstrates the rippling effect on many victims. Guinness shareholders were deprived of the millions of pounds which were used as payments in the cover-up of the initial dealings. Distiller's shareholders were deprived of a fair choice between merger partners. Stock market operators who bought or sold Guinness shares without the luxury of indemnities also lost out as did Argyll shareholders who were deprived of a victory which might have been theirs. Thousands of small investors, who, through their pension funds and insurance policies are also stakeholders in Guinness, were further victims (*The Guardian* 28/8/90). Finally, the credibility of the business and financial world is damaged by revelations of these kinds of activities (Clarke 1990). Therefore, their impact is wider than often assumed, and they are not properly described as victimless. They also provide further examples of the narrow borderline between the acceptable and unacceptable faces of capitalism, and of 'criminal' practices which are widely tolerated and regarded as normal and acceptable.

Computer crime

Computer fraud is more feared by management than any other kind of fraud (Levi 1988). Whether or not these fears are justified is difficult to assess, as computer crime is particularly resistant to any reliable measurement. Indeed, the term computer crime itself is misleading and difficult to define. In practice, much so called computer crime is essentially similar to the kinds of frauds which employees who handle financial transactions have always perpetrated – entering false figures into a computer is, for example, much the same as entering false figures into ledgers (*Independent on Sunday* 21/10/90). Many offences using computers are dealt with as theft by an employee (Wasik 1989; Lloyd 1990). Estimates of the amounts of computer crime are therefore highly suspect and depend on which definition is being used (*The Guardian* 1/3/90; Lloyd 1990). Some commentators prefer a definition which would restrict the use of the term to only those crimes which involve a direct manipulation of computer files (*The Guardian* 1/3/90). On the other hand, the essence of computer crime, in both popular and legal terms is that a computer is the means of the commission of the offence or provides the environment within which criminal conduct can occur (Lloyd 1990: 164).

Whatever definition is adopted, estimates of its amounts vary considerably and, despite the considerable fear of computer crime, recorded instances are relatively few. The Audit Commission, adopting a broad definition of computer crime as 'any fraudulent behaviour connected with computerisation by which someone attempts to gain dishonest advantage', discovered only 118 incidents in England and Wales in the years 1984–7, involving total losses of a little over two-and-a-half million pounds (Lloyd 1990: 165). However, other estimates have been much higher, ranging from £300 million to as much as £2 billion (*The Guardian* 1/3/90). As is the case with other employee crimes, much computer crime probably remains undetected and unreported. Lloyd (1990) speculates that banks in particular may be reluctant to report frauds for fear of losing public confidence, a suggestion also made by a Senior Police Officer from the City Fraud Squad (*Independent on Sunday* 21/10/90).

Management's fear of computer crime is probably based on feelings of vulnerability as it is notoriously difficult to detect – as one Senior Police Officer comments, 'every institution's nightmare' is a programme fraud by its own staff where the chances of detection are slim (*Independent on Sunday* 21/10/90). Banks may be particularly concerned about the possibility of fraud committed by their own employees who have considerable knowledge of and ready access to their computer systems. In addition, computerized systems enable the electronic transfer of vast sums of money across the globe in only a few seconds. Lloyd (1990) describes one case in which a bank employee transferred money from dormant accounts in Kuwait to the tune of £45,000, to be placed in accounts of his own once he had left the bank. In order to prevent detection, he programmed the computer to delete all records of these transactions.

Financial frauds are not the only offences in which computers are used, and both employees and outsiders can use or abuse computer systems for a variety of purposes. High-tech fiddles and perks may involve 'theft' of computer time, where employer's computers can be used for purposes as diverse as playing computer games, working out personal accounts or running a business (Wasik 1989). Many organizations are also concerned about the possible penetration of their systems by hackers. For most hackers the main challenge is entering the system, which has been likened to electronic trespass, or 'electronic burglary' (Wasik 1989: 261), and little damage is caused. However, some leave a signature on the system – a form of 'electronic graffiti', and others may damage systems – a form of 'electronic vandalism' (Lloyd 1990: 168). What worries organizations most is that hackers may abstract data which can be exploited for illegitimate purposes. Hacking can be associated with electronic espionage by competitors and some information (for example, lists of clients) could also be used by competitors for their own purposes (Wasik 1989; Lloyd 1990). Some have even suggested that professional criminals have become involved – some computer fraudsters are apparently the bank robbers of the 1960s! (*Independent on Sunday* 21/10/90). The potential impact of computer crime is therefore enormous, although essentially it differs little from other offences. It can also create considerable legal difficulties – particularly where what is at risk is information rather than goods (Wasik 1989).

Tax fraud

Tax fraud costs the Government and tax payers millions of pounds annually, but like many other offences is grossly under-represented in official figures. Not even the small number of Inland Revenue revenue prosecutions recorded annually involve solely tax evasion or white collar crime. Cook (1989a), for example, found that prosecutions were more likely for 'real' crime, involving the theft of payable orders and girocheques, than for business crime. Other prosecutions involve 'moonlighting', where regular PAYE taxpayers fail to disclose additional earnings from employment which is not their regular employment, and the many and various subcontracting 'fiddles' of builders. However, these are only a tiny proportion of known tax offences and an even tinier proportion of the real amount of tax evasion (see, for example, Clarke 1990). Studies of the Inland Revenue and other enforcement bodies have found, in common with other regulatory areas, that investigations are highly selective, target particular occupations, and that prosecution is relatively rare (see, for example, Cook 1989a; Clarke 1990; Chapter 5).

None the less, enormous losses have been attributed to unpaid income or value added tax. Levi (1987a), for example, reports that in 1979 the Secretary of State estimated loss of revenue from Value Added Tax at £300–500 million, and Uglow (1984: 129) reports a statement by the Chairman of the Inland Revenue that it is 'not implausible' that undeclared income is of the order of seven and a half per cent of GNP – a loss to the Revenue of upwards of three billion pounds per year. Others have calculated that tax evasion costs five or six times as much as all conventional crimes put together (Levi 1987a; Levi and Suddle 1989).

Opportunities for tax evasion are related to a person's occupation. Employees in regular salaried employment who are subject to PAYE taxation have very few opportunities for evasion, in contrast to the self-employed or those who provide services outside the confines of regular salaried employment. These earnings provide the basis for a host of tax fiddles, which are essentially similar whether committed by professional or blue collar workers. Examples include the undisclosed earnings gained by builders and manual workers who do jobs 'on the side', the 'ash cash' earned by doctors who issue cremation certificates, or the fees of academics who undertake guest lectures or examination marking (Cook 1989a). While those in both high and low paid occupations can benefit from these various fiddles, those who earn more have more to gain (Cook 1989a). In addition, both large and small businesses attempt in many and various ways to misrepresent the true state of their accounts in order to pay as little tax as possible.

Like employee theft, tax evasion is often euphemistically described as a 'fiddle' or perk, and the line between tax evasion and legal tax avoidance is extremely fuzzy. McBarnet (1987, 1988), for example, describes a host of complex tax avoidance schemes, which comply with the letter of the law but quite clearly contravene its spirit. Many writers report a general attitude that tax evasion is morally acceptable and that 'everybody does it', views which reflect the unpopularity of taxation itself (Cook 1989a; see Chapter 4). In addition, law abiding taxpayers implicitly condone some fraudulent evasion by happily paying for services in cash, knowing full well that the provider of these services is probably not declaring the payment. Tax evasion then provides yet another example of an offence which is widespread and culturally tolerated but which involves enormous losses to the Government and ultimately to the public in general. The moral ambivalence surrounding tax fraud can be sharply contrasted with the almost universal condemnation attracted by a very similar offence – social security fraud (Uglow 1984; Cook 1989a).

Crimes against consumers

Much of what is referred to variously as corporate, organizational or business regulatory crime is similarly under-represented in official figures, and its impact often underestimated. The prosecution of companies for what appear to be minor breaches of the many regulations covering the health and safety of production processes, or the quality, quantity and contents of goods on sale, appear somewhat mundane in comparison with the millions of pounds involved in the offences examined in previous sections. However, behind these apparently trivial prosecutions lies a concern with the protection of consumers, workers and the general public from a host of inherently fraudulent selling practices, and from the considerable dangers to health arising from modern industrial and manufacturing processes. Many of these statutes deal with the protection of consumers, which is the first main area to be examined. As Table 2.1 shows, offences under Trade Descriptions, Weights and Measures and Food and Drugs Acts account for a substantial proportion of prosecutions involving companies.

Trade descriptions offences

Table 2.1 shows that in 1988 a total of 864 men, 38 women and 463 companies were prosecuted under Trade Descriptions legislation. The Annual Report of the Office of Fair Trading (Director General of Fair Trading 1988) further records that in the year ending September 1987 there were 1428 convictions under the Trade Descriptions Act. The vast majority of these were for false descriptions of goods, with false descriptions of motor vehicles, including car 'clocking', constituting 556 of these – the largest single category. Other offences involve false price indications, misleading bargain offers and misleading descriptions of goods and services. As might be expected, these prosecutions represent only a small minority of offences. Even the most vigilant of consumers is unable to tell whether or not goods actually match up to their descriptions and even the most suspicious car buyer cannot verify the mileage of a second-hand car. Consequently, only a small proportion of offences are reported to Trading Standards Officers or Consumer Protection Departments. Detecting offences depends, in a large part, on enforcers who are severely constrained by available resources, and even where offences are detected, prosecution is not inevitable.

Many trade description offences may appear somewhat trivial, including the misdescription of roulette systems, 'clip joints' and the sale of cheap jewellery or perfume which are 'passed off' as expensive brand named products (Croall 1987). However, the law is directed at many inherently deceptive practices which yield substantial profits. A major concern of enforcement departments at present for example is the problem of counterfeiting – a highly organized and fraudulent activity. Another major problem is car 'clocking' and garage repair fraud which have been estimated to cost the consumer millions of pounds per year (Borrie 1984; Cranston 1984). In one case alone a trader is reported to have made £100,000 illegal profits in ten months (Croall 1987). This is not a problem unique to Britain, but has been found in both the United States (Leonard and Weber 1977), and in Australia, where Braithwaite (1978) estimated that there were 70,000 such frauds in one year in Queensland alone, compared to 80,101 crimes of all kinds.

Employees and employers can both benefit from trade descriptions cases, and some may involve employee fiddles. During the author's research a large catering company was convicted twice in one year following a number of offences involving the sale of drinks at a major sporting venue. This company was apparently in the habit of bussing in staff to 'one off' events, encouraging staff, who were poorly paid, to bring their own stock and placing few restrictions on the prices charged (Croall 1987). Other misleading practices include bogus sale offers, where the consumer can be misled into thinking that they are being offered a real bargain when in fact no higher price has ever been charged. In many instances, the borderline between legal and illegal bargain offers is extremely difficult to draw, as is the borderline between so called misleading offers and outright deception. All these marketing strategies are of course designed to persuade the consumer to buy goods, encouraging them with the carrot of an apparent saving. This illustrates the narrow borderline between acceptable and unacceptable commercial practices, a question also raised by Sutherland (1949) who pointed to the close relationship between advertising 'puffs', normal selling techniques and deception.

Weights and measures offences

There are very few prosecutions under the Weights and Measures Acts with only 121 men, 7 women and 81 companies being convicted in 1988. Around half of the Weights and Measures convictions recorded by the Office of Fair Trading in the year ending September 1987 involved the sale of goods with short weight or measure. Others involve the use of 'false or unjust balances'. As for Trade Descriptions offences, enforcers are hampered by scarce resources and the detection of offences, involving test purchases of food products or alcoholic drinks, is costly. In common with similar offences, offenders are often cautioned rather than prosecuted (Croall 1987).

Basically, these laws seek to protect the consumer from being deceived about the quantity of goods they are buying, and specific regulations cover foodstuffs, drinks, petrol and many other items. While most offences involve seemingly trivial cases of underweight coal, short measure drinks and underweight bread, the potential gains to offenders can be large. Even a tiny shortfall to any one consumer can be multiplied hundreds or thousands of times to produce enormous illegitimate profits. Weights and Measures offences can also involve the multifarious fiddles common in the Hospitality industry (Mars 1973; Mars and Nicod 1984). Employees may systematically adulterate drinks with water or sell them in smaller quantities than are required by regulations. Excess drinks can be abstracted for employees' personal consumption or subsequent sale. Beer drinkers may be familiar with the problem of ascertaining whether or not a pint glass contains a pint of beer – some glasses are too small to incorporate a full pint in addition to the froth which often accompanies it. While this may sound a trivial matter, publicans can profit considerably from the accumulated shortfall, as more pints can be sold out of one barrel. As revenue is paid on the basis of a fixed number of pints per barrel this practice can also be a means of paying less revenue (*Which?* April 1983).

Weights and measures legislation also attempts, rather inadequately, to control a number of rip offs and cons lying at the fringes of legality. Particularly controversial, for example, is the issue of deceptive packaging, where the size of packets may exceed and thus misrepresent the amount of goods which they contain. Consumers can be deceived by the use of labels such as 'giant size' or 'extra large' which imply that somehow or other more goods are being sold – when in fact they may be paying more for air or cardboard! (Clinard and Yeager 1980; Smith 1982). Many of these practices are not strictly offences, although some Trading Standards Departments have attempted test prosecutions under the Trade Descriptions Act on the basis that descriptions are misleading and cosmetics sold in double walled jars which look big but contain little have been the subject of prosecutions (Croall 1987). Yet again the narrow borderline between normal, illegal and deceptive selling practices is illustrated.

Food and drugs offences

The quality, quantity and ingredients of food are covered by the Food and Drugs Acts. Table 2.1 shows that a total of 268 men, 27 women and 747 companies were convicted in 1988 for offences described as 'adulteration of food'. The main offences involved are the sale of food generally described as 'unfit', and the sale of food 'not of the nature, quality or substance demanded by the consumer'. These include the sale of mouldy or decomposed food, food which is not what it appears – like beefburgers containing kangaroo or horse meat, and food containing what are charmingly described as 'foreign bodies' which can be chips of wood, metal, glass, sticking plaster or pens. In addition, labelling regulations regulate how foods can be described and which contents must be stated on the label. As is the case with other consumer offences, detection can involve complex scientific tests and probably only a tiny minority of offences are detected.

Offences can involve highly organized frauds on consumers and may also result in physical harm or illness. Most notorious were the meat rackets of the early 1980s in which kangaroo, horse, goat and condemned meat from knacker's yards were passed into the legitimate meat market. Indeed, a report of the Institute of Environmental Health Officers (1982) estimated that 'the majority of people have at some stage eaten products made from unfit or knacker meat'. Except of course for vegetarians! So widespread was this trade that the Institute estimated that it constituted about two per cent of the legitimate meat market, and while many prosecutions followed, recent inquiries suggest that these frauds are still prevalent (*The Guardian* 15/10/90). So vast and profitable is the meat trade that there are many kinds of organized frauds, including the importation of meat from outside the EEC for sale in member countries (Van Duyne 1991). These kinds of frauds are of course more properly described as organized, or 'enterprise' crimes, in that the businesses concerned are primarily set up with illegitimate intent (Van Duyne 1991).

Food laws also attempt to protect the consumer from being misled about what food contains, and to prevent the excessive use of water, additives and other substitutes for 'real food'. One of the oldest forms of food adulteration is the addition of water to food, which increases its apparent volume. Modern food processing techniques make it possible for water to be inserted quite legitimately at various stages in the manufacturing process, leading to a situation in which consumers can spend considerable amounts of money on water or ice. Along with the addition of additives, colourings and preservatives this, in the view of many commentators, amounts to 'legalized adulteration' (Cannon and Walker 1985). Consumers can also be misled by both pictures and labels, where words like 'wholesome' or 'natural ingredients' backed up with pictures portraying farmyards, fields or fruit can be used to give the impression of wholesomeness and nutritiousness. As is the case with other selling practices, the line between legitimate, illegitimate and deceptive descriptions is very narrow and the law leaves many loopholes (Croall 1987; see Chapter 8).

Food legislation also aims to protect consumers from possible illness, injury or disease. One of the most dramatic cases in recent years was the Spanish cooking oil incident where 259 consumers were killed and many more were seriously ill after using cooking oil which had been mixed with industrial oil (Croall 1987). Some wine drinkers still avoid Austrian and

Italian wine following revelations that some bottles contained a mixture of wine, methyl alcohol and anti-freeze! (Croall 1987; Levi 1987a). Other consumers have been hospitalized as a result of injuries caused by glass, metal or caustic soda which have been concealed in everyday foods (Croall 1987).

Food can also poison consumers, often as a result of inattention to hygiene regulations. Food poisoning can of course kill and an outbreak in the Stanley Royd Hospital in 1986 killed 19 patients and led to a review of the Crown immunity from prosecution enjoyed by hospitals at the time (Croall 1987). While it is often difficult in practice to link food poisoning outbreaks directly to offences against regulations the prevalence of both food poisoning and neglect of regulations is undoubtedly far greater than the small number of prosecutions indicate. Environmental Health Officers, for example, report that they find contraventions of regulations in as many as seventy per cent of establishments visited (Croall 1987) and a recent report by Environmental Health Officers further states that more than 12 per cent of the restaurants, canteens, hotels, school and hospital kitchens and food factories in England and Wales pose a 'significant and imminent' health risk to the public (*Daily Telegraph* 25/6/90). Food poisoning is not only extremely unpleasant to experience, but also has an economic impact. *The Times* (5/9/85), for example, cites an estimate that it cost over 23 million working days per annum.

Food is not of course the only dangerous product which can harm consumers and before completing this section on crimes against consumers, mention must be made of the serious impact of unsafe goods. Indeed the production and illegal international trade in goods and drugs which fail to conform to safety standards is in itself a major form of organized white collar crime (see, for example, Braithwaite 1984a; Box 1987). Children can be the victims of unsafe toys, as revealed in the many revelations around Christmas time of the hidden dangers of cheap and attractive toys (see for example *Which?* January 1986). Serious injuries and death can also result from the use of inadequately tested drugs. While many of the most serious instances have not led to prosecution, falsifying test results contributed to the Thalidomide tragedy (Box 1983; Braithwaite 1984a) and played a major part in the aggressive selling strategies for the Dalkon Shield contraceptive device which killed several women, left many childless and caused enormous suffering to countless others (Perry and Dawson 1985). In addition to the physical suffering caused by these cases, the high cost to the Health Service of dealing with resultant injuries and illnesses is another of the rippling effects of this form of organizational crime.

Employee and public safety

Neglect of safety regulations not only endangers consumers, but also threatens the lives of employees and the public in general. These effects have recently been highlighted by a number of accidents and disasters which have resulted in the death of workers and passengers. These have subsequently been found to have been avoidable, being caused by a neglect of and failure to prioritize safety precautions. Yet there are few prosecutions for these kinds of offences. Table 2.1 records that in 1988 a mere 302 men, 16 women and 741 companies were convicted under Health and Safety at Work legislation. Yet again, the small number of prosecutions reflects the compliance strategies of enforcers. Writers from Carson (1971) onwards have found that only a very small proportion of detected violations of safety regulations result in prosecutions and that even violations which have led to injuries may escape prosecution. In addition, the Health and Safety Executive, in common with many other regulatory agencies has had its resources reduced, meaning that fewer enforcement officers are responsible for more workplaces (Tombs 1990).

Other indicators of the neglect of safety regulations are the often alarming statistics on workplace accidents, injuries and deaths, many of which are the result of violations, although clearly not all are so caused. None the less, the high toll of industrial accidents does cause considerable concern. It has been calculated, for example, that workers are seven times more likely to be killed at work than by homicide (Box 1983) and accident rates have risen in recent years. Tombs (1990), for example, indicates that between 1981 and 1985 there was an increase of around 30 per cent in the rates of fatal and major injuries reported to enforcement authorities in manufacturing industries. Some indication of the association between accidents and the neglect of regulations can be found in the reports of the Health and Safety Executive which indicate that a sizeable proportion do result from offences and can be blamed on management. Reviewing these reports, Pearce and Tombs (1990: 426) conclude that:

> in at least two out of three fatal accidents, managements were in violation of the Health and Safety at Work Act 1974 in terms of their general duties to employees.

Similarly, Bergman (1990a: 1108) comments that:

> the HSE is replete with reports concluding that about three-quarters of deaths at the workplace are the fault of management.

Violations of safety regulations are therefore widespread and more common in some industries than others, in particular the construction industry. Most recently, the building of the Channel Tunnel has been associated with the death of seven workers (Bergman 1990a). Another particularly hazardous undertaking is the extraction of oil from the North Sea. Carson (1981) found that many fatalities, often attributed to the inherent dangers of working on the 'frontiers of technology', in fact resulted from routine breaches of safety regulations. Inattention to safety regulations also affects the public at large and especially passengers. Recent transport accidents and the ensuing legal inquiries and trials have highlighted the many problems of attributing blame and responsibility for accidents along with the complex issues involved in corporate manslaughter (see, for example, Wells 1988; Bergman 1990b).

Pollution

No list of corporate and organizational crime would be complete without mentioning the enormous costs of pollution, which threatens many sectors of the public who can be harmed by noxious emissions from factories, by chemicals in water supplies, or by the pollution of beaches and rivers. Pollution also damages the environment and kills wildlife. As with all the offences examined in this chapter, the scope of the problem is not reflected in prosecutions, and pollution is not even counted separately in official statistics. Table 2.1 reveals that a total of 660 men, 59 women and 399 companies were convicted in 1988 under Public Health legislation, which includes many offences other than pollution, and includes food hygiene offences. Other available data include the statistics of the Water Authorities reported in *Social Trends* (1989), which record that of 20,639 incidents reported in which pollution was found, a mere 318 prosecutions were undertaken, over half of which involved farm waste. This would appear to reflect increasing concern about the disposal of silage and slurry, which led to an increase of 27 per cent in prosecutions between 1986 and 1987, although the number of incidents has increased by only five per cent (*Social Trends* 1989: 158). More recently, new legislation is expected to produce more prosecutions, with at least five of the ten new water companies facing a possible total of 169 prosecutions for sewage dumping (*The Guardian* 11/10/90; *The Times* 11/10/90).

Studies of the many bodies responsible for the enforcement of aspects of Pollution Legislation reveal that they operate in a similar way to other enforcers (Richardson *et al.* 1982; Hawkins 1984). They face resource constraints and offences are difficult to detect, leading to a situation in which few offenders are prosecuted. Indeed the prosecutions of water companies are not necessarily of the worst polluters as a further 800 sewage works were, in 1989, dealt with by a relaxation of 'pollution consents' in return for promises to make improvements (*The Times* 11/10/90).

A few examples indicate the potentially enormous impact of pollution. Recently, much publicity has been generated by the unhealthy state of beaches throughout Britain and the possible prosecution of Local Authorities under EC regulations. These concerns were fuelled by revelations that children bathing from Blackpool were more than five times likely to be affected by diarrhoea and three times more likely to suffer from vomiting than children who played on the beach and did not go into the water. Affected children also suffered from itchy skin, fever, lack of energy and loss of appetite (*Independent* 28/1/91). In one of the most dramatic cases in recent years the South West Water Authority was prosecuted following the contamination of drinking water at Camelford, where aluminium sulphate entered the water supply after a driver had discharged his load into the wrong tank. A total of 500,000 fish were said to have been killed and many consumers complained of skin rashes, nausea and vomiting, and even brain damage (*The Times* 9/1/91; *The Guardian* 8/1/91). Noise pollution, littering and illegally dumping rubbish are other concerns covered by pollution legislation, in addition to illegal seepages of sewage and industrial waste into waterways and rivers.

Summary and discussion

These examples are necessarily selective. To the seemingly endless list of frauds and deceptive practices could be added the offences of professions, and the malpractices and corruption which take place in many public organizations, in the health service, the police force (Box 1983) or in Local and National Government (Doig 1984). International and cross-border frauds are also an increasing problem (Van Duyne 1991; Van Duyne and Levi 1991) as are the many frauds perpetrated on the institutions of the European Economic Community (Leigh 1980; Nelken and Passas 1991). In 1988, for example, reported frauds in connection with Agricultural Subsidies involved 120,315 million ECU, an amount which is generally felt to be an underestimate (Nelken and Passas 1991). The effects of unsafe consumer goods and pollution have only been touched upon, and to all the deaths, injuries and diseases caused by corporate crime could be added the effects of the Bhopal and Seveso tragedies. Pharmaceutical companies take advantage of the more lenient regulations in third world countries to market drugs and devices banned in Western countries with predictably disastrous results (Braithwaite 1984; Perry and Dawson 1985), manufacturers dump unsafe goods banned in one country into others (Box 1987), and the whole issue of toxic waste dumping is yet another problem which has also been found to involve organized crime (Van Duyne 1991; Levi 1991c).

No attempt has been made to estimate or even guesstimate the total amounts or costs of white collar crime in either financial or human terms, or to compare this with conventional crime, as both are equally as unmeasurable. According to Braithwaite and Pettit (1990: 186):

> there can never be a systematic comparison of the volume of white collar crime with that of common crime.

What is clear is that official figures grossly under-represent the real amount of both occupational or organizational crime. Much white collar crime remains undetected or unprosecuted, and it is also clear that its impact, both in physical and economic terms, is huge. Most citizens are probably multiple victims, however unaware they may be. Braithwaite and Pettit (1990: 186), considering whether or not it is reasonable to infer that white collar crime is more prevalent than conventional crime conclude:

> we think that the inference, even in the absence of systematic data, is not only plausible, but overwhelming.

From the examples given it is also clear that many offences are commonplace and widely tolerated in many occupational groups, from the shop floor subcultures in which pilfering is perceived to be a legitimate reward of work to the city wine bars where insider dealing is seen as a normal part of capitalist activity. This tolerance, and the moral ambivalence which surrounds many offences, is a major reason why they are not defined as 'crime' by victims and perpetrators alike. It has been seen over and over again that there is an extremely thin line dividing so called normal trading, selling and commercial practices from fraud and deception, and that there is a gap between social and legal constructions of crime. All of this has many implications for the analysis and regulation of white collar crime which will be explored in subsequent chapters.

3

WHO ARE THE CRIMINALS?

It has been seen that white collar crime tends to be associated with rich, wealthy and elite offenders, and corporate crime with the offences of the large, powerful corporation. However, it has also been argued that essentially similar offences can be perpetrated by high and low status employees, and that the status of the offenders should not be part of the definition of offences but should rather be empirically established. Exploring the class or status of even convicted offenders is, however, no easy task. There may be little consensus over what indicators of either status or class should be used, and many terms such as rich, powerful, elite or wealthy are often used somewhat loosely. In any case, official sources of information give few indications from which the social or occupational status of offenders can be inferred, and it cannot be assumed that all offenders in white collar crime categories are necessarily of high occupational or social status. Neither can it be assumed that the companies who constitute the 'other' category are the 'corporations' often associated with organizational or corporate crime. Companies may be large or small, supermarket chains or corner shops. As will be seen, the indications from the few researches which have looked at the social status of offenders is that they are drawn from a broad social spectrum (Croall 1989).

However, convicted offenders are not necessarily typical. Indeed, it has been argued that the high status of offenders in itself contributes to their relative immunity to prosecution. On the other hand, it could be argued that the rich and powerful do not need to commit offences and may have considerably more to lose if they are caught. Few corporations, for example, can be indifferent to the damaging effects of revelations that their inattention to safety has placed the lives of passengers, consumers or their own employees in danger. Therefore, high status executives or large corporations might avoid law breaking. This chapter will examine the rather sparse data on the status of offenders, and explore the questions raised by such an examination.

Blue collar and white collar crime

A possible objection to broadening the definition of white collar crime to include essentially all occupational crime is that the category then includes both 'blue collar' and 'white collar crime'. However, these terms, apart from nowadays being somewhat outdated, are extremely loose and difficult to define – where, for example, does blue collar stop and white collar begin? None the less, they retain a symbolic significance and are commonly used. Thus the term 'blue collar crime' tends to be associated with the offences of low status employees (Clarke 1990) and the term white collar crime with fraud, embezzlement and other offences associated with high status employees. This association has been reinforced by the many studies of fiddling and pilfering on the part of manual workers such as bread salesmen (Ditton 1977) or waiters (Mars 1973; Mars and Nicod 1984). In comparison we know little about the existence of or subcultural norms surrounding 'fiddling' higher up the occupational ladder. Employees at all levels of the occupational hierarchy have the opportunity to abuse or exploit aspects of their occupational roles, ranging from the seemingly trivial abuse of employers' telephones or computers, to more profitable and organized activities which are more readily definable as 'criminal'. Theoretically therefore it can be assumed that, given suitable opportunities, all kinds of occupational crime can be perpetrated by employees at all levels.

The millions of pounds involved in more serious and publicized frauds reinforces the image of fraudsters as high status offenders. However, as was seen in Chapter 2, categories of fraud encompass an enormous variety of both offences and offenders. One recent study for example concludes that:

> most frauds taken to court would be depicted more accurately as 'blue collar crime', being committed by people of modest social origin. (Levi and Pithouse 1989: 4)

While it is difficult to estimate exactly what proportion of frauds are committed by high or low status offenders, there are strong indications that while the frauds of high status offenders may involve the greatest amounts of money, reported frauds involve both junior and senior employees. In his survey of organizational victims, Levi (1988: 4) found that 73.8 per cent of reported frauds were attributable to employees, of which 29 per cent were attributed to managers and 19 per cent to accounts officials. A further 9.7 per cent were attributed to directors or partners. Lower level employees were responsible for the rest with salespersons and shopfloor operatives accounting for 12.9 per cent, computer operatives for 3.2 per cent and distributors and drivers for a further 6.5 per cent.

Frauds associated with financial dealings and institutions, while rarely prosecuted, might be expected to involve more high status offenders, and to include members of the financial elite or establishment, however defined. Certainly, many offenders need to be affluent to participate in such frauds, but this may not always be associated with social class or status. Levi (1987a) indeed suggests that prosecutions tend to involve 'mavericks' rather than 'elite insiders' or 'establishment' figures, claiming that between the Second World War and 1987, apart from one isolated exception, no elite insiders have been prosecuted for fraud. While some might quibble with his definition, as he dismisses the notorious cases of Lord Kagan, John Stonehouse and Jim Slater as not involving 'establishment men', it makes the point that even in an area assumed to be the preserve of the rich and powerful, they by no means dominate prosecutions. The celebrated 'Guinness four' might appear to be exceptions to this, as they were undoubtedly wealthy – one defendant was reported to be the fifteenth richest man in Britain – and mixed in elite circles. However, even these defendants were not all unambiguously 'establishment' figures in the conventionally accepted sense. While one defendant had been to Oxbridge, and another was from an affluent background, the two others have been described as 'classic self-made entrepreneurs', representing 'new money' and the 'much vaunted Thatcherite enterprise culture' (Levi 1991b). In other areas of fraud the businesses involved are hardly the most prestigious. Many insurance frauds occur in the motor trade, where inflated claims are regularly made following accidents. Businesses who resort to arson are likely to be small businesses with a history of problems and current financial difficulties, often from the garment and fabric trades (Clarke 1989).

The small number of prosecutions and absence of research makes it difficult to explore whether these observations apply to other groups of offenders. Some offences by their very nature appear to involve wealthy offenders – for example, out of thirteen prosecutions for insider dealing, ten offenders are described as 'brokers and other professionals in the securities industry', others being wives, relatives and other professionals (Naylor 1990: 4). Inspectors who were interviewed by Naylor described three main categories of insider dealers. First, there are highly sophisticated rings of professionals dealing with trust and personal portfolio management who trade inside information amongst themselves. These are the most difficult to detect and their numbers difficult to estimate. The second group consists of opportunist offenders, most likely to be heads of family firms who stumble on usable information. Finally, there are those described as professionals, largely corporate officers, outside accountants, lawyers and investment bankers who actively pursue inside information on behalf of a company. These descriptions seem to indicate high status and respectability but again they may not be, in Levi's terms, 'establishment figures'. Indeed, the broadening social base of those involved in the financial services market has been identified as one of the factors underlying arguments for tougher regulatory controls (Clarke 1986).

Research in other countries also reveals that offenders cannot always be described as high status. In the United States, where it is accepted that more white collar criminals do conform to the conventional stereotype (Levi 1987a), research reveals that many offenders are in fact of relatively low status. For example, Hagan *et al.* (1980: 809) found that:

> in none of the districts does the prosecution of white collar crimes predominantly involve what might conventionally be regarded as white collar persons.

In Ontario, Hagan (1988) divided all offenders referred for prosecution for securities violations between 1966 and 1983 into categories using class as opposed to status indicators. 27.09 per cent of offenders are described as employers, 19.7 per cent as managers, 9.36 per cent as petty bourgeoisie – defined as those working in the legitimate sector and owning a business, but with no employees – and 43.85 per cent as workers – located in either the illegitimate or legitimate sector. Thus employers and managers formed a minority of offenders, although the scope of their offending was greater.

It was seen in Chapter 2 that opportunities for tax offences are spread throughout the occupational hierarchy and that many prosecutions involve low rather than high status offenders. Cook (1989a) identifies five occupational categories in which distinctive techniques of fiddling are found – the building trade, the 'one man band' and small commercial traders, auction and street market traders, the hotel and catering trade, and highly paid employees, directors and professionals. These techniques included moonlighting, ghosting, subcontractor frauds and fiddles associated with the construction industry, fiddling expenses, allowances and benefits in kind and fiddling accounts. Tax evasion provides an excellent example of how different patterns of offending are strongly associated with the 'alternative opportunity structures' associated with different kinds of occupations, which cross-cut class or status boundaries. Thus, doctors, lawyers, academics and journalists may engage in essentially similar activities to builders, plumbers and electricians.

While information about the social status of offenders is far from satisfactory, it is evident from research that employees at all levels of the occupational hierarchy are found amongst offenders. While this may be hardly surprising when the definition of white collar crime incorporates most occupational crimes, it is, none the less, significant that such a diversity of offenders is encountered among offence categories normally associated with white as opposed to blue collar crime, such as fraud and tax evasion. Even when offences assumed to involve wealthy and establishment figures are closely examined, less wealthy and 'maverick' figures appear likely to dominate the ranks of those prosecuted, however much the media may focus on the 'fall from grace' of the rich and famous.

The myth of the corporate criminal?

Corporate crime is often portrayed as involving the large and powerful corporation, prioritizing profits and neglecting the interests of powerless workers or consumers. However, the consumer can be misled by the corner shop or the large supermarket, poisoned by the local fish and chip shop or by the local branch of a multi national chain of five-star hotels. Employees can be killed on small building sites as well as in the Chunnel, and rivers can be polluted by small farms or large oil companies. What is often known as corporate crime therefore can equally well be small business crime.

Studies which have examined the enforcement of many business regulatory statutes indicate that enforcers are concerned as much, if not more, with small traders and manufacturers than with large corporations. Research into the work of Consumer Protection Departments and Environmental Health Officers, for example, reveals that butchers, bakers, coal merchants, second-hand car dealers and small building firms feature strongly among the businesses where problems are found (Cranston 1979; Hutter 1988).

In the author's research (Croall 1988, 1989), smaller businesses in fact constituted the majority of those prosecuted. In around half of fifty cases observed in court under consumer protection legislation, offenders were described as companies. Many were small concerns, owned and run by one individual, often with very few employees. Sufficient details were available in court to further distinguish medium sized companies, which had more than one outlet but which operated primarily on a local or regional level, and large corporations who operated at the national or even international level. Often these latter were household names. Only nine cases involved these large companies. Six cases involved medium-sized companies, and a total of 33 out of 57 defendants represented small businesses, some being prosecuted as companies, and others being proprietors or individual traders. A further 12 offenders were employees and managers. The term 'manager' normally referred to individual branch managers of supermarkets or other multiple retail outlets (Croall 1987, 1989). A similar distribution of offenders was also found in the case files of enforcement departments.

The largest single group of offenders was made up of restaurants prosecuted under food hygiene regulations, followed by a variety of food stores, bakeries, bars and butchers. Other studies have noted a predominance of garages and coal merchants among those prosecuted (Cranston 1979). Large companies could be prosecuted under many statutes but were most likely to appear as manufacturers of food containing foreign bodies, or owners of restaurant and hotel chains. Many small business proprietors were from ethnic minorities. Fifteen individual offenders or small business proprietors were Asian, and fifteen English. Hutter (1988) also reports that many offenders were from ethnic groups and specialist journals confirm that ethnic businesses feature strongly among those prosecuted (*British Food Journal* Mar/April 1984).

Some offenders came from what could more properly be described as 'criminal businesses' (McIntosh 1974). As was seen in Chapter 2, offenders involved in the meat rackets ran businesses primarily set up to pass unfit, illegally slaughtered and other unacceptable meat into the legitimate food chain, and this has also been noted in the Netherlands (Van Duyne 1991; Van Duyne and Levi 1991). Their activities are therefore closer to organized crime, and the police as well as Environmental Health Officers were involved in investigations (Croall 1987). Other offenders could be readily described as 'shady operators' (Sutton and Wild 1985), such as market traders selling falsely described or counterfeit goods. The borderline between white collar and organized crime, between business crime and criminal business is often therefore somewhat blurred, which has led to use of the term 'enterprise' crime (Van Duyne and Levi 1991).

Employees, from barmaids and waiters to branch managers, may also be prosecuted for consumer crimes, and occasionally both employees and companies were prosecuted for the same offence. Both legally and morally, companies sought to pass the blame for offences to other employees (see Chapter 6). In some cases offences resulted from employee fiddles, where for example, short measure or watered down drinks are served to consumers. Other companies often attribute production problems to sabotage by disgruntled employees (Croall 1989). While ultimately it may be the company's responsibility to ensure that these incidents do not happen, in some cases companies may be unable to prevent them and their excuses may have some basis (Clinard and Yeager 1980). This means that any clear cut distinction between what is generally seen as occupational or employee crime and corporate crime is difficult to make empirically. As will be seen in Chapter 4, organizational systems and the social organization of work may be associated with many organizational offences.

Other studies of regulatory enforcement have also noted a proliferation of small business offenders. While few give details of the types of establishments prosecuted, the descriptions given of businesses by enforcement officials reveal that many offenders are small traders. Officers describe some kinds of businesses as more likely to be 'rogues' or 'cowboys', a term more often used to describe small businesses. Nelken (1983), similarly found that small residential landlords were more likely to be prosecuted for illegal eviction. In the United States, while research has often focused on large corporations, some studies reveal the significance of small business offending. Leonard and Weber (1977) found car repair frauds to be more prevalent among smaller operators, and Rothschild and Throne (1976) describe criminal consumer fraud as a product of 'fly by night' operations and 'shaky businesses'. In Australia, Sutton and Wild (1985) indicate that for both environmental and consumer complaints, large corporations form a minority of offenders, with smaller and medium sized firms predominating. Indeed, they argue that

> when prosecutions are compared with estimates in actual numbers and types of enterprises operating in the Australian economy, they seem to suggest that the larger a company becomes, the more likely it is to be law-abiding. (Sutton and Wild 1985: 249)

Thus, many offenders in offence categories normally associated with corporate crime are likely to be small companies and individual proprietors of small businesses – in class terms the petit bourgeoisie (Hagan 1988). Others are virtually indistinguishable from what might be called professional criminals – and many such businesses operate at the margins of the irregular economy. However, to dismiss small business offending as the product of 'shady operators' or 'fly by night' illegitimate business is to deny its significance and likely persistence (Sutton and Wild 1985). In addition, not all small business offenders are shady operators. Second-hand car dealers, while attracting a negative stereotype (Braithwaite 1989), are none the less engaged in primarily legitimate businesses.

It might readily be objected that many of these studies have looked primarily at convicted offenders who are likely to be a far from typical group, and may be partly selected by enforcement officers as easier targets for detection and prosecution. It has to be asked therefore whether and to what extent high status offenders are able to avoid the detection and prosecution of their offences.

Selective enforcement

Analyses of policing suggest that young, lower class, unemployed males are more likely to be stopped, searched or arrested partly because they are more likely to be subject to police surveillance, and thereby become 'police property' (see for example Reiner 1985; Smith and Gray 1985). In contrast, white collar offences take place in private, offenders are not subject to intense surveillance and offences are difficult to detect. However, the contrast between the policing of conventional crimes and the law enforcement process characteristic of white collar crime can be overdrawn. Regulatory enforcement officers and the police alike operate with high amounts of discretion and face resource constraints. They both have to prioritize particular offences or areas for attention, and may concentrate on offences which are easier to detect and less costly to prosecute. While law enforcement will be examined in more detail in Chapter 5, this section will consider the extent to which particular groups may be relatively vulnerable to detection and prosecution.

It is perhaps obvious that if offences are clearly visible, they are more likely to be detected and if offenders are regularly encountered by enforcers, they may be more likely to be investigated. The presence in larger numbers of lower class, unemployed and black youth 'on the streets', means that they are there to be stopped, searched and arrested (Smith and Gray 1985; Reiner 1985). This can also be the case with many white collar offences. When carrying out their inspection functions, enforcers are very much like 'bobbies on the beat' (Cranston 1979), and may be drawn to high street and corner shops and especially to market stalls and street vendors, whose offences are, literally, 'street crime'. Environmental Health Officers, for example, report that their attention can be alerted by immediately recognizable breaches of regulations. These could include the height of fruit boxes off the ground, misleading price indications, visibly unsafe building work or even a 'bad smell' (Hutter 1986; Croall 1989). Further inspection may reveal more serious violations. On the other hand, large manufacturers or employers generally do not carry out their business in the public eye and inspection of premises is often by prior arrangement.

Similar considerations could affect offences within organizations. While fraud by its very nature is often not obvious, the activities of the less skilful and especially the incompetent fraudster may be more obvious. The more complex the fraud, the more difficult it is to unravel. Senior employees are generally trusted more and probably have more opportunity to cover up their offences, whereas lower level employees are more subject to immediate surveillance (Scraton and South 1984). Clarke (1989: 15) found that the insurance frauds of amateurs are easier to detect, as they are more likely to contradict themselves in their account of events and more often produce evidently false documentation. Indeed, he comments that 'one wonders whether it is only the incompetent fraudsters who are detected.' The professional fraudster, in particular the professional arsonist, is more likely to employ lawyers and accountants to ensure that documentation is in order. The more serious forms of insider trading are also more difficult to detect. Generally, the activities of amateur, one off, insider traders are easiest to detect, whereas very little is known about the activities of the rings of insider traders, who are largely made up of professional groups. In these cases, detection is largely dependant on information supplied by someone with personal knowledge of their activities. Detection and subsequent prosecution may take several years. Thus, it is hardly surprising that even enforcement agencies know little about the extent of such activities (Naylor 1990).

Like police, enforcement agencies involved in white collar crime develop stereotypes of likely offenders, and a knowledge of where offences are most likely to occur. Cranston (1979) found, for example, that secondhand car dealers were seen as rogues and along with coal merchants were perceived to be likely offenders. Officers interviewed in many researches give accounts of 'typical' offences and offenders in their area (Croall 1987), and often describe less respectable businesses in an area as 'rogues' or cowboys (see, for example, Richardson *et al.* 1982). Where officers associate particular groups of traders or businesses with offending they will inevitably subject these groups to more intensive inspection, and may be more likely to prosecute them (Chapter 5).

It has often been suggested that enforcers could be sympathetic to businesses whose proprietors and managers are their social equals or superiors. Hutter (1988) notes, for example, that fewer officers defined the activities of higher status offenders as 'crimes'. However, she also found that officers sympathized with many small businesses who were defined as respectable. In Britain at any rate there has been little evidence that enforcers are any more likely to be sympathetic towards larger concerns although they may treat them in a different way. Cranston (1979) for example, found that one consumer protection department only prosecuted large companies, whereas another fought shy of such prosecutions. In departments visited by the author, different approaches were used towards larger concerns. In one department, if one outlet of a chain of restaurants was found to have problems, all outlets would be visited. If they were found to be unsatisfactory, the company itself would be approached. If conditions showed no immediate improvement, the company would be prosecuted. This strategy did not imply leniency, nor did it appear to arise out of any sympathy. Indeed, officers could express considerable satisfaction when large companies were involved. One senior officer related with pride how he had confronted a well-known businessman, in his kitchen, about repeated violations of health and safety and food hygiene regulations. This department was also criticized by magistrates for the prosecution of several well-known establishments (Croall 1987, 1989).

While there is therefore little evidence that large companies are treated more sympathetically, they may be less likely to be prosecuted. Large companies and indeed wealthy individuals can and do use their considerable resources to prevent prosecution and, if prosecuted, to defend themselves. Consequently, prosecutions may be seen as more risky, particularly in view of the high costs of an unsuccessful prosecution. One senior officer interviewed by the author commented that officers were afraid of being 'grilled' in court by skilled barristers, and another department employed barristers to prosecute major cases involving large companies. Wealthy defendants may use accountants and lawyers specifically to prevent prosecution, particularly where investigations take a long time (Mann 1985; Levi 1987a). This may deter agencies from undertaking lengthy investigations where evidence is difficult to obtain. Other companies may attempt to lobby Local Authority council committees who approve all prosecutions (see

Croall 1987; Hutter 1988). Larger concerns may also be better placed to negotiate out of court settlements. Within organizations some employees may be able to bargain with employers, as they may be able to offer information leading to the detection of other offences (Shapiro 1990). In addition, companies may be more unwilling to prosecute senior employees, as more loss of face might be involved, whereas they may be more willing to prosecute manual workers.

The high cost of detection and prosecution may also protect corporate or high status offenders. Major international frauds and the operations of large multi-national corporations are more costly to investigate, especially in situations where the individuals or corporations concerned have something to hide and refuse to co-operate. Therefore, agencies may focus their attention on offences which are less complex and costly to investigate (see Chapter 5). Levi (1987a: 174), for example, comments that in the Fraud Squad, 'the task of senior allocating officers is to try to judge which cases are most likely to "produce a result"'. This may lead to the neglect of particularly complex cases and international frauds. The Inland Revenue also may be more likely to concentrate its limited resources on particular occupational groups like builders, where offences are assumed to be widespread, and where detection and prosecution are less costly (Cook 1989a).

It could be argued therefore that the frauds of more senior executives or the regulatory offences of large corporations may be less likely to be reported or detected. High status or corporate offenders may also be less likely to be prosecuted. In Canada, for example, Hagan (1988) found that employers were less likely to be prosecuted under the criminal code, as a result of their power and influence over enforcers, the complexity of their offences and the costs of prosecution. Thus, it is very likely that selective enforcement does lead to some under-representation of the crimes of larger concerns and the offences of high status offenders amongst convictions, despite the fact that their crimes may be more serious.

Do high status executives and corporations need to break the law?

It could also be argued that the relatively small number of convictions involving high status and corporate offenders could reflect a lower rate of offending on their part. Analyses of conventional crime suggest, for example, that while the greater vulnerability of young working class males to police attention and prosecution may produce disproportionate amounts of these groups in court and prison, these groups are also more likely to commit street crimes (Lea and Young 1984). Therefore, the possibility that high status or corporate offenders are less likely to commit 'suite' crimes must be examined. There are indeed strong arguments that they may be better placed to use their resources to prevent and avoid not only detection but also law breaking.

In the first place, establishment figures and large corporations may not wish or need to break the law (Levi 1987a: 255). They may not need to offend as they already have considerable wealth or may not want to offend because they have more to lose if they are caught. For the high status executive, loss of status, prestige, reputation, income and life style are real considerations (Levi 1987a). For the corporation, prosecutions can lead to a loss of reputation, loss of sales and low morale amongst employees (Braithwaite 1989). Some corporate offences may indeed result in economic loss rather than increased profits. Clarke (1989) points out, for example, that it is more likely to be smaller companies in shaky financial positions who resort to arson as larger businesses have more to lose by a fire than they have to gain. In addition products may have to be recalled at considerable expense if they are found to be unsafe (Braithwaite 1984a). Naylor (1990: 54) suggests that professional insider dealers have been deterred by the criminalization of insider dealing.

Larger and more successful businesses also have more resources at their disposal to prevent offences occurring in the first place, and to ensure that they are not held liable for the offences of their employees. In many business regulatory statutes, a defence is provided if a company can establish that it has instituted 'systems' for preventing the occurrence of offences (Cranston 1984; Croall 1988). These include quality control systems, the use of technological 'scanners' in food production, computerized pricing systems, and arrangements for instructing managers about the information which they must provide about products. These systems require both capital investment and the employment of professional personnel. All these resources are more likely to be available to large businesses who are more likely to have appropriate quality control, legal and accounting departments along with appropriate professional staff.

Smaller, less successful businesses have fewer systems and are less able to afford professional advice. This can be seen most clearly in the example of very small businesses and individual retail outlets. Individual traders may be ignorant of the precise details of regulations. Written instructions to staff about pricing, stock rotation or checking goods for damage would be inappropriate in smaller concerns, whereas it is the existence of a system of written instructions which enables large concerns to avoid liability for the offences of their staff. The small manufacturer may also not be able to afford sophisticated scanning machinery to check the quality of goods. Where food hygiene and health and safety offences are involved, small premises may be old and ill suited to the purposes for which they are being used. Structural alterations may be necessary to improve compliance but many small businesses may simply not possess the necessary capital (Croall 1987, 1989; Hutter 1988). Small retail concerns are also more likely to purchase goods from the local cash and carry, which, according to Environmental Health Officers may result in the purchase of substandard stock (Croall 1987). These considerations are closely related to the different market positions of small and large concerns. Especially in times of recession smaller businesses are more likely to be engaged in a 'struggle for survival' which may create pressures which make law breaking a more likely and rational response (Box 1987; see Chapter 4).

This is not to argue that large concerns are necessarily more 'socially responsible' as the same resources that can be used to prevent breaking the law can also be used to evade it (Box 1987). Thus, both rich business executives and large organizations can use both their financial resources and professional expertise to comply with the letter of law but at the same time to engage in activities which quite evidently contravene its spirit. Nelken (1983), for example, found that it was mainly small landlords who were prosecuted for offences involving the harassment of tenants. Large landlords were relatively immune from the effect of the law because they could use their greater resources to vet tenants, and to pay tenants large sums of money to vacate their properties, a practice known as 'winkling'. They could also afford to carry out structural alterations to premises which justified increasing rents to amounts which tenants could not pay. Large landlords therefore did not need to use illegal tactics to evict tenants.

Laws can also be manipulated as seen in the example of taxation, where lawyers, accountants and financial advisers are employed specifically to advise wealthy clients how to avoid paying taxes without resorting to illegal evasion (McBarnet 1987, 1988). It has already been seen that there are ambiguities and loopholes in many laws, and many instances where the law regulates one practice which is then replaced by another similar practice. Large food manufacturers, for example, can use their considerable technological and scientific resources to develop new and more complex ways to reduce the amounts of 'real' food in food products, and to increase the use of additives, water and other substitutes, practices often described as 'legalized' adulteration (Cannon and Walker 1985; Croall 1987; see Chapter 8). Drug manufacturers may continue to sell dangerous drugs in third world countries, whose regulations are less severe (Braithwaite 1984a; Box 1987). Thus,

> corporations facing contraction in industrialised countries are able to avoid breaking the law by acting immorally and exporting their 'illegal' behaviour to where it is legal. (Box 1987: 55)

There are convincing arguments therefore that large successful corporations and top executives may be less likely to commit offences as they have less need to offend and can pursue their goals legally. As Box (1987: 55) argues, 'corporate crime need not occur', as the superior resources of large organizations can be used both to prevent offending and evade the law.

Summary and discussion

White collar crime therefore cannot automatically be assumed to be the preserve of the rich and powerful. Employees at all levels of the occupational hierarchy have many opportunities to abuse their occupational roles, and both large and small businesses can indulge in many dangerous and deceitful activities. Examination of the occupational or social status of convicted offenders fails to expose the widespread criminality of elite groups, high status executives or large multinational corporations, however loosely defined these terms may be. Instead, the offences of butchers, bakers, restaurateurs, porters, manual workers and small businesses are found to be equally, if not more prevalent. While it is likely that high status and corporate offenders may be more immune to detection and prosecution, at the same time there are structural factors which make them better able to avoid breaking the law. This may not arise from superior morality or social responsibility, but from the use of their considerable resources to remain on the right side of the law.

This has profound significance for many of the issues raised in analyses of white collar crime. It adds strength, for example, to the arguments outlined in Chapter 1 that the definition of offences should be separated from the status of offenders. It also challenges analyses which, assuming that offenders are by definition high status, attribute the special status of white collar crime to the class of offenders, and assume that the apparently favourable treatment which offences and offenders receive in the criminal justice process results from class bias. This is not to deny that issues of class status and power are important in exploring these issues, and these will be major themes of subsequent chapters. However, the high status or power of offenders cannot be taken for granted and analyses of white collar crime must take the social heterogeneity of offenders into account.

4

UNDERSTANDING WHITE COLLAR CRIME

It has already been indicated that much research and analysis of white collar crime has focused on law and its enforcement rather than on attempts to explain patterns of offending. There are, for example, very few studies of the attitudes and motivations of fraudsters, the subcultures of insider dealers, or the attitudes to health and safety amongst corporate executives. In addition as was seen in Chapter 1, theoretical perspectives on crime and deviance have tended to neglect white collar crime. Sutherland, attempting to correct this, advanced his own theory of crime, which was applicable to both white collar and conventional crime. Criminality, he argued, was learned in association with other offenders, and resulted from an excess of criminal definitions over non-criminal ones (Sutherland 1949). Despite some attempts to apply this theory of differential association to white collar and conventional crime, it has now been largely superseded, being dismissed by one noted commentator as a theory whose 'generality borders on a platitudinous restatement of social learning theory' (Braithwaite 1985: 3).

Popular analyses, which assume the high status of offenders, often portray offences as motivated by greed rather than need, a motivation supported by the selfishness and individualism inherent in the values of capitalist society. This association with the values of capitalism is also used to interpret corporate crime, often seen as representing the self-seeking prioritization of profits over the requirements of legislation which protects the interests of consumers, workers or the public in general. Sweeping though these generalizations may be, they can provide a starting point for analysis, and are paralleled in many sociological perspectives on crime and deviance. To some, the conflict between profit goals and the public interest indicates the potential value of anomie or strain theory (Box 1983, 1987; Passas 1990), and it has already been seen that many offences are culturally and subculturally tolerated.

A broadly similar range of approaches can be applied to the study of white collar and conventional crime, focusing on individual offenders, cultures, subcultures and the social structure. As offences occur within occupations and organizations, attention is also drawn to the social organization of work (Shapiro 1990) and to organizational structures, some of which have been described as criminogenic. This chapter will begin by looking at individual offenders, followed by an exploration of the illegitimate opportunity structures found in different occupations and organizations. The significance of organizational structures and cultures will then be discussed, followed by an examination of some of the arguments relating white collar crime to cultural values. Finally, the relationship between crime, business and the wider political and economic environment will be explored.

Rotten apples in the barrel?

Early criminological theorists focused almost entirely on the individual offender and attempted to associate criminality with a variety of biological and psychological pathologies, personality traits, and the adverse effects of environmental and social conditions. Individual offenders were compared with non-offenders in an attempt to isolate what made some individuals criminal and others not. This was a major reason why Sutherland felt they were inapplicable to white collar crime. Thus he argued, those suggesting a link between personal pathology and crime,

> would suggest only in a jocular sense that the crimes of the Ford Motor Company are due to the Oedipus Complex, or those of the Aluminum Company of America to an Inferiority Complex, or those of the U.S. Steel Corporation to Frustration and Agression, or those of Du Pont to Traumatic Experience, or those of Montgomery Ward to Regression to Infancy. (Sutherland 1949: 257–8)

In addition as white collar crime has tended to be interpreted as economically rational behaviour, it is not easily explained by irrational impulses or personality problems.

None the less, there is a tendency in popular accounts and official reports to individualize white collar crime, and to attribute it to the personality traits or personal problems of individual offenders. Doig (1984), for example, notes that official reports on corruption tend to blame the 'rotten apples in the barrel', a phrase which, by placing the blame on individuals within an organization, diverts attention away from ethical standards and the organization itself. There have also been attempts to discover what, if any, characteristics distinguish these 'rotten apples'. Assuming, as Box (1983: 38) does, that 'the vast bulk of corporate crime is initiated (if not always implemented) by high ranking officials', the majority of these approaches have focused on middle to senior executives. Some have linked the personality traits required for success in business to those associated with crime. Often quoted, for example, is Gross's (1978: 71) characterization of top executives as 'ambitious, shrewd and possessed of a non-demanding moral code'. Box argues that one of the consequences of success may be a lessening of the moral bind of conventional values. Success brings with it power and a sensation that everything and anything is possible, thus:

> numerous corporate executives, having already responded to the situational demands necessary for career mobility within an organization by displaying sufficient degrees of competitive ambition, shrewdness, and moral flexibility will experience a further development of these characteristics when they have to respond to the relatively unaccountable and unconstrained power of being at or near the top of a large national, but especially transnational corporation. They are then in a high state of preparedness to commit corporate crime should they perceive it as being necessary 'for the good of the company'. (Box 1983: 41)

But not all successful business executives resort to law breaking. Can those who do be distinguished from those who do not? Clinard (1983: 136–7), from interviews with middle management, associates a propensity to engage in 'unethical practices' with two distinct 'types' of managers. Some managers were seen to be more interested in financial prestige and quick profits in comparison with more technical or professional 'types'. 'Entrepreneurial' managers, who prioritize profit maximization were contrasted with 'fiduciary' managers who displayed a stronger ethical commitment to service. Finally, mobile executives, recruited into the corporation from the outside were described as more aggressive, interested in their own reputation and less concerned with the corporation's long-term reputation. In contrast, those promoted from the ranks tended to be more indoctrinated into the company's values and to show more loyalty. Those more likely to engage in unethical practices came from the financially orientated, entrepreneurial and mobile group.

While these observations are interesting, they are very generalized, and many amount to little more than what Box (1983) describes as 'Dallas type sketches'. In addition, the focus on successful high level executives takes for granted that offenders are drawn from the ranks of the successful, an assumption which, as seen in Chapter 3, can be questioned. It could equally well be argued that comparative failure, frustration or financial problems could provide the motivation for offences, as might a desire to improve career chances and to get to the top (Passas 1990). Cressey (1986), for example, suggests that embezzlement may originate in personal, non-shareable, financial problems. Therefore failure as well as success may be linked to offending.

Ultimately, a focus on the individual characteristics of offenders provides only a very partial view of criminality. Indeed it can divert attention from wider organizational or structural problems by 'emphasizing the rotten apple rather than the barrel' (Doig 1984: 383). White collar crime by its very nature is located within organizations and occupational roles. Thus Mars (1982) argues that while personality factors cannot be ignored, variants of personality must be seen in the context of the work situation which is a prerequisite for participation in fiddles. As Schraeger and Short (1977: 410) point out

> preoccupation with individuals can lead us to underestimate the pressures within society and organizational structures which impel those individuals to commit illegal acts . . . recognizing that structural forces influence the commission of these offences does not negate the importance of interaction between individuals and these forces, nor does it deny that individuals are involved in the commission of illegal organizational acts. It serves to emphasize *organizational* as opposed to *individual* etiological factors, and calls for a macrosociological rather than an individual level of explanation.

Criminal organizations?

The occupational nature of white collar crime raises the question of whether certain occupations or organizations are likely to be more crime prone than others. The language of the pathological approach can even be extended to organizations and corporate bodies. Hopkins (1980), for example, attributes offences to 'organizational defects' and the Sheen Inquiry following the Zeebrugge disaster stated that 'from top to bottom the body corporate was infected with the disease of sloppiness' (cited in Wells 1989: 934). BCCI was similarly described by the Governor of the Bank of England as 'rotten right through' (*Reuter* 23/7/91). This section will explore some of the characteristics of occupations and organizations which have been associated with offences.

Illegitimate opportunity structures

It is perhaps evident that potential offenders can only benefit given suitable opportunities. Employees can only profit economically if they have access to money, goods or other assets which can readily be misappropriated. These opportunities are in turn related to the way in which a particular occupation is organized, to levels of supervision and to the nature of the trust which exists between providers and consumers of services. These relationships constitute what is described as the social organization of work and the social organization of trust (Shapiro 1990). As Shapiro explains, 'trustees' (providers of goods and services or employees) are entrusted to carry out functions by 'principals' (clients or employers) – who are unable to supervise trustees or who may lack the appropriate expertise to judge their performance. Opportunities for trust violation derive from these basic arrangements.

Shapiro (1990: 350–2) further analyses the many and various opportunities open to trustees to exploit this trust. Theoretically, she argues, most offences can be reduced to lying and stealing. Most obviously employees can lie about the time they spend on jobs, claiming payment for more work than they have done, or can steal goods or money. However, lying can also be indirect, as for example, where relevant information is withheld – as would be the case in a cover-up. Those involved in marketing and advertising can lie indirectly through the skilful use of language and pictorial images to give a misleading impression of products or services. Stealing need not be restricted to goods or money, but can also, as has been seen, involve time or equipment. Given suitable opportunities, employees may also steal information which can be used for their personal benefit or which is saleable. Insider dealing, for example, amounts to the misappropriation of information obtained by virtue of a trusted position, subsequently misused for illegitimate gain (Shapiro 1990). Trustees can also allow others to benefit from their positions of trust – corruption for example can be interpreted as the selling of trust to outsiders for mutual benefit (Shapiro 1990).

Some occupations clearly provide more of these opportunities than others, and Mars (1982) categorizes occupations on the basis of the opportunities they provide for fiddling. 'Hawk' jobs, examples of which are sales and professional jobs, give workers a high amount of freedom and autonomy, producing many opportunities for systematic fiddling, as supervision is minimal. On the other hand the scope for fiddles is greatly reduced in 'donkey jobs', where workers have very little freedom, are closely supervised, and are isolated from colleagues – like, for example, the supermarket cashier. These jobs leave little scope for anything other than small amounts of individual cash fiddling or 'time fiddling' through day dreaming or absenteeism. 'Wolfpack' jobs rely on team work and, where goods or money are involved, provide opportunities for collective and highly organized fiddles. Dock work before containerization was an example of this kind of work and highly organized fiddles were prevalent. Finally, 'vulture' jobs are characterized by competition and uncertainty which is exploited by both management and workers to carry out collusive fiddles. This is the case in, for example, the hotel and catering industry.

Some occupations are particularly 'fiddle prone' (Mars 1982). For example, occupations which involve direct economic exchanges with 'passing trade', customers who are never likely to return, are particularly fiddle prone as no relationships between workers and consumers can be built up. Tourists, for example, are especially vulnerable to the fiddles of hotel and restaurant workers. Professional occupations are also highly fiddle prone as the client may be unable to determine the kind of service they need, let alone whether or not it has been provided. Similarly, the ignorance of customers makes car servicing and repairs especially fiddle prone, as consumers are assumed to be ignorant about which parts or services they need. Other fiddle prone jobs are those where employees act as gatekeepers between suppliers and consumers, as is literally the case with gatekeepers collecting money. Many jobs involve gatekeeping, which exists in situations where a third party introduces consumers to suppliers, acting as a mediator or broker. Those who are responsible for arranging contracts for Government and Local Authorities are gatekeepers, a situation which provides ample opportunities for corruption and bribery. Different jobs, therefore, provide different 'illegitimate opportunity structures'. However, clearly not all of these opportunities are exploited and whether they are or not may well be related to other aspects of the social organization of work.

Criminogenic organizations?

The assumed tendency of organizations to prioritize profitability has led to their being described as inherently criminogenic (Gross 1978). However, offences do not occur in all organizations and law breaking is not necessarily profitable. Braithwaite (1984a), for example, disputes that there is any conflict of interest between consumers and corporations, as customer satisfaction is ultimately associated with long-term profitability. Many corporations or large organizations may therefore try to avoid offending. None the less the conflict between goals of profits and compliance can be relevant. Writers attempting to apply anomie theory to the study of corporate crime argue, for example, that the conflicting demands of achieving production or sales targets and complying with regulations can create strains throughout large organizations (Box 1983; Passas 1990). Sales and marketing departments, for example, may find that pressures to increase sales may be so great that they might encourage or at least not discourage misleading advertising campaigns. Production departments may find that cutting corners on safety is necessitated by demands to maximize productivity.

These pressures can create conflict between departments, the outcome of which may depend on which department has more power. Therefore, the delegation of responsibilities within organizations can affect patterns of law breaking. Stone (1978), for example, describes an automobile plant where attempts to minimize quality defects were resisted if their implementation threatened to slow down production. In this way the short-term goals of production were placed above the long-term interests of the company. This makes the status of quality control departments in the company hierarchy crucial. Braithwaite (1984a), in his study of the pharmaceutical industry, suggests that pressure to cut corners is more likely where quality control managers are answerable directly to sales departments. If, on the other hand, quality control managers are answerable directly to the Board, by passing sales pressures, they may be able to operate more effectively. Thus, in industries where safety is essential, quality control departments must carry organizational 'clout'.

The role of legal departments is also important. Some American research, for example, suggests that lawyers can be isolated from other departments. Stone (1978) found that they could be seen as 'no men', frozen out and deprived of important information. Lawyers in organizations may also experience a conflict of interest between professional ethics and corporate goals, and some may prioritize the latter. Braithwaite (1984a) found that in some pharmaceutical companies the role of lawyers monitoring sales information became one of advising marketing staff 'what they can get away with'. McBarnet (1984) points to the significant role of lawyers in tax evasion, when they are employed to advise clients how to legally avoid paying taxes. Other organizational problems may involve staff supervision and the monitoring of sales departments. Hopkins (1980), studying companies convicted of trading offences, attributes offences to 'organizational defects'. The most common of these was a failure on the part of management to check the accuracy of promotional material. Other convicted companies paid insufficient attention to complaints or failed to give sales staff full information about products, encouraging them to invent information in sales pitches.

The diffusion of responsibility within organizations may also create a situation in which individual employees do not feel directly responsible for the consequences of their actions. Those working in a production department cutting corners on safety are likely to see this as a rational response to pressures from above. Therefore, individuals directly responsible for offences can quite justifiably argue that others were to blame and that the consequences are not their fault. Individual employees are therefore unlikely to suffer from a guilty conscience, which in itself may make rule breaking more likely (Braithwaite 1989). Classic instances of serious corporate offending reveal a complex web of interlocking responsibilities, and cover-ups at all levels which combine to conceal where responsibility ultimately lies. Thus, as Clinard and Yeager (1980) argue, the size, delegation and specialisms associated with large organizations can combine to produce an organizational climate favourable to the commission of illegalities.

This climate may depend on senior executives' attitudes to compliance and on the extent to which they are aware of what actually goes on in the organization (Clinard and Yeager 1980). Research so far has provided conflicting evidence about how far top management are implicated in offences and about how well informed they tend to be. Clinard (1983), for example, found that middle managers generally felt that senior managers did know what went on, and that rule breaking was related to their attitudes. On the other hand, others suggest that senior management may be deliberately shielded from unethical or law breaking practices, and may indeed prefer to remain in ignorance (Clinard and Yeager 1980). Stone (1978) argues, for example, that there is a natural tendency for bad news not to rise to the top. Where offences are deliberate, as in price fixing conspiracies, it may even become someone's job to ensure that top executives are not told. Indeed, Braithwaite (1984a) refers to the existence of the 'vice-president responsible for going to jail'. There is probably considerable variation between top management, but their attitudes are clearly important.

This is perhaps reflected in the common finding that offences are not found in all organizations. Indeed, Clinard and Yeager (1980) found that around 40 per cent of large corporations had no record of offences. From this they suggest that the culture within organizations is crucial. Law breaking and inattention to regulations can become a 'normative' pattern within a company, with top management setting a moral tone into which middle management are socialized. A stringent or sloppy attitude can therefore permeate the organization. In addition, subcultures can arise in response to particular aspects of the technological and social organization of work.

Workplace subcultures

It was seen in Chapter 2 that fiddling and pilfering may be widely tolerated in what are often described as workplace subcultures. These are often related to wider industrial relations issues (Scraton and South 1984; Clarke 1990) and, in addition to employee theft, have been associated with a variety of practices including restriction of output, absenteeism, sabotage and other informal manifestations of industrial conflict. This suggests that they can also be relevant to organizational crime. These subcultures are often interpreted as a more or less organized response on the part of employees to organizational structures, managerial policies or payment systems.

Many economic fiddles derive from a variety of organizational systems. Ditton (1976, 1977), for example, in a study of bread roundsmen, found that fiddling the accounts was necessary to balance the books, to meet the demands of an extremely complex formal accounting system. As employees became accustomed to this kind of fiddling, fiddles of a more self-interested nature developed, justified on the grounds that they represented an attempt to secure a 'fair day's pay for a fair day's work' (Ditton 1976). Both legitimate 'perks' such as tips and illegitimate fiddles can also be justified as attempts to supplement low incomes (Mars 1973). Therefore, in industries characterized by low pay such as retailing and catering, where many jobs are 'fiddle prone', fiddling may become an accepted part of a taken for granted total reward system. Management may be tacitly aware of this and tolerate a certain amount of fiddling to avoid demands for pay increases. Indeed, if tolerance levels change and a tougher stance towards fiddlers is adopted, workers may respond to what is perceived as a pay cut by adopting more militant strategies. This was illustrated by the incidence of strikes and working to rule by baggage handlers at Heathrow Airport which followed prosecutions for theft (Mars 1982).

Some aspects of organizational crime can also be associated with workplace subcultures. Management regularly attribute organizational offences to 'human error' and to individual cases of sabotage or other forms of indiscipline. While this can readily be interpreted as an attempt to deny managerial responsibility, many offences do originate in the acts or omissions of lower level employees (Clinard and Yeager 1980). Workers themselves may neglect safety regulations, can quite literally 'throw spanners in the works', and 'time' theft through absenteeism or inattention to the job can affect the quality of products and compliance with safety procedures. These kinds of activities are often widely tolerated by both workers and management, and derive from aspects of the technological and social organization of work.

In many jobs, workers have little discretion or freedom. The pace and nature of work may be determined by technological requirements, which can have far reaching consequences. Assembly line work, for example, has often been associated with absenteeism, poor industrial relations and poor quality products (see, for example, Beynon 1973). The potential significance of this for organizational offences is indicated by Braithwaite (1984a), who suggests that the tight regulations surrounding the manufacture of drugs can lead to alienation, carelessness and even sabotage. Another illustration is provided in Ditton's (1972) vivid description of the boredom of working on a mass production line producing cakes and bread. Workers frequently resorted to day dreaming as a reaction to the deadening monotony, and as a means of escape, occasionally dipped other workers in the confectionery mix! Although Ditton himself does not make the point, this could result in the presence of 'foreign bodies' in the food products. Sabotage can also be a result of boring work or of the pressures of production. Taylor and Walton (1971), for example, interpret some kinds of sabotage as a search for fun in an otherwise boring and deadening work environment, and others as responses to frustration or the pressures of production.

Such responses can be individual or collective, and the development of subcultural and organized, as opposed to individual and unorganized responses is also related to the work itself. Subcultural responses are more likely where employees work in groups and where the tasks they perform require co-operation. Where workers are isolated, responses are more likely to be of an individual variety, like the donkey jobs described by Mars (1982). The form of response in turn depends on the existence of legitimate avenues for dissatisfaction with work or pay. In industries where trade union activity is recognized and organized, grievances are likely to be expressed through negotiation, collective bargaining or other institutionalized avenues. However, where these avenues are blocked, informal conflict, including fiddling, absenteeism or sabotage, may be more prevalent (see for example, Hyman 1977). Taylor and Walton (1971) further demonstrate that sabotage can become a more organized tactic of resistance on the part of workers where there is no formal trade union organization. Many offences, both occupational and organizational, can therefore be associated with workers' individual or collective responses to many aspects of the organization of work or pay.

However, just as opportunities for offending are not always exploited, oppressive or pressurized work environments do not always produce individual or subcultural rule breaking. It is generally accepted that workers' attitudes to and behaviour at work result from an interaction between the organization of work and cultures and subcultures outside the workplace (see, for example, Goldthorpe *et al.* 1969). Fiddling and pilfering are only likely to persist where they can readily be justified according to pre-existing norms and values. Similarly, fiddling expense forms, evading taxes and many other offences are more likely to be prevalent where they can be justified as not really deviant or criminal. Cultural values outside the organization must also therefore be explored.

Enterprise, entrepreneurship and crime

It has already been seen that many white collar offences are culturally tolerated and have been linked to the values of capitalism. Indeed, Mills (1956: 138) portrayed business as operating in a 'subculture of structural immoralities', and Mars argues that the ambiguous attitude of society towards many fiddles means that

> there is only a blurred line between entrepreneuriality and flair on the one hand and sharp practice and fraud on the other. (Mars 1982: 49)

This fine line was well illustrated in Chapter 2, and gives ample scope for offenders to argue that their activities fall on the right side of that line. In addition, many activities are not greeted with widespread disapproval or defined as really criminal. There is, for example, a ready market for goods which 'fall off lorries', and participants in such trading are not generally seen as 'thieves' or 'handlers of stolen goods'. Other offenders regularly dismiss their offences as 'technical' rather than criminal and distinguish their actions from those of 'real' criminals (Benson 1985; Croall 1988).

This moral ambivalence is illustrated in offenders' accounts and justifications. Many of these are similar to the 'techniques of neutralization' described by Sykes and Matza (1957) in which offenders seek to neutralize any guilt implied by their offences (Rothman and Gandossy 1982; Box 1983; Benson 1985; Croall 1988). While these are inevitably *post hoc* justifications, they can, as Benson (1985) argues, help the understanding of crime at an individual level. Cressey (1986: 201) also argues that these 'vocabularies of motive' reflect cultural ideologies which justify the commission of crime in certain circumstances. The tacit assumptions inherent in many of these accounts also illuminate offenders' views of the borderline between acceptable and unacceptable activities. As might be expected offenders routinely deny that they intended any harm, argue that offences were someone else's fault, and that they are isolated incidents in an otherwise respectable career (Box 1983; Croall 1988; see Chapter 6). Another major theme in the remarkably similar accounts of very diverse groups of offenders is that after all, they are in business, thus revealing their interpretation of acceptable business values (Benson 1985; Croall 1988).

This latter argument was put at its simplest by a car dealer convicted for turning back an odometer, who protested that he was 'in the business of buying and selling cars' – as if no further elaboration was necessary (Croall 1988: 307). Similarly, Cressey (1986) highlights the ideological significance of the type of excuse which claims that 'honesty is the best policy but business is business', and Benson (1985) found that anti-trust offenders frequently argued that their activities were necessary given the realities of the business world. Thus, he argues, two sets of rules were applied – the legislative rules and a higher set of rules based on concepts of profit and survival. If therefore:

> one is not trying to make a profit or trying to keep one's business going, then one is not really 'in business'. (Benson 1985: 593)

Box (1983: 57) makes a similar point when he argues that:

> free enterprise – the pursuit of fair profit, the generator of wealth and employment, the backbone on which social welfare is possible – can be viewed, at least by corporate officials, as the primary ethic for and of an industrial society and conformity to this neutralizes any obedience to the law merely because it happens to be the law.

These kinds of arguments implicitly or explicitly imply that the law unfairly interferes with the pursuit of legitimate business goals. Offences can therefore be presented as 'technical' or not really criminal as the moral basis of the law can be challenged. As Benson (1985: 588) argues:

> the widespread acceptance of such concepts as profit, growth, and free enterprise makes it plausible for an actor to argue that governmental regulations run counter to more basic societal values and goals . . . criminal behaviour can then be characterized as being in line with other higher laws of free enterprise.

Any possible blame attaching to offenders can also be neutralized on the grounds that 'everybody does it', an excuse regularly offered by tax evaders (Benson 1985; Cook 1989a) and anti-trust offenders, an attitude which further challenges the moral basis of the law.

These justifications may in turn reflect ideological conflicts over the criminalization or regulation of business activity. Thus, Cressey (1986: 205) notes that many justifications come close to a rationalization that 'government regulation of business is socialistic and counterproductive'. Tax evasion, generally agreed to be widely tolerated and morally acceptable, provides a good illustration of this point (Deane 1981; Cook 1989a; Clarke 1990). Its acceptability, argues Cook (1989a), reflects political and ideological conflicts over the principle of taxation. Thus, taxation is often portrayed in political and public discourse as an intolerable burden which stifles incentives, a discourse reflected in offenders' justifications. Offenders regularly argued that offences were simply an attempt to restore perks, or were part of a battle to 'beat the taxman'. This 'sporting' theory of tax evasion assumes the fundamental unfairness of taxation, an assumption which makes 'taking on the Inland Revenue' a legitimate activity. Offenders also argued that 'everyone does it' and that it is 'natural' to want to pay as little tax as possible. She concludes that these justifications

> must be located within the context of the contradictory principles which underlie our understanding of taxation (and welfare). (Cook 1989a: 70)

At the same time, the 'as yet unresolved contradictory principles of citizenship and free market individualism' set normative boundaries – few, for example, argue that tax evasion should be unlimited and most accept a distinction between 'acceptable fiddles' and 'shrewd business practice'.

Given that so many offences appear to be morally acceptable, it could be argued that there is little need for white collar equivalents to oppositional delinquent subcultures. As Box (1983) argues, white collar criminals, unlike delinquents, do not face a war against their activities. In certain circumstances, however, regulatory regimes can be responsible for creating oppositional subcultures. Braithwaite (1989: 128), for example, found that the stigmatization of car dealers facilitated a criminal subculture among Queensland dealers, which 'transmitted expectations that the only way to survive in business was through dishonesty'. Similar subcultures are discernible in the United States, where some businesses resist law enforcement by contesting all enforcement actions as a response to punitive enforcement. While examples of such subcultures are rare, there may well be deviant subcultures within particular industries or occupations or indeed among businesspeople in general (Passas 1990).

However, business values are not universal, and many have pointed to a conflict between business and professional values, a conflict likely to be experienced by occupations who define themselves as professional. Clinard's (1987) contrast between the financially orientated, entrepreneurial and mobile manager with the technical and professional, fiduciary and less mobile manager is one example of this kind of analysis. Others have also found such distinctions. Quinney (1963) found that pharmacists with what he describes as a professional orientation committed virtually no offences compared with more business orientated pharmacists. Within organizations, Braithwaite (1984a), in the pharmaceutical industry, found a difference between the orientation of medical staff and quality control managers who lacked professional standards or ethics. Others have pointed to a conflict between the values of business and those of public service. Doig (1984: 353), analysing corruption, argues that an increasing interaction between public and private sectors:

> saw many politicians either overwhelmed by, or anxious to emulate the brash, singleminded and self confident commercial world that appeared to be achieving success, growth, and profits in their own activities.

A clash between the two standards was, he argues, inevitable, especially in view of the 'potential for misconduct . . . inherent in traditional commercial activities'.

The moral ambivalence surrounding offences means that offenders have a set of ready made justifications for their activities. This arguably makes law breaking more likely, as offenders rarely risk massive disapproval or, as Braithwaite (1989) suggests, are unlikely to experience feelings of shame. Thus, potential offenders can more readily exploit the opportunities for offending provided by their occupational role, a response which may also be affected by structural pressures from outside the organization – the final set of factors to be considered.

Crime and the business environment

Environment and market conditions can affect white collar crime in a number of ways (Box 1983; Passas 1990). Particular economic conditions may produce specific pressures to which law breaking can appear a rational response, a response which may also be affected by the regulatory environment which affects calculations about the potential costs of offending. In turn, both economic conditions and the regulatory environment may be affected by political and governmental policies and priorities. These links will now be explored.

Some writers argue that anomie theory, which interprets criminality as a response to the structural strain created when goals cannot be achieved by pursuing legitimate means, is particularly appropriate to corporate crime. Box (1983) argues, for example, that the main goal of corporations is to maximize profits. If environmental uncertainties create a situation in which legitimate means of profit making are blocked or threatened, pursuing profits by illegitimate means becomes a rational choice. Thus,

> contradictions between corporate goal-achieving behaviour and... environmental uncertainties creates a strong strain towards innovative behaviour. (Box 1983: 36)

The cultural ambivalence towards white collar crime makes these illegal solutions more likely, as

> the cultural accent on success and money... makes for 'innovation' rather than 'conformity', particularly in competitive conditions. (Passas 1990: 162)

Competition itself creates uncertainty, and offences like price fixing, corruption, bribery or insider dealing can be interpreted as attempts to reduce the many uncertainties created by competition. Braithwaite (1979) illustrates this in relation to transnational corruption. In order to secure important expansion business executives may face what he describes as a structural strain. In an environment where corruption is seen as normal, and competitors resort to illegal behaviour, law breaking may be the most economically rational choice.

Law breaking is not, however, the only option. As was seen in Chapter 3, many businesses have the option of pursuing their goals, not by breaking the law, but by evading it. Law itself is therefore an important aspect of the business environment and some businesses may be able to manipulate the law thereby reducing its potential threat (Braithwaite 1979; Box 1983, 1987). As Box (1987) points out, corporations, unlike conventional criminals, have sufficient political muscle to influence the law itself, either by lobbying to secure the repeal of laws they dislike or to prevent new and tougher laws being enacted (see Chapter 8). Where regulation is weak, law breaking may be more economically rational, as the chances of being detected are small and penalties may be trifling. Thus, Box (1987) argues that corporate crime may increase as a result of what he describes as the deregulatory stance of Governments on both sides of the Atlantic in the 1980s. Such an increase might, he argues, be expected particularly in industries and sectors of the economy in which law evasion and law manipulation is not an option, and where there is little chance of being either detected or prosecuted.

It is difficult to estimate the extent to which these factors affect patterns of offending, or whether certain kinds of offences are likely to increase in particular economic situations, for example recession. One of the few studies to explore these effects found that industries in which intense competition and inelasticity of demand were combined did show higher amounts of collusive behaviour such as price fixing (Clinard and Yeager 1980). They also found that firms with poor financial performances were more likely to violate the law, as were those in depressed industries. Box (1987) argues that during a recession, competition and environmental uncertainties are likely to increase, on the basis of which he argues that some corporate crime may increase. He also noted an increase in fraud by company directors and bankruptcy offences.

These observations direct attention to market conditions which could be specially relevant to smaller businesses, who may have fewer opportunities or resources to benefit from law evasion (Box 1987). Some writers have described 'criminogenic markets', in which higher levels of offending have been associated with specific market conditions. In the United States, the liquor industry (Denzin 1977) and the car industry (Leonard and Weber 1977) have been so characterized. In their analysis of garage fraud, Leonard and Weber (1977) found an oligopolistic market in which large motor manufacturers controlled dealers through franchises, exerting strong pressure for sales. However, little profit was gained by dealers from the sale of new cars, leaving servicing and second-hand car sales as the main avenues for enhancing profits. This encouraged a variety of illegal activities such as altering odometers and giving false accounts for servicing and repairs. These offences are therefore 'coerced occupational crime' resulting from a criminogenic market. Braithwaite (1978) offers a similar analysis of used car fraud in Australia, where salesmen pressured mechanics to alter odometers in order to boost sales, and intense competition encouraged false or deceptive advertising. Given the fiddle proneness of car servicing and the absence of a code of ethics (Braithwaite 1978, 1989), the car industry, and in particular garages, could therefore be expected to be associated with higher levels of offending. It was also seen in Chapter 3 that small retail businesses, lacking the resources of larger concerns may be more preoccupied in a 'struggle for survival', given the high failure rate of small businesses (Aldrich *et al.* 1981). This may lead to pressures to ignore regulations as they must maximize sales and may be more tempted to sell substandard or out of date items. In addition, they are less likely to be able to raise the capital necessary to improve old and out of date premises.

In other industries similar combinations of technological and economic factors may produce particular patterns of offending. In the food industry, for example, authors have commented on the struggle between 'health and wealth' (Cannon and Walker 1985; Croall 1987). The food industry is highly competitive and faces a relatively inelastic market. In order to expand, food manufacturers must secure a competitive advantage. This leads to continual diversification and 'value adding' practices, in which basic foods are converted into attractive convenience foods. Thus, the potato is turned into a dazzling variety of crisps, chips or baked potatoes, all with different ingredients and flavours, which result in the consumer paying much more for smaller amounts of 'real' food. To assist the marketability of these products, manufacturers use a variety of flavours, colours, and additives –

many of which are inadequately regulated, and have been associated with a number of undesirable side effects (Cannon and Walker 1985, Miller 1985; London Food Commission 1988).

Along with the car industry, the Pharmaceutical Industry is often associated with high levels of corporate crime (Braithwaite 1984a; Clarke 1990). Yet again, intense competition appears to be a factor. New drugs can yield enormous profits and companies try very hard to be first in the market with a new product. Typical offences involve the falsification of test results on new products, unethical sales techniques to persuade doctors to use particular drugs and the exporting of drugs failing to meet one country's standards to other, mainly third world countries (Clinard and Yeager 1980; Braithwaite 1984a; Box 1987). Perry and Dawson's (1985, 1987) account of the Dalkon Shield case illustrates how these factors can combine. Global concerns over population control in the 1960s led to efforts to find a cheap and safe form of contraception, and intra-uterine devices were speedily developed. The original inventors of the Dalkon Shield carried out highly questionable tests on an early version of the device, on the basis of which they made grossly exaggerated claims about its effectiveness and safety. It was then bought by a large drugs company, and despite many doubts on the part of production supervisors, scientific officers and many others, it continued to be widely marketed, despite an increasing number of septic abortions, infertilities and deaths being associated with it. As regulations on devices were less stringent than those on drugs, regulatory authorities took a long time to react. No prosecutions were ever made; however, this case reveals the complex relationship often found between market pressures, organizational priorities and the regulatory environment.

The combination of economic, market and regulatory factors can in turn be affected by political considerations, as is shown by Carson (1981) in his study of fatalities on North Sea Oil Rigs. Many fatalities in the North Sea were routinely dismissed as 'accidents' caused by 'freak waves' and their incidence seen as inevitable in an industry operating at the 'frontiers of technology'. Carson, however, found that many resulted from routine breaches of safety regulations which would have constituted offences had they occurred in factories on shore. However, regulation was slow to develop on off-shore installations and legislation was not originally applicable to the Continental shelf. Despite the efforts of the Health and Safety Executive, Governments were slow to react, as they were concerned to develop the fields as speedily as possible to maximize their revenue. Thus, a 'political economy of speed' was associated with a lenient regulatory regime which was exploited by oil companies reluctant to institute tougher safety procedures.

Summary and discussion

It is clear, therefore, that many approaches can usefully be applied in the search for a fuller understanding of white collar crime. As is the case with conventional crime, a combination of individual, cultural and structural factors must be considered and white collar crime cannot simply be attributed to greed, acquisitiveness or even capitalism and its associated values. Greed or a desire for success may well provide initial motivations, but white collar crime is uniquely dependant on occupational roles. Occupations provide a range of 'illegitimate opportunity structures', and the structure of organizations produces many situations in which rule breaking may be an individual or collective response to the many strains and pressures of work, originating within organizations or from outside. However, opportunities are not always exploited, and employees do not respond like automatons to the many pressures towards rule breaking. Offences are, however, facilitated by a moral ambivalence, which means that they can be readily justified and that offenders experience little guilt. This may be exacerbated in situations where a combination of economic factors and a favourable regulatory environment make law breaking an economically rational solution to ensure the survival or profitability of a business.

Not all of these approaches are equally relevant to all varieties of white collar crime, although most can be applied to both occupational and organizational crime. However, an analysis of environmental pressures rather than strains within organizational structures may be more applicable to small business crime, where there is less delegation and diffusion of responsibility. Furthermore, small businesses may not be able to afford the skilled technical, legal or financial advice which enables larger businesses to legally avoid law breaking. In addition, not all offences are culturally tolerated. Offences which more readily approximate 'real crime', such as embezzlement, can less readily be justified as being not really criminal and commonplace, although embezzlers do employ verbal neutralizations similar to other offenders. They may claim, for example, that their offences are less harmful than other crimes because they are purely economic or that they were merely borrowing the money (Benson 1985; Cressey 1986).

The social class or employment status of offenders is also important and approaches which relate patterns of offending to the differential distribution of illegitimate opportunities irrespective of employment status may gloss over several important differences between the offences of high and low status employees. Scraton and South (1984), for example, criticize theories which attempt to analyse workplace crime without recognizing the significance of social class and occupational position. While opportunities for crime may well be spread throughout the occupational hierarchy, deviant responses arise from the very different pressures, working conditions and pay experienced at different levels. It has been argued, for example, that the criminal and deviant activities of lower level employees can be a response to oppressive working conditions and low pay. This kind of explanation can scarcely be applied to the albeit similar activities of senior executives, who face substantially different pressures. Scraton and South (1984) further argue that lower level employees are subjected to higher levels of surveillance, and that their offences are less publicly sanctioned and tolerated than those of managerial and professional employees. Furthermore, lower level employees and small businesses may be more adversely affected by economic conditions and are less likely to be able to cushion their effects.

II

WHITE COLLAR CRIMINAL JUSTICE

5

LAW ENFORCEMENT

Many of the issues surrounding the treatment of white collar crime in the criminal justice system have already been outlined. It is often assumed that white collar offenders are more leniently dealt with than their conventional criminal counterparts, and that this results from the operation of class bias. When these taken for granted assumptions are unpacked, however, a number of separate questions emerge. In the first place it has to be established whether the treatment of white collar offenders is fairly described as lenient, and if so, whether it can meaningfully be compared to that given to any other group. It will be seen, for example, that it is not always easy to compare the very different kinds of offences and offenders involved. Comparisons with other offenders can also divert attention away from the somewhat different but equally important issue of whether their treatment is appropriate or effective. It has been argued, for example, that the difficulties of detection, prosecution and trial make a different set of law enforcement policies and practices necessary, but that this need not involve any greater leniency.

More questions are raised by the issue of class bias. On the one hand, following Sutherland's analysis, class bias has been associated with the 'cultural homogeneity' assumed to exist between offenders and criminal justice personnel. On the other hand, given the widespread tolerance of many offences illustrated in Chapter 4, it is possible that any favourable treatment reflects a view on the part of law enforcers and sentencers that the offences in question are not really criminal and therefore do not require the same levels of prosecution and punishment as other crimes.

Broadly similar questions are raised in relation to all stages of the criminal justice process, from law enforcement to eventual punishment. The way in which offenders are dealt with has to be outlined and some assessment made as to whether this can be interpreted as favourable, either in relation to other groups or the perceived goals of legislation. In examining these questions, along with the vexed issue of class bias, it is important to explore the attitudes, assumptions and underlying rationales of the decisions and policies of legal personnel. It must also be recognized that the different stages of the criminal justice process are interconnected, with earlier stages having an effect on later stages. Selective prosecution for example, means that only a small and possibly atypical group of offenders are taken to court and subjected to public punishment. Some groups of offenders may therefore be less likely to be detected, prosecuted and severely sanctioned.

Law enforcement, which represents the first stage of the criminal justice process, is clearly a crucial area for investigation. It is generally accepted that arrangements for law enforcement and prosecution differ considerably from those which apply to many other crimes. Laws are enforced not only by the police, but by a host of specialist enforcement agencies, and prevention and detection is the responsibility of both these public agencies and the many self-regulatory organizations which oversee particular sectors of business and commerce. Many of these agencies have been the subject of research, which includes studies of the Factory Inspectorate (Carson 1971), Consumer Protection Officers (Cranston 1979), Environmental Health Officers (Hutter 1988), aspects of the enforcement of Pollution legislation (Richardson *et al.* 1982; Hawkins 1984) and the Inland Revenue (see, for example, Cook 1989a). Much of this research has involved observing and interviewing officers, and analysing how agencies, individual departments and officers approach their work. Far less empirical work has covered the many agencies involved in the regulation of financial services and company fraud. Much emphasis in this chapter will accordingly be on the former areas, with reference where relevant to the latter. Less is also known about the 'private policing' which takes place within companies, in relation to both compliance with regulations and the detection and prosecution of employee crime (see, for example, Shearing and Stenning 1987).

Despite the large number of agencies involved, many common themes emerge from these studies. Most confirm that agencies operate with a distinctive set of priorities and policies, often described under the general heading of compliance strategies, which are often contrasted with the more punitive strategies associated with the police. The rationales underlying compliance strategies are also broadly similar, and focus on their greater effectiveness in securing high standards of compliance and thus public protection. This chapter will first outline the nature of compliance strategies and their underlying rationales. Variations between individual agencies and departments will then be explored along with the different styles of enforcement adopted. The environmental constraints and influences on enforcement policies will be outlined, followed by a discussion of the questions raised at the beginning of this chapter.

Compliance strategies

The basis of compliance strategies lies in the formal role of agencies which is generally interpreted as being to establish and maintain high standards of trading, commerce, safety, health or the environment. Allied to this is the protection of the public, whether as consumers, investors, employees, residents or other businesses. Enforcing the criminal law is therefore only one part of this broader role, and it tends not to be seen as a major part. Agencies and individual officers therefore do not define themselves as industrial 'police officers' whose main concern is to detect and prosecute the guilty. Rather they see themselves as impartial, expert advisers who aim to secure the highest possible standards by balancing the interests of both the industries concerned and the general public. This role is generally built into the laws which give agencies their powers, and is routinely re-iterated in a variety of official statements and reports and in the records of agencies themselves. Thus, the first task of the Health and Safety Commission is to secure the willing compliance of employers and workers in safety measures (Leigh 1980). A typical description of Weights and Measures Inspectors is that they are:

> not simply . . . law enforcement officers engaged to identify offences and institute prosecutions, but . . . to secure a fair balance between traders and consumers. (Dickens 1970: 625)

Similarly, the Inland Revenue sees its main goal as 'the collection of taxes which Parliament says are due' (Cook 1989a: 150). The many distinctive features of compliance strategies emerge from this overall role and its practical interpretation.

Persuasion and prevention

Many agencies place a high priority on their preventive role, feeling that this best protects the public. The majority of agencies proceed by making routine inspections of regulated businesses, seeing their role in these inspections as being to advise and educate businesses about how they can best comply. If violations are found, the first course of action is normally to ask them to remedy matters and to advise them as to how this can best be done (Cranston 1979). In carrying out their advisory function, officers assume the role of experts, whose task is to isolate the particular problems faced by an individual business and to devise, with the co-operation of the business, the best way of solving these problems (Richardson *et al.* 1982). In addition, some agencies organize educational programmes, with the aim of making businesses aware of the requirements of legislation and current applications of 'best practice' (Richardson *et al.* 1982; Croall 1987). Prosecution tends only to be considered if such advice or help is ignored, or where it is seen as inappropriate.

This approach is perceived to be preferable to prosecution for a number of reasons (Cranston 1979; Richardson *et al.* 1982; Hawkins 1984; Hutter 1988). Many argue, for example, that high standards can better be achieved where businesses co-operate with agencies. Such co-operation is felt to be more forthcoming if agencies and officers are respected and seen as helpful experts rather than interfering and threatening law enforcement officers. On the whole, individual businesses are generally felt to be willing to comply, an assumption which further justifies the use of persuasive, rather than punitive strategies. Where violations are discovered therefore the assumption tends to be that the business in question will respond to advice and help. It is also felt that these strategies better protect the public by preventing future offences and maintaining high standards. As one Chief Trading Standards Officer put it simply, 'prevention is better than cure' (Croall 1987).

Administrative sanctions and out of court settlements

Persuasive and preventive policies are not the only alternative to prosecution, and may not in themselves be sufficient to ensure compliance. Where offences persist or are serious enough to warrant immediate action, agencies may employ a variety of strategies before resorting to prosecution. Many use what Richardson *et al.* (1982) describe as the 'graded letter system', in which a series of letters containing various implicit and explicit threats of further action are sent to firms where offences have been found. These are followed up by further inspections, advice and negotiation. A formal caution may be given and only if this is not followed by remedial action does prosecution follow. In many cases therefore protracted negotiations precede and prevent prosecution.

Some agencies have powers which they regard as more effective and indeed as more draconian than prosecution. These can involve the closure of an offending business, which clearly constitutes a powerful weapon, as it threatens its very survival. Environmental Health Officers, for example, can force the closure of food premises if they pose a direct threat to the public health. While these powers are rarely used, many officers feel that they can be more effective than prosecution and some departments negotiate agreements with firms to close for specified periods of time while essential improvements are undertaken (Croall 1987). Other agencies can grant or withdraw licences, and the threat of using these powers is another important weapon which is used in negotiations with offending firms (Richardson *et al.* 1982; Croall 1987). Similar powers can also be used in the regulation of financial fraud, where self regulatory organizations have the power to disqualify company directors (Levi 1987a) and professional bodies also have powers of disqualification. Other agencies can negotiate out of court financial settlements – the Inland Revenue may not prosecute if taxes are paid and can also impose financial penalties (Levi 1987a; Cook 1989a). Self-regulatory organizations like Lloyd's and the Stock Exchange can also take disciplinary action against offenders and order that compensation be paid to investors without initiating criminal proceedings (Levi 1987a). The use of such out of court procedures and sanctions therefore further limits the numbers of prosecutions.

Cost effectiveness

Arguments surrounding the relative benefits of compliance as opposed to prosecution policies also reveal a pragmatic concern with cost effectiveness. Thus, enforcers often argue that their scarce resources are better employed preventing future offences, rather than pursuing the lengthy and time consuming investigations which may be necessary to gather evidence for a successful prosecution. Indeed, some prosecutions can involve enormous sums. The recent unsuccessful prosecution of those involved in the Zeebrugge disaster, for example, is estimated to have cost ten million pounds (Bergman 1990b), and the total cost to the taxpayer of the prosecutions in the Guinness case has been estimated at around three million pounds (*The Guardian* 28/8/90). On one occasion an extra vote of funds from the treasury was required to pay for the prosecution of tax frauds (Levi 1987a). Therefore, cost considerations affect decisions to prosecute, especially in cases of financial frauds and insider dealing (Naylor 1990). The DPP balance the sums of money involved in the offence against the cost of investigation and trial, prosecuting only where the former exceeds the latter (Clarke 1986). Studies of enforcement departments in the areas of public health, consumer protection and health and safety legislation have also found that prosecutions may be avoided on the grounds of cost (Cranston 1979; Hutter 1988).

Agencies must also consider whether prosecutions are likely to lead to convictions and some may only be willing to prosecute cases with a high chance of success. The DPP, for example, only prosecute where there is an even chance of success (Clarke 1990), which is also the case with the Inland Revenue (Cook 1989a) and the Police Fraud Squad (Levi 1987a). This is particularly important where it is necessary to prove *mens rea,* which requires a high standard of evidence, particularly in cases of complex financial frauds and insider dealing. Other prosecutions may be considered too risky, particularly where agencies themselves have to bear the cost of unsuccessful prosecutions. In Local Authority departments cost considerations limit the use of inherently risky test prosecutions, which can be used to clarify ambiguities in the law (Croall 1987).

The cost of prosecution is also balanced against its likely effectiveness as a means of securing compliance. Unlike persuasive strategies which are considered to be effective, prosecution can alienate businesses, and thereby make them less open to persuasion (see, for example, Braithwaite 1989). Prosecutions can also be seen as counter productive, as money spent on fines could be better spent on improving compliance. Others argue that fines are generally so small that they have little deterrent value (see, for example, Cranston 1979; Hutter 1988). On the other hand, most accept that some prosecutions are necessary, as they can act as a deterrent and make threats of prosecution realistic. Under what circumstances therefore is prosecution likely to be considered?

When to prosecute – the big and the bad

In practice, a mixture of considerations underlies decisions to prosecute. Prosecution is often used as a last resort where all other efforts have failed, and is therefore reserved for persistent offenders or those who are clearly unwilling to comply. In addition, offences which involve particularly large sums of money or serious breaches of regulations which attract media and public attention may be more likely to be prosecuted. Hawkins (1984), for example, noted a tendency to prosecute 'big' cases involving particularly serious pollution incidents, and prosecutions under safety legislation are more likely where there have been fatal accidents involving members of the public (Hutter and Lloyd Bostock 1990). The seriousness of the offence is therefore important, although seriousness in itself has not been found to be a sufficient criteria for prosecution (see, for example, Carson 1970; Richardson *et al.* 1982; Croall 1987).

Evidence of intent or apparent blameworthiness also underlie many prosecution policies. This is illustrated by the Inland Revenue's criteria for prosecution, which indicate that the following kinds of cases are more likely to be prosecuted.

1 'Heinous' cases.
2 Cases where individuals have already enjoyed a negotiated settlement.
3 Cases where taxpayers have made incomplete disclosures.
4 Status prosecutions – for example, where accountants have been involved (Cook 1989a: 150).

Imputations of blameworthiness are reflected in the term 'heinous', and in the inclusion of cases where individuals have already been warned and where a position of trust has been abused. Other agencies also use implicit notions of moral blame. Where prosecution is used as a last resort following the long history of visits, warnings and persuasion characteristic of much enforcement, continued offending in itself is considered to indicate blameworthiness (see, for example, Carson 1971; Cranston 1979; Richardson *et al.* 1982; Hawkins 1984; Hutter 1988). In addition, persistent offenders are more likely to be defined as 'criminal' and prosecution justified on moral grounds (see, for example, Hutter 1988). A mixture of moral and strategic arguments therefore affect choices between prosecution and persuasion strategies, leading to the prosecution of the 'big and the bad' (Hawkins 1984).

Thus far, prosecution and persuasion have been discussed as alternative strategies. However, the distinction between them can be overdrawn and as Braithwaite (1989: 131) points out, neither 'fits the situation that business regulators confront in the field'. Persuasion strategies are only one part of the armoury of enforcers, who may be better characterized as 'walking softly while carrying a big stick' (Braithwaite 1984). In practice, departments may strategically choose a variety of persuasive and prosecution strategies and use their powers of prosecution as an ultimate threat. Hawkins (1983), for example, describes the day-to-day negotiations between enforcers and business as a process of 'bargaining' and 'bluffing'. Within the overall umbrella of compliance strategies therefore a mixture of approaches are possible, and very different emphases may be found.

Policing business

Strategies and styles of law enforcement

A major difference between departments is the relative emphasis placed on prosecution or persuasive policies. Cranston (1979), for example, in his study of consumer protection departments identifies three different approaches. Some departments used prosecution sparingly and only prosecuted the most serious cases. Others were 'prosecution minded' and a third group, the largest, neither encouraged nor discouraged prosecution. Hutter (1988) found that Environmental Health departments adopted both 'persuasive' and 'insistent' strategies, the latter involving higher levels of prosecution. In the author's research (Croall 1987), differences between Environmental Health departments were readily obvious, and were reflected in the language and attitudes of officers. For example, in a department described by a senior officer as an 'action department', officers talked of a 'firm' attitude to prosecution, described themselves as being 'a bit like detectives', and referred to 'nicking' offenders. In another department officers were keen to point out that they rarely prosecuted, as prosecution was a 'waste of time'. These departments were geographically close and these different approaches could be a source of complaint. Officers in one borough, for example, criticized those in another of 'never doing anything' and of adopting the 'writing one letter, then another' approach. In certain circumstances they felt that this could undermine their efforts, as some firms operated in both areas and might become aware of their very different chances of prosecution.

Other aspects of the enforcement role can be emphasized. One department visited by the author was decribed by a senior officer as a 'campaigning' department, and had played a leading role in lobbying for changes in legislation. Other departments focus on particular kinds of offences, and departmental priorities and strategies may change over time. A common strategy in many departments is to initiate 'crackdowns', 'blitzes' and 'purges' on particular offences or groups of offenders (Braithwaite and Vale 1985; Croall 1987). Inland Revenue departments, for example, target particular sectors where they suspect the existence of widespread offending. Cook (1989a) found that particular trades or occupations including video shops, street markets, auctions and taxi ranks were regular targets of local offices. One Environmental Health department deliberately introduced a strategy of visiting all food premises and prosecuting in all cases where offences were detected in an attempt to 'clean up the area' (Croall 1987). This was backed up by a policy of seeking publicity, and a collage of publicized cases was compiled and sent to all food premises. This was considered to be a temporary policy, the intention being to return to a primarily persuasive approach. These crackdowns may be instigated at local, regional or national levels in response to specific problems, and can also be seasonal. One Trading Standards department, for example, launched crackdowns on unsafe toys at Christmas, and blitzed greengrocers in the summer when they were particularly concerned about the amount of strawberries contained in different sizes of 'punnets' (Croall 1987).

Law enforcement in the field

Officers in the field use a variety of tactics which are affected by their attitudes towards individual businesses and how they interpret their role. It has already been seen that officers have been likened to 'bobbies on the beat' and they develop a knowledge of their 'patch' and the businesses with whom they come into contact. Preventive, proactive work largely consists of inspection visits to premises. In choosing which premises to inspect, officers often talk of following 'hunches' (Cook 1989a) and rely on their knowledge of the local area. Generally speaking, officers assume that the majority of businesses are willing to comply, and that their job is to encourage co-operation, not to detect offences or to pursue the guilty. Hutter (1988), for example, found that officers did not see themselves as fighting the 'crime problem', and felt that most businesses were respectable and reputable. Offences were often attributed to ignorance, and the officer's role was seen as advising businesses and helping them to understand regulations. Thus, one officer commented that

> we aren't dealing with criminals; most of the people we see don't even know the law. You've got to educate them. (Hutter 1988: 63)

Similar attitudes were found by Richardson *et al.* (1982) who found that officers often attributed non-compliance to a combination of practical and economic difficulties, ignorance and 'bad housekeeping'. Officers, therefore, regularly interpret non-compliance as a 'technical' rather than a criminal matter (Hutter 1988), and prosecution is often felt to be inappropriate and possibly counter-productive. Many officers share the view expressed earlier that fines can make the financial problems of a business worse and make eventual compliance less likely (Richardson *et al.* 1982; Croall 1987).

While the majority of businesses are considered to be reputable, a minority are felt to be unco-operative and, as was seen in Chapter 3, particular businesses can attract negative stereotypes and be defined as 'unscrupulous' (Cranston 1979), or described as 'rogues' or 'cowboys' (Richardson *et al.* 1982). These groups may be more readily defined as criminal, a perception which may be heightened when information about their activities comes from the police (Hutter 1988). These 'unscrupulous' offenders are more likely to be prosecuted, and individual decisions to prosecute reflect officers' judgements of both offences and offenders. (Richardson *et al.* 1982), for example, found that following accidents, officers tended to look for evidence of negligence or previous warnings.

Some offences may be considered to be inherently more blameworthy than others. Environmental Health Officers, for example, felt that food offences were more criminal than pollution offences. In their view, food offences were more likely to result from a lack of attention to detail, whereas pollution offences could be very costly to prevent and there was some sympathy for the small business who could not afford improvements (Hutter 1988). In addition, they, like other enforcers, were more likely to label offenders as criminals in cases where there were clear indications of intent or where offences were serious or persistent. In practice, therefore, officers have an intuitive notion of offenders who 'deserve' prosecution, which contains elements of *mens rea* (Richardson 1987).

Different aspects of the enforcement task may present particular problems which require different policies and strategies. Preventive work, which involves the regular inspection of premises, amounts to what Hawkins (1984) describes as a 'continuous state of affairs' in which officers build up relationships with individual firms in order to encourage co-operation. Prosecution could damage these kinds of relationships. Therefore, where officers have to deal with offenders on a regular basis, prosecution may be less likely (see, for example, Carson 1970; Richardson *et al.* 1982; Hawkins 1984; Hutter 1988). On the other hand, 'one off' cases, in which serious or dangerous situations are discovered either by the public or agencies themselves may be more likely to be prosecuted. Such is the case, for example, in the 'big' cases discussed above, particularly following accidents, serious pollution incidents or outbreaks of food poisoning. In these kinds of situations, enforcement is largely reactive and prosecution may be justified in order to maintain the public credibility of the agency (Hawkins 1984; Hutter and Lloyd Bostock 1990).

Other agencies face different situations. What might be described as classic detection work is required, for example, in the discovery of tax evasion, and the Inland Revenue may adopt 'cloak and dagger' surveillance tactics (Cook 1989a). Trading Standards Officers deal with offences which are more like 'real crime' when they are dealing with counterfeit goods or the illegal importation of unsafe goods. This may necessitate the use of surveillance tactics, involve the police and lead to a more 'sanctioning' style of enforcement (Croall 1987).

In practice, therefore, enforcement departments adopt a variety of different approaches and the choice of particular strategies may depend on a number of different considerations. Clearly the nature of the enforcement task and the attitudes of officers towards different offences and offenders is important, as are the attitudes of Chief Officers, who are responsible for setting priorities and who can affect the style of a department (Hutter 1988). In addition, individual agencies and departments operate in a wider environment which may influence and constrain their choice of alternative approaches. This will be explored below.

Law enforcement in context

All agencies must of course work within the constraints imposed by the particular laws for which they are responsible. The law and its associated regulations specify the duties of the agency itself, the nature of the offences and the powers which agencies have at their disposal. All of this can significantly affect their choice of policies. As Levi (1987a: 192) points out,

> whereas to the Health and Safety Executive, the alternative to prosecuting or closing down factories owned by unco-operative management may be doing nothing, the Revenue departments may take the money and run rather than prosecute.

While enforcement agents must work within the law their discretion gives them some freedom to choose between different policies. As is the case with studies of policing, studies of white collar law enforcement reveal considerable gaps between the law in action and the law in books. The use by officers of implicit notions of *mens rea*, even where the law requires only strict liability, is one illustration of such a gap.

The law can also be used as a resource, and legal powers can be used strategically (Richardson *et al.* 1982), as in the 'bargaining and bluffing approach' (Hawkins 1984). In general, the 'big stick' of prosecution and other sanctions can be used as an ultimate threat to encourage compliance. Richardson *et al.* (1982), for example, found that in situations where a test was necessary in order to initiate a prosecution, the testing procedure itself was used as a threat. When the fines for individual offences under the Food and Drugs Acts were a mere £100, Environmental Health officers strategically increased the number of summonses for individual offenders in order to increase potential penalties. Thus, a dirty restaurant could receive up to 100 individual summonses relating to cookers, cooking surfaces or individual implements, rather than one summons relating to the entire kitchen (Croall 1987). Where possible, statutes which carried heavier fines, such as the Trade Descriptions or Health and Safety at Work Acts, could be used. Thus, selling meat which failed to meet the standards required under the Food and Drugs Act could be interpreted as using a 'misleading indication' under the Trade Descriptions Act. Large restaurants or hotels could be charged under the Health and Safety at Work Act where, for example, dirty light switches were found in dirty kitchens (Croall 1987). In addition to using the law, many agencies seek actively to change it, by campaigning for law reform and seeking representation on the Committees which set the standards which accompany regulations (Croall 1987).

Agencies must also work within available resources. The effect of resource constraints on both detection and prosecution has already been seen, and economic stringencies have severely threatened the ability of many agencies to fulfil their inspection programmes. Budget reductions often mean that there are fewer trained staff available to conduct routine inspections, a problem reported in many agencies including Consumer Protection Departments (Croall 1987), the Inland Revenue (Levi 1987a; Cook 1989a) and the Factory Inspectorate (Tombs 1990). This reduces the amount of preventive work which can be undertaken, and results in longer intervals between routine, proactive inspections. Annual Reports and public statements of enforcement bodies routinely re-iterate the adverse effects of staff shortages on their ability to adequately monitor compliance (Croall 1987). Other policies may also be affected. Hutter (1988) found that in some departments there was pressure to employ formal legal methods rather than persuasive strategies, some of which were considered to be more time consuming and therefore costly. Any reduction in prevention work also means that fewer offences are detected and any deterrent value is thereby reduced.

Many public enforcement agencies are run by Government Departments or Local Authorities who may attempt to influence departmental policies and may also intervene in individual cases. While little is known about the specific influence of Government Departments, it can be assumed to be significant. In some serious cases both Ministerial and Governmental intervention is evident. The issue of prosecution can indeed become politically controversial as was seen, for example, in the many questions asked about the non-prosecution of those involved in the Harrod's takeover, and the considerable discussion about possible prosecutions which often follows scandals and major accidents. Very little is known about the criteria underlying these decision making processes, however. The DPP, for example, are concerned primarily with the 'public interest', but rarely is this precisely defined (Clarke 1986).

Other agencies are answerable to Local Authorities, and legally can only prosecute with the approval of the appropriate Local Authority Committee (Croall 1987; Hutter 1988). These committees may also attempt to influence policies and priorities. Hutter (1988), for example, found that one department had been asked to prioritize high profile environmental and housing issues over preventive public health inspections (Hutter 1988). Prosecutions are often made by Local Authority legal departments, who may seek to influence the amount and kind of cases which are prosecuted (Hutter 1988). In one of the 'action' departments visited by the author, the encouraging attitude of the legal department was mentioned as a factor supporting a high prosecution policy as was their willingness to employ barristers where complicated defences were expected (Croall 1987). Council Committees may either rubber stamp decisions to prosecute or may intervene in individual decisions. Environmental Health Officers in Hutter's study, for example, complained about individual councillors' ignorance about environmental health matters in general.

To date, there is little evidence to suggest that the political persuasion of the majority party consistently affects the kind of influence exerted by Local Authorities (Croall 1987; Hutter 1988). The author studied five enforcement departments, and both the most prosecution and the most persuasive orientated departments were located in Boroughs with strong Conservative councils. All Chief Officers recognized the significance of Local Authority influence, which was transmitted via council solicitors and individual councillors, however, only one felt that party politics had a specific influence. This officer felt that a Labour Council did exert more pressure for prosecution. On the other hand, a strong prosecution policy in another department was strongly supported by a radical right wing Conservative council, on the grounds that high standards of trading had to be maintained (Croall 1987).

The nature of the local community and the businesses within it may be a stronger influence on policy than political considerations. Hutter (1988), for example, found that departments adopting persuasive strategies were more likely to be found in smaller, rural areas and in more closely knit communities, where officers were likely to interact with people they knew both professionally and socially. These relationships also mean that officers are more likely to see businesses as honest and law abiding. On the other hand, businesses who tend to be seen as 'rogues' or 'racketeers' are more likely to be found in metropolitan and urban environments where officers have less opportunity to develop social relationships with regulated businesses. The industrial complexion of an area may also affect enforcement priorities and policies. In areas reliant on tourism, for example, pollution control, hygiene and trading standards may be seen as particularly important. The action department studied by the author was in an area noted for tourism and this was mentioned in discussions of their policies (Croall 1987; see also Richardson *et al.* 1982).

These considerations may appear less relevant to financial fraud, although as Cook (1989a) points out, Inland Revenue departments are locally based and officers develop a knowledge of their particular area. In the financial world also, regulators and the regulated form social relationships and develop mutual trust. Indeed, the regulation of the city in the past was built on the mutual trust between insiders, who were drawn from a restricted social background (Clarke 1986). While it may seem a long way from images of community policing, a study of the regulation of city fraud and insider dealing might well reveal the significance of similar community factors.

A final external influence is 'public demand' and the need to maintain the public image of departments (Richardson *et al.* 1982). This can make some departments more likely to prosecute where public concern is evident, as in 'one off' major incidents (Richardson *et al.* 1982; Hawkins 1984; Hutter and Lloyd Bostock 1990). Many agencies indeed may respond to public complaints at the expense of prevention work, in an attempt to foster public relations. In some Environmental Health departments, relatively routine offences discovered as a result of public complaints were more likely to be prosecuted than those discovered through inspection work (Croall 1987). These influences cannot be separated from others, as maintaining a favourable public image can be justified on the grounds of legitimizing the organization, and bolstering claims for increased resources (Richardson *et al.* 1982). Hutter and Lloyd Bostock (1990) comment that accidents do result in greater attention being paid to the work of Inspectorates and can also be used to support arguments for extra resources.

Summary and discussion

It can, therefore, be seen that compliance strategies reflect agencies' and individual officers' perception of their role, which prioritizes public protection and the maintenance of standards. While individual departments may emphasize different aspects of this role, and adopt different policies and strategies in response to a variety of legal, economic and local considerations, prosecution tends to be seen as costly and cumbersome and only necessary for the minority of more serious offences and more blameworthy and persistent offenders.

It is difficult to assess objectively whether this amounts to favourable treatment, especially in comparison with conventional offenders. The often made distinction between compliance strategies and the more 'sanctioning' or 'punitive' strategies assumed to characterize the policing of conventional crime can, for example, be overstated. The police also have considerable discretion in relation to prosecution, can also bargain and bluff, and have been described as 'street corner politicians' (Brogden *et al.* 1988). Different styles of policing are also affected by resources and the nature of the local community, and crime prevention is an important aspect of police work (see, for example, Reiner 1985; Brogden *et al.* 1988). Regulatory enforcers can employ a mixture of strategies and some can use their powers punitively. The way in which, for example, the Inland Revenue 'get their money back', levy financial penalties and adopt 'cloak and dagger' tactics has been criticized (mainly by those caught) as draconian and aggressive (Leigh 1980; Cook 1989a). Therefore, compliance strategies need not necessarily be lenient, and are in any case justified as representing the most effective way to secure compliance and thereby protect the public.

None the less, it has been seen that on the whole, regulatory enforcers tend to avoid prosecution, which could, in itself, be interpreted as favourable treatment. Sanders (1985), for example, argues that the police legally display a propensity to prosecute whereas agencies dealing with the middle class legally display a propensity not to prosecute. But does this necessarily amount to class bias? As indicated in Chapter 3, few studies have found evidence of conscious or consistent sympathy towards businesses on the basis of their class or status (Hutter 1988). In addition, British studies have found little evidence of the 'capture' of the regulators by the regulated (Hawkins 1984; Hutter 1988). Allegations of agency bias are, therefore, difficult to sustain.

However, as was seen in Chapter 3, the outcome of compliance strategies may well be that high status offenders are less likely to be prosecuted. Levi (1987a: 191), for example, argues that the case for class bias 'remains to be made out' if class bias is defined as 'the intentional discrimination against one group and in favour of another'. On the other hand, he argues, if bias is judged not by intent but by consequences, 'the allegation of "structural bias" is considerably more convincing'. The tendency of some agencies to select 'easy targets' for detection and prosecution does mean that certain occupations, trades and businesses are more likely to be investigated and prosecuted. These groups are more likely to be of lower status. Thus, Cook (1989a: 117) argues that:

> the richer pickings which are available through the investigation of highly paid taxpayers, directors and trading accounts are largely ignored in favour of the type of investigations which are quick (and cheap) to undertake.

Other agencies target businesses who are labelled as 'unscrupulous' or 'rogues' and who are often smaller, more marginal businesses. The use of administrative sanctions which involve out of court negotiation and financial settlement can also amount to structural bias. These are not available options for many conventional offenders, many of whom would be unable to 'buy themselves out' of prosecution, even if such a possibility existed. The very existence of these options in itself amounts to treating one group of offenders differently from another.

The rationales underlying compliance strategies can also be challenged, particularly the stress on cost effectiveness. As Cook (1989a) argues, it might well be more cost-effective in the long-term to direct Inland Revenue investigations and prosecutions at the offences of wealthier taxpayers as these would produce higher income from settlements, and could act as a greater deterrent. The economic constraints on public enforcement agencies further reflect political priorities in the allocation of resources for crime control. Thus, Levi (1987a) queries the rationale underlying the employment, in 1986, of more social security investigators on the grounds that more fraud would be prevented, when at the same time, no more staff were employed in Customs and Excise departments despite strong arguments that the increased revenue collected would exceed the extra staffing costs. And the ability of enforcement agencies to protect the public is, as has been seen, hampered by economic constraints.

Justifications for compliance strategies also underplay arguments that offenders *should* be prosecuted and receive their just desserts. The preference for persuasive strategies rests on an assumption that many 'violations' or 'infringements' are not really 'criminal offences' and that many businesses are in need of advice and help rather than being defined as 'offenders'. Cook (1989a: 105) argues that the word 'compliance' is itself significant – comparing Inland Revenue with Social Security investigations she points out that:

> the language used to refer to taxation is altogether more obliging, equivocal and morally neutral than the vocabulary of welfare benefits. A crucial factor in obtaining the taxpayer's compliance is an unspoken agreement that financial reparation, not official punishment, is sought by the Revenue when an 'omission' from returns of income is discovered.

Therefore, while allegations of agency bias may have little foundation, white collar offences and offenders do appear to enjoy structural advantages, and the outcome of the policies pursued by law enforcers is that many avoid public prosecution and punishment, which could be justified on deterrent and retributive grounds. In addition, the justifications for compliance strategies reflect the moral ambiguity surrounding white collar offences. Subsequent chapters will explore how this also affects later stages of the process.

6

DEFENDANTS IN COURT

While under-researched in comparison with law enforcement and sentencing, an examination of courtroom proceedings is highly relevant to the issues raised in Chapter 5. It can, for example, further explore the extent to which white collar defendants are advantaged by their higher status and resources, and the arguments they use to defend themselves can reveal how they attempt to gain the sympathy which they are often assumed to receive. The distinctive characteristics of white collar crime strongly affect legal proceedings, although the proceedings typical for different groups of offenders vary considerably. Complex cases of insider dealing, tax evasion and financial frauds, for example, are generally heard in higher courts, involve complex legal issues, and evidence of intent or *mens rea* is required. Some, like the recent Guinness trials, are surrounded by considerable media attention (Levi 1991b). Regulatory offences, on the other hand, are often seen as routine and trivial. Many are offences of strict liability, in which no proof of *mens rea* is required, and they are generally, though not exclusively, heard in lower courts and attract little publicity (Croall 1987, 1988). The use of strict liability has been criticized on the grounds that it appears to be unduly harsh, as the 'honest' business person can receive a criminal conviction for a 'mistake' (see, for example, Hadden 1970; Richardson 1987). However, as will be seen, defendants can use strict liability to their advantage, as it enables them to present their offences as 'technical' rather than 'criminal', and to minimize their apparent blameworthiness.

This chapter will outline the distinctive features of white collar criminal proceedings which provide the context within which defence arguments and strategies are constructed. This will be followed by an exploration of the extent to which the ability of high status defendants to employ skilled legal advice can work to their advantage. The many strategies used to 'defend white collar crime' (Mann 1985) will then be described, focusing on the content of strategies of defence and mitigation (Croall 1988).

White collar crime on trial

In any criminal trial, legal rules structure the proceedings and determine the amount and kinds of information which are relevant. The arguments offered by both prosecutors and defendants are shaped by the requirements of rules of evidence and by the nature of the offence or offences in question. Defendants, for example, cannot simply claim that offences were not their fault, they must provide legal arguments which deny their legal responsibility. In white collar crime trials, the law itself and the specific characteristics of offences strongly affect the tactics and strategies which are available to both prosecutors and defendants.

The task of the prosecution in a criminal trial is to present sufficient evidence that the defendant did commit the offence in question and, where *mens rea* is required, that the defendant intended to commit the offence. It has already been shown that meeting this 'burden of proof' may be particularly difficult for many white collar offences, difficulties well illustrated in the example of complex financial frauds. Many frauds have been going on for several years before they are discovered, and trials may involve several defendants, each of whom may have participated in only some of the activities, and some of whom may be only indirectly implicated. Complex frauds may involve a number of different kinds of offences, all of which are the subject of separate indictments, and some of which may be easier to prove than others. In the Guinness trials, for example, a total of 24 different charges included separate counts of conspiracy to defraud, unlawful purchase of shares, false accounting and theft of over two million pounds. Each of the four defendants were tried for a different combination of these offences (*The Guardian* 28/8/90). The evidence in these kinds of cases can involve mountains of documentation, detailed examination of corporate and personal bank accounts, and requires the testimony of many witnesses, some of whom may be unavailable or unwilling to testify.

The high cost of these kinds of trials has already been referred to, and they may even require special organizational arrangements – the court used in the Guinness trial, for example, had to be specially converted to accommodate the army of lawyers involved – at an estimated cost of around £15,000 for this alone (*The Guardian* 28/8/90). Fraud trials may fail because key witnesses die or move abroad and don't wish to come back, especially where their evidence could incriminate themselves (Levi 1987a). Trials may last for weeks or even months. Levi (1987a) found that on average, contested conspiracy to defraud trials lasted for five and a half working weeks, and even relatively simple fraud cases lasted an average of three weeks. Apart from the high costs involved, it may be difficult to find a jury – especially one that is representative as few can make themselves available for such long periods of time (Levi 1991b). The interpretation of complex and detailed evdence creates technical legal problems, and many cases involve activities where the line between legal and illegal activities is difficult to establish. All this makes major fraud trials difficult for the lay person to comprehend, which has led to suggestions that complex financial frauds require a different set of procedures, that the use of juries should be limited, or that rules of evidence should be streamlined (Levi 1983, 1987a; Clarke 1986).

It has already been seen that prosecutions may only be undertaken where they have a reasonable chance of success (Chapter 5) and therefore it might be expected that cases would be watertight when they are prosecuted. In the United States, for example, prosecution follows intensive pre-trial review and negotiation between prosecution and defence attorneys. To defence attorneys, prosecution in itself represents failure, as their first aim is to prevent it (Mann 1985). Where cases are taken to court therefore it is likely that there is strong evidence and defendants may secure some advantages by plea bargaining. Therefore, few cases are contested (Mann 1985). However, this does not mean that defendants cannot attempt to minimize their guilt by denying intent and culpability. Rather than use these arguments to contest guilt, they can be used in an attempt to reduce the sentence. Consequently, in white collar trials substantive legal arguments are often used not in defence, but in an 'adversarial sentencing process' (Mann 1985). Pleading guilty has the additional advantage that it reduces the amount of evidence provided by the prosecution, as they do not have to establish intent or *mens rea*. Therefore, evidence which might indicate dishonesty and blameworthiness is not provided, which enables defendants to deny their existence in mitigation (Mann 1985; Wheeler *et al.* 1988).

See Also Levi in Evans

In England and Wales, where the powers of regulators to secure 'out of court settlements' and conduct pre-trial negotiations are very different, these considerations may not apply (Levi 1987a). Of more concern in England and Wales has been an apparently high rate of acquittals, often attributed to the inability of juries to comprehend proceedings. Whether or not acquittal rates are too high is impossible to judge in the absence of any standard which indicates how many acquittals can reasonably be expected (Levi 1987a), but it is clear that many acquittals result, not from jury decisions, but from judges' directions on legal technicalities, which may result from the prosecution's failure to provide sufficient evidence (Levi 1987a).

The burden of proof is less onerous in offences of strict liability, where it is sufficient to establish that an offence took place and that the defendant is the legally responsible person. The use of strict liability was adopted for business regulatory offences largely because it was found to be extremely difficult to secure convictions and to prove, for example, that sellers knowingly sold defective goods, or that factory owners knowingly broke safety regulations (see, for example, Paulus 1974; Carson 1979). The justification for strict liability is that it is necessary in the interests of protecting the public to waive *mens rea*. Therefore, strict liability offences, and by extension much corporate crime, are placed in a separate legal category in which offences are perceived of as not really criminal (Carson 1979). Defendants, as will be seen, can use this distinction to great advantage, particularly as it means that the prosecution do not need to provide evidence of intent (Croall 1988).

In practice, what is often seen as the harshness of strict liability is softened by the provision of statutory defences. In consumer protection offences, for example, a defendant may plead not guilty on the grounds that the offence was the fault of a third party, provided that the defendant can establish that he or she exercised 'due diligence' and did all that could reasonably be done to prevent offences occurring. Defendants can therefore be found not guilty if they can establish that they have instituted systems for checking that offences do not occur (see, for example, Cranston 1984). Thus, the proprietor of a shop who has sold mouldy food can claim that it was mouldy when it was received from a supplier. Provided that defendants can further establish that they had no way of knowing that it was moudly and had kept it under the required conditions for no longer than the specified period of time, they may escape conviction. Other statutes provide broadly similar defences. Most defendants in practice plead guilty, but may then use these arguments in mitigation, claiming, for example, that offences were not their fault, and that they had taken all reasonable steps to avoid them (Croall 1989).

Criminal proceedings are structured by legal rules and conducted in legal language in which everyday accounts of events are transformed into legal categorizations, and information is shaped and truncated by the requirements of evidence. This can at times appear absurd, where, for example, the court is asked to disregard incriminating evidence about a defendant because it fails to comply with rules of evidence (Carlen 1976). Therefore, in any criminal trial, accounts of what really happened are artificially structured, and everyday rules of language and interaction are suspended (Garfinkel 1956; Carlen 1976). In an adversary system, prosecution and defence select those aspects of the circumstances surrounding the offence which best fit their strategic interests. In addition, their arguments and accounts must fit the rules of evidence and be expressed in language acceptable to the court. In this way participants play information games (Carlen 1976), as each side is concerned to present only that information which supports their argument. Information control, therefore, becomes a crucial part of successful defence strategies (Mann 1985). Prosecution evidence tends to be 'denunciatory', based on a selection of information which inculpates defendants, whereas the defence select information which exculpates them. Defendants may also try to control the amount of damaging information provided by the other side. In this way, a plea of guilty can be a strategic attempt to limit the amount of damaging information provided by the prosecution (Mann 1985).

In all criminal trials therefore information control and a comprehension of legal language and proceedings is crucial. In white collar crime trials, opportunities for information control are strongly affected by the nature of the offence and the law itself. The control of any information which indicates blameworthiness, intent or responsibility is particularly significant. As seen in Chapter 5, many prosecutions follow a long history of visits, warnings and negotiation, and prosecution in itself may indicate blameworthiness. However, the criminal law deals with individual offences, committed at specific times, and many prosecutions select a sample of individual offences for which evidence is available. Prosecutions for tax frauds, for example, may cover only certain dates, even though the fraud itself may have lasted for much longer and may indeed still be going on (Mann 1985), and for regulatory offences, summons normally relate to the situation found on one inspection, or with one incident. The long history which may have preceded prosecution is not, therefore, relevant and is not offered in evidence. This gives defendants the opportunity to present offences as 'one off' isolated incidents. Where organizational crime is concerned, individual offenders may be able to claim that offences were not really their fault. The 'ideology of individualism' (Braithwaite and Condon 1978) of the criminal law, therefore, gives many white collar offenders the opportunity to deny elements of intent and blame, an opportunity which, as will be seen, many defendants exploit to their advantage.

Defendants and legal representation

Given the importance of legal rules and language, the use of legal representation is likely to be beneficial and indeed studies of courtroom proceedings have revealed the considerable problems which unrepresented defendants can face (see, for example, Carlen 1976; Bottoms and McClean 1976). It could, therefore, be assumed that white collar offenders who can more readily afford legal representation would be advantaged. More resources can secure more legal advisers who can spend more time disputing prosecution evidence, collecting and preparing counter evidence, interviewing witnesses and devising strategies of information control (Mann 1985). An illustration of the kinds of resources which could be required is provided by the admittedly atypical example of the Guinness trials, where the total defence costs for one defendant were said to be around two million pounds, and were reputedly over one million pounds for two other defendants (Levi 1991b). One firm employed was thought to charge around £200 per hour for the services of partners (*The Guardian* 28/8/90).

However, not all white collar defendants are wealthy, and many are small business proprietors who may not be able to afford such extensive or skilled legal advice. This was evident in the author's study of cases under Consumer Protection legislation. In 58 per cent of cases, legal representatives were present or defendants pled guilty by letter, usually from a firm of solicitors. In addition, all large companies were represented (Croall 1987, 1988). While it is difficult to gain figures for lower courts as a whole, Bottoms and McLean (1976) found that only 19 per cent of cases were legally represented. Therefore, in general, business defendants were more likely to be legally represented. However, many others, normally small businesses or lower status employees were unrepresented, and it was readily obvious that they suffered some disadvantage as a result. Some small businesses demonstrated in court that they misunderstood the law, which prevented them using the more skilled defence strategies used by the legal representatives of larger companies (Croall 1988).

Strict liability presented particular problems to unrepresented defendants. Some attempted to plead not guilty, using 'commonsense' notions of criminal law by arguing, for example, that 'I didn't mean any harm' or 'I didn't mean to . . .', but in order to plead not guilty, defendants must notify the court in advance of their intention to use one of the statutory defences. Attempts to plead not guilty were therefore likely to be ruled out of order by the magistrates' clerk, as happened in two cases where defendants indicated that they wished to use a mixture of guilty and not guilty pleas in an extensive list of charges. These kinds of problems could lead to much confusion. As some of these defendants were Asian, the issue of whether or not they understood the proceedings was raised. In one such case, the magistrates' clerk exclaimed, 'as they are all businessmen . . . they should understand'. Indeed, for business defendants, ignorance of the meaning of strict liability could in itself become incriminating.

This could happen when defendants appeared to misunderstand their legal responsibilities. An off-licence proprietor, charged with selling out of date beer, claimed that he relied totally on the brewery representative to check the sell by date. The magistrates' clerk reiterated several times that it was the proprietor's responsibility to ensure that stale beer was not sold and delivered a long homily about the nature and purpose of strict liability. By revealing that he never checked the date stamps, the proprietor made the offence appear far more serious than it might otherwise have done, and incriminated himself by appearing ignorant of his legal responsibilities.

Ignorance of rules of evidence and procedure could further incriminate defendants who on occasion revealed, by arguing with enforcers, the long history of visits preceding prosecution. A group of three co-defendants in a food hygiene case claimed that they had been 'picked on' unfairly by the

Environmental Health department. After all, they argued, they had improved their premises, as their last prosecution had involved more summons than this one. At this stage the magistrates' clerk attempted to invoke 'order' (Carlen 1976) by advising them to 'keep quiet about that matter', but by this time the defendants had revealed their previous history. Other defendants made statements when they should have been asking questions, attempted to engage witnesses in a dialogue, and continually reiterated their reliance on suppliers or their lack of intent from the very beginning of the proceedings. These interventions provoked the 'out of order, out of place, out of time' responses found by Carlen (1976), in which the court rules the arguments inappropriate and inadmissible. When asked eventually if they had 'anything to say', some defendants often felt they had said it all, thus depriving themselves of the chance to offer legitimate mitigation. Unrepresented defendants were therefore less able to control the amount of damaging information available to the court.

These confused responses were very different to the skilful tactics of legal representatives, who similarly claimed lack of intent, reliance on suppliers or other third parties, but who accepted, in the majority of cases, their client's responsibilities. They also used more arguments and made more substantive points, which were typically offered not in defence, but in mitigation. Indeed, a plea of guilty in itself could skilfully be turned into mitigation. Following a guilty plea, for example, it was often claimed that 'my client' had pleaded guilty as the offence was one of strict liability . . . but wished the case to be seen as an isolated incident, not really my client's fault, and that 'my client's' responsibility and willingness to comply is demonstrated by an acceptance of liability and a plea of guilty (Croall 1987, 1988). Some, often corporate defendants, used their resources in other ways. Independent 'experts' could be called to testify, teams of senior managers were brought into court to demonstrate the seriousness with which the company regarded the case and in some cases quality control managers gave evidence of the systems used by the company to ensure compliance.

Therefore, while some white collar offenders are more likely to employ skilled legal representation to good effect, others, particularly small business offenders, may not be able or willing to employ such resources and may be disadvantaged as a result. On the other hand, the large company, which can more easily prevent both offending and prosecution, further benefits from the ability to present its activities in a better light. This is further illustrated when specific strategies of defence are examined.

Strategies of defence

Defendants offer many arguments which aim to secure an acquittal or reduce the severity of the eventual sentence. Arguments offered in defence aim to persuade the court that, despite evidence to the contrary, defendants did not commit the offence in question, or were not really 'guilty'. If this fails or is inappropriate in view of a strong prosecution case, defendants, in mitigation, attempt to excuse their behaviour and make themselves appear less 'guilty'. They may claim, for example, that personal or other circumstances beyond their control led to the offence, that the offence did little harm, was not terribly serious or was an isolated occurrence. These strategies of defence are similar to the techniques of neutralization described by Sykes and Matza (1957) in which juvenile delinquents seek to neutralize their guilt, and they are also similar in content to the accounts, excuses and justifications described in Chapter 4. Their use in court, however, is largely strategic, as their aim is not simply to justify activities, but to minimize defendants' blameworthiness in a way which is acceptable to the court.

This determines which kinds of strategies and arguments are most appropriate. Thus, for example, pleading not guilty may be particularly risky as it appears to challenge the evidence of law enforcers. In addition, if it fails it can make it more difficult for defendants to show appropriate remorse and may reduce the credibility of mitigation. It has already been seen, for example, that white collar defendants can use a guilty plea to their advantage, as it reduces the amount of damaging information which is likely to be provided by the prosecution, allowing them to deny blameworthiness in mitigation. In addition, while business offenders often justify their actions by arguing that the law itself is unfair, it would be ill advised to use this kind of argument in court, as it amounts to challenging the law which it is the court's duty to uphold. Nelken (1983) for example, found that landlords in court were unlikely to express their real disapproval of the law, stressing instead their acceptance of its importance. Other defendants may stress their support for the law but deny that it applies in this particular instance (Croall 1988).

The specific nature and circumstances of white collar offences make particular kinds of defence strategies particularly appropriate. The organizational nature of many offences allows defendants to claim that they were really someone else's fault, or that they were unaware that offences were being committed by other persons, provided that this strategy does not make them appear to be ignorant of their own responsibilities. The technical, financial and legal complexities of offences can also be exploited to underline a defendant's lack of culpability. The ambiguity of many laws gives considerable scope for arguments that particular offences are very close to the line between legitimacy and illegitimacy (Mann 1985). The ambiguous criminal status of offences can also be used to minimize their seriousness and to stress that they are 'not really criminal'.

These kinds of arguments may not be appropriate for all offences. For example, embezzlers can scarcely claim that their offences are merely 'technical', nor can they readily claim that someone else was to blame (Benson 1985). They may, therefore, rely on mitigations which stress personal or financial problems. In addition, small business proprietors have fewer opportunities to blame someone else in the organization, as they themselves are responsible for the majority of tasks and supervision. However, they can claim that the law has an unfair impact on their business in comparison with the large corporation. Strategies of defence therefore will be used where they are likely to be most credible. Despite the wide variety of offences and individual circumstances many common themes can be discerned in the kinds of arguments offered. The most common strategies will now be described using the categories developed from the author's observation of offenders prosecuted under Consumer Protection legislation (Croall 1987, 1988).

'Someone else's fault'

Where organizational offences are involved, defendants often attempt to blame someone else, even where they themselves accept legal responsibility. Therefore, it is argued that offences are *really* someone else's fault. This can be lower level employees or company executives – depending on which position the defendant occupies. Even where statutory defences are not used and defendants plead guilty, third parties are blamed in mitigation. Suppliers blame manufacturers, manufacturers blame staff or suppliers, employees blame employers and employers blame employees. Even victims may be blamed. Attributing offences to some other person is a very common strategy and in cases observed in court, 60 per cent of defendants used these kinds of arguments (Croall 1988).

Where 'companies' are defendants, lower level employees are often directly or indirectly blamed for offences. Offences can be attributed generally to sabotage or to the activities of disgruntled and unreliable staff. Inferences that individual staff were to blame could on occasion be accompanied by an implication that they no longer worked for the company, indicating that the 'problem' had been solved and was therefore not likely to occur again. One representative of a catering firm argued that there had been a 'degree of carelessness' among the staff and that therefore 'my clients are absolved from responsibility'. General staffing difficulties could also be blamed, implying that the carelessness of staff was due, not to management's inefficiency, but to labour problems in general.

Higher officials are another target for blame (Box 1983), as are many others in the organization, about whose activities individual defendants frequently claim ignorance. This may be the case in anti-trust offences or major frauds involving more than one conspirator. Offenders may claim that other defendants were 'really' to blame and that they have become the 'scapegoat' (Benson 1985). This is especially likely where offences are highly organized, and involve the collusion and co-operation of many participants.

In offences which involve the sale of substandard, unsafe or underweight goods, or unfit food, the blame may lie at different stages in the chain of production and sale. While the onus of the law often falls on sellers, statutory defences provide the opportunity to pass legal responsibility onto third parties. Anticipating such defences, manufacturers or suppliers or even both can be prosecuted, which allows each to blame the other. Sellers routinely blame suppliers for providing them with unsatisfactory goods, or not giving them sufficient information. Suppliers, in turn, blame sellers for ignoring instructions, for storing food incorrectly or otherwise tampering with goods. In other cases, victims were accused of ignoring instructions or damaging goods. In one case seen in court, a supermarket chain claimed that mouldy patches on pre-packaged cheese were caused by customers with long nails handling and puncturing the packets (Croall 1988). Companies may also argue that workers ignore safety precautions or that customers themselves are to blame for injuries inflicted by dangerous goods as they have ignored instructions (Braithwaite and Condon 1978).

Technological factors – problems are 'inevitable'

Another common argument is that offences are inevitable results of the technology of specific production processes. This can be the basis of a statutory defence, provided that all possible steps have been taken to prevent an offence by, for example, the introduction of systems of checking that abuses have not occurred (Cranston 1984). Proving the existence of such systems may be difficult, but these kinds of arguments were offered in mitigation in cases where defendants or expert witnesses provided details of the technological processes involved in the business concerned. Thus, the court could receive lengthy descriptions of the technicalities of baking bread, or the machinery required to scan foodstuffs for the presence of 'foreign bodies'. One expert witness, following a long explanation of the scientific and technical principles underlying bread production, concluded that 'bread making is not an exact science', and that it was therefore impossible to ensure that all loaves in a batch would weigh exactly the same.

Following these kinds of detailed explanations it was regularly concluded that 'no system could be perfect', that 'freaks' could occur or that 'human error' or 'accidents' could not be ruled out. Milk companies routinely detail the intricacies of scanning machinery, and stress that millions of bottles of milk do not contain foreign objects which are often, they argue, left in bottles by customers who don't wash them adequately. Occasional problems are therefore inevitable. In one case, a producer of meat pies outlined in laborious detail the conditions under which his pies were produced, and presented in court the results of his own experiment to determine the conditions under which they could become mouldy. After passing round a number of pies in various stages of decomposition, he concluded that, 'one cannot escape the possibility . . . of a rogue pie'. In another case, much debate centred around the incubation period of fly larvae, to determine at what point in the chain of supply insect infestation had originated. After this, a Magistrate commented that perhaps one needed a degree in biology to determine where the apricots had been contaminated.

Similar strategies are used where systems of monitoring arrangements for price marking, stock rotation or quality control are involved. Defendants in these kinds of cases took great pains to describe such systems. In one case, a senior manager in charge of pricing goods for a supermarket chain gave lengthy details of how pricing instructions were passed to individual store managers about price changes and special offers in order to demonstrate that the fault lay with the store manager. Other offences involve failure to carry out improvements, as was the case where hygiene regulations were involved. Restaurateurs often elaborated on the technical difficulties of the particular business, on occasion providing technical drawings and builder's estimates to underline their case. The structure of the premises, or the difficulties of keeping particular parts of it clean would be described in detail to demonstrate that compliance was particularly difficult for the defendant concerned.

There have been few detailed studies of the mitigations offered in financial frauds (Levi 1987a), but it is likely that the technicalities of corporate finance provide scope for similar arguments, and offences attributed to inevitable accounting 'mistakes'. Tax evaders, for example, claim that offences occur 'by mistake' or oversight, and that failure to disclose earnings are merely 'omissions' (Cook 1989a). It is also possible that these kinds of excuses may be offered by defendants in other regulatory areas where the technicalities of production processes are similarly complex and scientific and technological knowledge is required to ensure that offences do not occur. Carson (1981), for example, comments that after listening to official accounts of accidents in the North Sea it appeared that all waves causing accidents were 'freak waves'. Officials also argued that the industry was operating at the 'frontiers of technology' - defying the institution of adequate safety precautions.

Business values and business practice

As was seen in Chapter 4, many offences are justified on the grounds that they are part and parcel of business practice. In court, these kinds of justifications could be offered in mitigation and, where appropriate, defendants argued that occasional offences were inevitable outcomes of the need to maintain profit levels or were necessitated by competitive pressures. These arguments tend to accompany descriptions of the technical difficulties of compliance faced by the particular business. While they did all they could to prevent offences, to eliminate them altogether could be extremely costly. These costs might involve a reduction in profit margins or be passed onto the consumer. Similar arguments were also used by small businesses who claimed that they could not afford complex machinery. The representative for a bakery, responding to a prosecution argument that following the precedent set in the case of *Tesco v Nattrass* [(1972) A.C. 153] it was the baker's responsibility to make sure metal did not enter his products, exclaimed, 'this is a small bakers, not Tesco's'. He went on to argue that the law could surely not require all bakeries to install metal detectors.

Appeals to profit margins imply that of course businesses are there to make a profit and anything which threatens profits is therefore unacceptable. Practices necessitated by the interests of profit and competition are justifiable, even where they might lead to the occasional offence. Thus, the legal representative of a chocolate manufacturer explained that the company used plastic moulds, which unfortunately were less reliable than metal moulds and occasionally chipped, leaving plastic chips in the chocolate. The use of these moulds was, none the less, necessary as they were cheaper and used by major competitors. In this way, arguments fall short of criticizing the law itself. Rather, the law is supported but its application in particular circumstances is questioned.

The narrow borderline between acceptable and unacceptable business activities, and the difficulties of defining at what point a particular activity is illegal can also be used in defence strategies. In financial cases, defence attorneys frequently exploit the ambiguities of the law by arguing that offences lie on the boundary of legitimacy rather than illegitimacy (Mann 1985). In commercial fraud cases, 'custom and practice' defences have been accepted by Judges and led to acquittals (Levi 1987a). Thus, a defendant in an alleged commodity broking fraud was acquitted following evidence by experts that his activities were established market practice, and defendants accused of 'window dressing' accounts were acquitted on the grounds that this was common practice in the City of London at the time. Similarly, defence counsel in a case involving multiple share applications in the British Telecom flotation argued, amongst other things, that such applications were 'hallowed practice in the City of London' (Levi 1987a: 231). These are of course more complicated ways of saying, as tax evaders do, that 'everybody does it' (Benson 1985; Cook 1989a).

'It's not so serious', 'It's not really criminal'.

These strategies all implicitly involve denials of blameworthiness and intent, which also underly the common tactic of arguing that offences are merely 'technical' or trivial matters in comparison to other imaginary really serious or 'criminal' offences. Defendants, who are almost always portrayed as honest, reputable and reliable, are compared with images of the unscrupulous businesses against whom the law is really directed. Even where fraudulent intent is implied by the nature of the offence, where, for example, goods may have been sold in short measure, or blatantly misleading descriptions have been used, any dishonesty is almost always ritually denied. It is argued that while some traders unfortunately use 'sharp practices' and deliberately 'con' consumers, this is not the case in this instance.

Others claim that their offence is trivial, compared with what they might have done if they were *really* dishonest. Thus, a car dealer claimed that if he had intended to defraud he would have turned back the odometer to read 40,000 miles, not 2,000 as he had been charged. A publican argued that he would have put more water in his gin if he had really wanted to make more profits. Where no dishonesty is implied, defendants point out that their case is not as serious as others. Restaurateurs in hygiene cases on occasion argued that their restaurant was not really very dirty, that no-one had complained of being ill and that after all the many summons related to only one room. A version of this argument was provided by counsel for the South West Water Authority in the prosecution following the Camelford water pollution incident. In this case it was argued not only that there had been a 'witch hunt' against the authority, but also that the contaminated water, which caused long-term illness in some consumers, had 'never been more acidic than many household fizzy drinks' (*The Guardian* 8/1/91).

This all leads to the inevitable conclusion that while the law is directed at unscrupulous or persistently negligent traders, the offence in question is only 'technical' and not terribly serious. Thus, counsel for a coal merchant argued that this was merely a 'commercial offence' and another counsel referred to the matter as a 'purely technical offence'. This would appear to be a common argument for many other white collar offences. Levi (1987a: 230), for example, recounts a case involving a defendant on a charge of fraudulent trading who had apparently legitimately traded for some time before becoming insolvent. Counsel argued that 'this is not a case where a company was set up with the deliberate intention of defrauding', thereby distancing the defendant from real culpability and attempting to move the judge away from a focus on the harm done. Similarly, Benson (1985) found that anti-trust offenders justified offences as merely harmless business practices that happen to be 'technical violations' and argued that offences were very different from those of street criminals. Similarly, Mann (1985) describes cases in which attorneys stressed the technical as opposed to criminal nature of violations, coupled with arguments that elements of intent were absent. Embezzlers argue that their offences were not as serious as they might have been, given the large sums that they could have embezzled (Benson 1985).

Business reputation and personal characteristics

Defendants in all criminal cases tend to appeal in mitigation to their good character, family situation and reputation, in an attempt to present offences as 'uncharacteristic' and out of the ordinary (Benson 1985). While white collar offenders more often deny culpability using the strategies outlined above, they are in addition more likely to be able to claim respectability and blame-free records (Mann 1985; Wheeler *et al.*, 1988). In addition to other strategies therefore white collar defendants often claim that their offences are isolated incidents in an otherwise blame-free career. The reputation of businesses was often stressed in court, and defendants cited their experience, their lack of previous offences, or the absence of consumer complaints (Croall 1988). Defendants in the Guinness trials produced witnesses and evidence to testify to their good character and business records prior to the ill-fated take over battle (Levi 1991b). Witnesses can also be called to confirm their continuing faith in establishments and the long-standing reputation of businesses in the community could also be brought out.

Where these kinds of arguments are not appropriate, either due to the seriousness or nature of the offence, more conventional mitigations appealing to family, domestic and personal pressures could also be used. Some defendants were clearly not very experienced in business and this inexperience in itself could be cited in mitigation, as could financial pressures and domestic problems. This was an evident attempt to attract sympathy for the struggling small business. Of course, embezzlers may have few options other than to claim personal or financial difficulties. The likely adverse effects of conviction can also be used in mitigation, and defendants often point to the damaging publicity, loss of reputation and custom that may follow, arguing that this in itself is a sufficient penalty (Mann 1985; Levi 1987a, 1991b; Croall 1988, 1991). The significance of this and other mitigations for sentencing will be explored in Chapter 7.

Many defendants use a combination of arguments and represented defendants in court used more than unrepresented defendants (Croall 1988). Basically, strategies aim to present the defendant as an honest, reputable and compliant business person, who regrets the offence and who has taken all reasonable steps to prevent offences occurring. Therefore, while technically guilty, defendants are not really to blame and certainly should not be treated as criminals. Law is rarely directly criticized, but is implicitly portrayed as being unfair in its demands on individual businesses. In this way defendants aim to secure the sympathy of the court, and strategies reveal defendants' perceptions of what they think the court wants and expects. Therefore, they reflect an assumed consensus of values about the application of the criminal law to the regulation of business.

Summary and discussion

Studies of courtroom proceedings therefore further illustrate the structural advantages enjoyed by white collar offenders discussed in Chapter 5. The superior resources of some, though not all defendants, can be used to present more credible defence strategies, many of which exploit the many ambiguities in the law itself and the ambiguous criminal status of offences. This enables many defendants to deny imputations of blame or intent, to present themselves as fundamentally honest and reputable business persons and thus, of course, as undeserving of harsh punishment.

These advantages are not simply a consequence of the class and status of offenders. While it has been seen that the greater ability of offenders to employ more, and presumably better, legal representation is an undoubted advantage, it has also been seen that not all offenders can so benefit. Indeed, some may experience the 'plight of the unrepresented defendant'. Simple contrasts between the wealthy business defendant and the poor street criminal can therefore be overdrawn. In addition, resources alone cannot guarantee a credible defence as this depends on the nature and circumstances of the individual offence. Mann argues, for example, that while client resources are crucial in determining the strength of defences, resources in themselves are not sufficient. Where there is little ambiguity in statutes, and where the client's behaviour cannot be portrayed as lying on the margin of legality, these kinds of strategies cannot be used even where the client may have considerable resources. Thus,

> client wealth always can be translated into a vigorous defense, when defense opportunities are available. The interesting question is where, when and how the resources can be applied. (Mann 1985: 236)

None the less, the nature of criminal proceedings and the law itself provide space for many white collar defendants to deny imputations of responsibility, intent or blameworthiness. They may be able to control potentially damaging information about the persistence and seriousness of their offences, even though this may be a factor precipitating prosecution. While it was seen in Chapter 5 that cases prosecuted are likely to represent the more 'heinous', serious or persistent offences, this is not evident in court as the long history of warnings and negotiations that typically precedes prosecution is not relevant. Defendants are, therefore, able to portray offences as trivial, technical matters, which are isolated incidents or unavoidable accidents. The strategic nature of these presentations can be seen in the reactions of enforcement officers in court, who are often cynical and critical when hearing defences (Cranston 1979; Croall 1988). Many complain that magistrates may be taken in by what they see as posturing, and may misunderstand the nature of enforcement policies.

Strict liability further allows defendants to deny dishonesty and intent and to compare themselves favourably to hypothetical *really* guilty parties. Strict liability, therefore, far from being 'hard' on businesses may have the opposite effect by allowing them to deny the *criminal* nature of their offences. Where on the other hand *mens rea* is required, the organizational nature of offences and the complexities of the law can allow defendants to minimize their apparent culpability. In the United States, guilty pleas can further prevent potentially incriminating evidence being revealed in a full trial (Mann 1985; Wheeler *et al.* 1988). In England and Wales, a high acquittal rate is often attributed to the inherent difficulties of convicting complex offences, which are difficult for lay persons to comprehend. Thus, the jury has arguably become a scapegoat for the inherently 'risky' nature of fraud trials (Levi 1983).

The credibility of defence presentations further reflects the ambiguous criminal status of white collar offences. Levi, for example, points out that there is a fundamental distinction between 'excusing' the activities of fraudsters as 'common practice', when similar attitudes would certainly not prevail towards lower class defendants. He asks:

> on what basis would we distinguish accepting the right to carry out window dressing of accounts from the right of young unemployed blacks to extract 'street rent' from passers-by, or from the right of Rastafarians to smoke cannabis, or even from the 'customary right' of employees to take home 'spare' produce from the workplace? (Levi 1987a: 209)

Defendants' arguments are therefore made more credible because their offences are assumed to be less criminal than others. Appeals to business values assume that business offences are *not* really criminal. As Levi (1983) points out, suggestions that the jury be abolished in complex fraud cases are more acceptable because fraud is not seen as 'real' crime. If this were to be suggested for real crimes it could be seen as infringing a basic principle of criminal justice.

7

SENTENCING WHITE COLLAR OFFENDERS

The study of the sentencing process raises similar issues to those explored in Chapters 5 and 6. In the first place it has to be asked whether, and on what grounds, sentences can be described as lenient. This involves looking at the range of sentences commonly used for different offences. Assessing whether this represents leniency, however, is a complicated question. Leniency assumes, for example, some kind of comparison – but what kind of comparison? Are sentences to be compared to those given to burglars or rapists? On what basis might such a comparison be made? Given the different nature of the offences, and the very different characteristics of offenders, it is unlikely that offences and offenders could be 'matched' as they are in much sentencing research. On the other hand, arguing that sentences are lenient could imply that they are insufficiently deterrent or punitive.

The issue of class bias also raises complex questions. In the first place it cannot be assumed that offenders are from high class or status backgrounds, which makes any simple association between sentencing patterns and class bias questionable. In addition, some offences may attract tougher sentences than others. The argument that 'anti-capitalist' offences are treated more harshly than offences which are more evidently 'in the pursuance of capitalism' (Pearce 1976), for example, suggests that frauds could be dealt with more severely than business regulatory offences (Leigh 1982). In addition, sentencers may not be consistent, and may have different views of the toughness or leniency of any particular sentence. Therefore, leniency, let alone class bias, cannot be inferred on the basis of outcomes alone.

Therefore, it becomes essential to explore the underlying rationale of sentences. There are, however, many difficulties facing researchers. The small numbers of prosecutions in white collar categories has tended to rule out large scale comparative studies (Hagan *et al.* 1980), leading to an over-reliance on individual cases or media accounts. Thus, Benson (1985: 584) argues that too much discussion has been based on anecdotal evidence and on 'famous' cases where the individuals concerned 'most likely do not represent typical white collar offenders'. A large part of the relevant research is American and may not be readily applicable to England and Wales (Leigh 1982). There is a scarcity of official information, particularly for business regulatory offences (see also Chapter 2). While some information can be obtained from individual Government Departments, for others, not even enforcement departments collect the relevant data (Levi 1987a; Cook 1989b).

This chapter will start with a brief description of the range of sentences common for different categories of white collar offences, along with a discussion of whether or not they can be described as lenient. This will be followed by an account, based on available research, of the many factors which have been found to affect sentencers, and of how sentencers assess offences and offenders. The role of class and status will then be explored. This chapter will focus on the sentencing process itself leaving broader questions of the aims of sentencing policy for discussion in Chapters 8 and 9.

Derisory sentences?

The view that white collar offenders are lightly sentenced is based on the general finding that few are sent to prison, and that even if they are, they are not imprisoned for long periods of time. White collar offenders more commonly receive fines, many of which have been described as 'trifling' or 'derisory'. Thus, Levi (1987a: 213) comments that 'commercial fraudsters are not creating the crisis of overcrowding in the English penal system', and that fines are 'far from draconian' (Levi 1989a). A brief outline of the range of sentences given to offenders in different offence categories is given below.

Employee theft, fraud and tax evasion

Starting with employee theft, the Supplementary Criminal Statistics for 1988 reveal that 40 per cent of men and 24 per cent of women sentenced in Crown Courts received a sentence of immediate imprisonment, in comparison with 39 per cent of males in all theft categories, and 19 per cent of women. In magistrates' courts, where more offenders were sentenced, a total of 2743 men and 776 women, representing three per cent and one per cent, respectively, were given a sentence of immediate imprisonment, compared with six per cent of men and two per cent of women in all categories of theft. In Crown Courts, therefore, imprisonment rates for employee theft were close to the average, whereas in magistrates' courts, theft by an employee was among those theft categories least likely to be dealt with by immediate imprisonment. Theft categories most likely to attract imprisonment were theft of a motor vehicle, theft in a dwelling and theft from the person. Offenders were also given community service and probation orders, fines and suspended sentences. No breakdowns are given which relates these sentences to the amounts of money involved in the thefts, although it could be assumed that more serious and organized thefts would be sentenced in Crown Courts, where prison was used more often.

During the 1980s an increasing number of fraudsters received prison sentences (Levi 1987a, 1989a). Between 1979 and 1987 the numbers of male fraudsters imprisoned rose from 1300 to 2100, representing between 48 and 51 per cent of those convicted. This increase is, according to Levi, more likely to be a result of the increased numbers of convictions and the introduction of partially suspended sentences, than of toughening Judicial attitudes. In general, sentences of imprisonment are not especially long – only 19 offenders in 1987 received sentences of more than four years, generally regarded as the 'cut off' point for long-term prison sentences (Levi 1989a: 422). The main alternative to prison for fraudsters is a fine, and the average fine for fraud and forgery in 1987 was £89 for men and £69 for women in magistrates' courts, and in Crown Courts, £316 for men and £128 for women. In 1985, only 13 men and two women were fined in excess of £1000 for fraud and forgery (Levi 1987a, 1989a). If £200 is taken as a 'notional cut-off' for a substantial fine, Levi's conclusion that fines are far from draconian would appear to be justified. Few sentences other than fines and imprisonment are recorded – in 1988 in Crown Courts, 377 men sentenced for fraud were given community service orders, and a further 251 were given probation orders (Supplementary Criminal Statistics 1988), although fraudsters are more likely than other property offenders to have to pay compensation (Levi 1989a).

Very little information is available about other financial offences. Until recently in England and Wales insider dealers were rarely if ever imprisoned, and before 1988 only two fines for multiple share applications and insider dealing exceeded £10,000 (Levi 1989a). Like fraudsters, tax evaders can expect to be imprisoned, although it is not clear which kinds of offenders are more likely to receive prison sentences. Deane (1981) found that principal as opposed to subordinate offenders were likely to be imprisoned, and Cook (1989a) suggests that financial advisers are more likely to receive harsher sentences. Levi (1989a) records that in 1986–7, 133 offenders involved in fraudulent evasion of VAT, 15 per cent of the total, were imprisoned, and in 1987–8, 163 offenders were fined an average of £25,438 for this offence. Unfortunately for researchers, however, imprisonment figures are no longer available (Levi 1989a).

Business regulatory offences

Details for business regulatory offences are especially difficult to obtain, and official sources, such as reports of the Office of Fair Trading, indicate little more than the total amounts of fines imposed on the total number of offences in individual offence categories. None the less, it is immediately evident that in comparison with tax evaders and fraudsters fewer business regulatory offenders are imprisoned (Croall 1991). For cases under consumer protection legislation, including trade descriptions, weights and measures, and food offences, prison sentences are rare, and almost exclusively reserved for car dealers involved in 'clocking' cases. Between 1985 and 1987, according to the Annual Reports of the Office of Fair Trading, a total of 45 offenders were imprisoned and a further 34 received suspended sentences. Overall, this represents a prisonization rate of between one and two per cent, much lower than the figures quoted for tax and fraud cases (Croall 1991).

The most common sentence used in these and other regulatory offences is the fine, and the maximum fines during the 1980s ranged from £1000–£2000, although some have now been raised considerably. Actual fines imposed generally fall short of these maxima, although some offences can attract substantial fines. In 1986–7, for example, average fines under the Trade Descriptions Act were £561, under the Weights and Measures Act £300, and under the Food and Drugs Acts £368. Trade descriptions cases involving motor vehicles tend to attract higher sentences as do Food Hygiene cases, where fines exceeding £2000 are now more regularly recorded, on occasion exceeding £10,000 (Croall 1991).

Fines are virtually the only sentence used for other business regulatory offences. In 1988, only one offender received a sentence of imprisonment in the Public Health category and without exception all regulatory offences listed in the Supplementary Criminal Statistics in 1988 were dealt with exclusively by fines. Levels of fines are not widely publicized, although they can, in some cases, be substantial. For example, a 'record' fine of one million pounds was imposed on the Shell corporation following the escape of crude oil into the River Mersey (*Independent* 24/2/90), but Richardson *et al.* (1982) found that average fines under Public Health, Clean Air and Alkali Acts were only 50 per cent of the maximum. Fines for offences under safety legislation are also relatively low – even following fatal accidents, for example, typical fines tend to be between £200 and £400 (*Independent* 14/12/90).

In very broad terms, therefore, a different pattern of sentences can be discerned for different kinds of offences. Offenders in the categories of employee theft, fraud and tax evasion can be imprisoned, given community service or probation orders, as well as being fined. On the other hand, offences in the business regulatory area are almost exclusively dealt with by fines, which tend to fall short of legal maxima. In the relatively few instances where regulatory offenders are imprisoned, offences are more readily equitable with 'real crime', as is the case, for example, with car clocking. Thus, the broad distinction between crimes against and crimes in the course of capitalism appears to have some substance, in that imprisonment is more often used for offences of employees as opposed to employers. However, it is extremely difficult in the absence of sufficient detail about the offences and offenders involved to make any more than broad comparisons. In addition, sentencing levels are constrained by legal maxima, which tend to be lower for business regulatory offences. Where companies are concerned, imprisonment is not an option and few alternatives to the almost universal fine are considered.

Are sentences derisory?

The next question to be considered is the extent to which these sentences can be described as lenient or derisory. In general, white collar offenders do seem to be sent to prison less often than some other groups. For example, fewer of those convicted for fraud and forgery are imprisoned than the equivalent figure for burglary and, given the higher sums of money typically involved, this could be interpreted as amounting to leniency (Levi 1989b). However, sentencers in practice take into account many factors, the harm done by offences being only one amongst many. To compare fraud or employee theft, let alone organizational offences, with burglary or robbery is simply not comparing like with like, as the nature of the offences is very different, let alone the characteristics of typical offenders. Fraudsters and employees convicted of theft, for example, often claim in mitigation that they have lost their jobs have therefore been punished already and have little opportunity to repeat their offences. As Levi (1989b: 99) asks, how do we weight the loss of *em*ployment prospects for the convicted fraudster against the continued *unem*ployment prospects of the typical burglar? Drawing any inferences about leniency in comparison with other offences and offenders is therefore likely to be highly subjective and possibly misleading.

None the less, there are other grounds for arguing that sentences are 'derisory'. In the first place, even substantial fines of £2000–£3000 imposed on wealthy offenders or multi-national corporations could be interpreted as trifling when the offender's ability to pay is taken into account. It has also been argued that fines often bear little relationship to and may well not exceed the illicit profits from offences. Levi (1987a: 217), for example, analysing Customs and Excise data for 1985–6, comments that income from settlements and court fines amounted to just over four million pounds, whereas tax arrears amounted to £23 million. Similarly, the Keith Committee which reported on aspects of Revenue offences concluded that – 'compared with the scale of culpable arrears, the fines imposed in the larger cases (of tax evasion) are modest' (cited in Levi 1987a: 217). Sir Gordon Borrie, Director General of Fair Trading, has described the typical fines given in car clocking cases as 'pinpricks' – arguing that whereas as much as £500 could be added to the value of a car, fines rarely match this extra profit (Borrie 1984).

Some argue that these kinds of fines amount to a licence to break the law, as the benefits of law breaking exceed the likely costs (Box 1983; Braithwaite 1984a; Cranston 1984). Cranston (1979), for example, argues that too often fines can be treated as a minor business expense. The costs of conviction may also be far less than the cost of preventive action. Thus, Levi (1989b: 106), citing a 1988 case in which British Petroleum were fined £750,000 following the deaths of three workers, queries whether such an apparently large sum is really substantial in relation to the cost of preventing such accidents, particularly in view of the financial assets of the corporation. Morris (1976: 115) provides an amusing example of this kind of reasoning in his description of the case of a building contractor who was fined £20 on two separate occasions for failing to erect a protective boarding around his works. When asked on his third appearance how much a boarding would cost, he estimated that it would cost £100. According to Morris, he was then fined £150, and 'the boarding erected forthwith'.

These arguments reflect concerns that sentences have little deterrent value. Borrie (1984) for example, has complained that the Trade Descriptions Act is undermined by 'laughably' inadequate fines which deter nobody. Similarly the Keith Committee, in the passage cited above, continues, 'given the circumstances and scale of the larger frauds, it is questionable whether such sentences have significant deterrent value' (Keith Committee 1983: 357 cited in Levi 1987a: 217). Enforcers regularly voice similar doubts, and further argue that low fines undermine their activities (Cranston 1979; Richardson *et al.* 1982; Croall 1987; Hutter 1988). One department studied by the author complained publicly that fines of only £10 given to establishments who had broken hygiene regulations or sold unfit food jeopardized the council's enforcement efforts (Croall 1991). Similar sentiments were expressed by the Health and Safety Executive (1988: 30) who argued:

> it is sometimes disappointing for inspectors, and more seriously it gives the wrong signal to management, when serious failures in health and safety attract relatively trivial fines... we sometimes wonder whether such fines sufficiently reflect the importance which society attaches to the prevention of accidents and ill health. (Cited in Levi Levi 1989b: 106)

There is, therefore, a general consensus amongst many commentators that sentences for many white collar offences are too light. This is particularly the case for many business regulatory offences, especially where large corporations are concerned. For such offenders, even seemingly enormous amounts may be relatively trivial expenses. The rationales underlying these sentences have therefore to be explored.

The paradox of leniency and severity

In practice, sentencers consider a large number of factors relating to both the circumstances of the individual offence and the characteristics of the individual offender. In addition, sentences may reflect a number of different aims – they may be directed at deterrence or rehabilitation, or be based on considerations of retribution or 'just deserts'. Serious offences would normally be expected to attract a heavy penalty on the grounds of either retribution or deterrence, but these considerations can be outweighed by the particular circumstances of individual offences and offenders. First offenders, the very young or old, some women and offenders who appear less culpable may be likely to receive lighter sentences on such an individualized basis (see, for example, Thomas 1978). Sentencers may, however, have different views about which offences are more or less serious, and which characteristics of offenders are significant. They may also have different views about which sentences can best achieve their preferred aims (see, for example, Hood and Sparks 1970; Hogarth 1971; Thomas 1978). This produces considerable disparities and inconsistencies when the sentencing patterns of different courts for similar offence categories are compared (Tarling 1979). In addition, sentencers are likely to be influenced by the information they are given about both offences and offenders, information which is provided by a number of different participants in the system (Hood and Sparks 1970; Wheeler *et al.* 1988).

All these factors affect the sentencing of white collar offenders (Wheeler *et al.* 1988; Levi 1989a, 1989b; Croall 1991). This was evident in a major study carried out by Wheeler and his colleagues who interviewed judges about their decisions in white collar cases (Wheeler *et al.* 1988). Three 'core legal norms' – harm, blame and seriousness, emerged as the main factors affecting judges' assessments of offences. In addition, judges also took into account the often blame-free records of offenders and the likely effects of prosecution and punishment. Similar considerations are reflected in the sentencing guidelines for fraud in England and Wales (Levi 1989a), which indicate that sentencers should take into account the defendant's character, whether or not the defendant has pleaded guilty, the length of time over which frauds have been perpetrated and the amount of money involved. Disparities emerge largely because individual sentencers weight these factors differently in individual cases (Wheeler *et al.* 1988; Levi 1989a).

The seriousness of the offence

The harm done by offences and their effect on victims are crucial factors underlying sentencers' assessments of seriousness. This can mean that many white collar offences are regarded as less serious than others as they are unlikely to involve violence. Even where physical harm is involved, defendants can rarely be accused of intending to harm individual victims. The 'rippling effect' (Sutherland 1949) of many white collar crimes also, of course, means that individual victims may lose very little, even though the illegal profits may be considerable. In addition, the harm done is often difficult to quantify or is concealed, particularly where only one or two offences are the subject of an individual prosecution (see Chapter 6).

Wheeler *et al.* (1988: 63) found that all these factors were significant to judges, particularly the absence of physical injury in financial offences. For example, one judge commented that 'the most distinctive thing about white collar crime is the lack of violence'. Consequently, assessments of harm revolved around the amounts of money involved. A judge in Wheeler's study commented – 'these guys had stolen a million dollars. You just can't ignore stealing a million dollars' (Wheeler *et al.* 1988: 66). In England and Wales, Court of Appeal guidelines suggest a sliding scale of sentences according to the amounts involved. In the leading case of *Barrick* [(1985) 7 Cr App. R. (S.) cited in Levi 1989a: 424], the Court argued that while the sum involved in a fraud is not the only factor to be considered, terms of imprisonment up to 18 months were appropriate for sums of less than £10,000, whereas 2–3 year sentences were appropriate for sums of between £10,000 and £50,000. Sums in excess of £100,000 justify sentences of up to four and a half years.

The nature of victimization is also significant. In fraud cases, for example, judges distinguished between individual and organizational victims, the latter being generally considered as 'less victimized' (Wheeler *et al.* 1988). On the other hand, individual victims were seen as relatively defenceless and offences were likely to be considered more serious if they involved poor victims. British guidelines similarly indicate not only that the effect of fraud on the victim should be considered, but also that they are considered more serious where private individuals are concerned (Levi 1989a).

Unlike fraud, some business regulatory offences have an actual or potential physical impact. While it is difficult to estimate how this affects sentencers, there are some indications that it may be a consideration. Concerns about public health, for example, may underlie the heavier sentences given to food hygiene cases. In court, magistrates did indicate signs of disgust and distate when long lists of summons detailing filth, dirt and insect infestation in food preparation areas were read out (Croall 1991). In addition, nearly all cases found in reports in the *British Food Journal* which had directly resulted in food poisoning received larger than average fines

(Croall 1987). It was seen in Chapter 2 that other offences can result in injuries or physical harm, such as those involving 'foreign bodies' in food, as a result of which some victims have been hospitalized. There is no clear indication, however, that these consequences lead to heavier sentences, and many continue to attract fines of under £200 (Croall 1991).

Similar inconsistencies can be found in relation to other offences, although it is difficult to assess relative severity or leniency. The uneven effects of injuries can be seen in the many complaints about the low fines which follow fatal accidents at work, but at the same time, Hutter and Lloyd Bostock (1990) suggest that fines can be higher following accidents and cite the case referred to above, where BP were fined £750,000 following seven deaths, as an example of this tendency. None the less, this same case is cited by Levi (1989a) as an example of a fine which can be considered lenient in view of the vast resources of the company concerned. Similarly, fines in cases of pollution are difficult to interpret. Is, for example, the fine of £10,000 imposed on the South Western Water Authority following the pollution of the water in Camelford, which affected 20,000 consumers, to be considered as high or low? It is very probably the case that while injuries and dangers to health are taken seriously, their effect is considerably lessened by the defence strategies described in Chapter 6, where defendants argue that they are not to 'blame' and that these unfortunate occurrences are isolated incidents.

Also significant is the extent to which offences appear to involve a serious breach of occupational trust. Thomas (1978), in his study of Court of Appeal judgements, found that breaches of occupational trust were more likely to be severely dealt with even where mitigating factors such as regular employment or possible loss of status were present. This was especially the case with public servants. Wheeler *et al.* (1988) similarly found that breaches of occupational trust were regarded more seriously, particularly where politicians, public servants, professionals, and senior executives were involved. In such cases judges could argue that violations damaged the fabric of society. One judge, for example, expressed the opinion that tax evaders were 'simply stealing public money', whereas in political corruption offenders 'are endangering the very foundation of government itself' (Wheeler *et al.* 1988: 79). British judges have also expressed such sentiments. In the leading case of *Barrick*, referred to above, the quality and degree of trust reposed in the offender, including his rank, is cited as a ground for aggravating the sentence (cited in Levi 1989a: 425).

Similar considerations may affect business regulatory offences where individuals can be directly implicated. A recent case involved the conviction of a train driver for manslaughter following the Purley rail crash in which five people died and eighty-seven were injured. Sentencing the driver to eighteen months imprisonment with twelve months suspended, Mr Justice Kennedy stated that

> those who provide services to the public should do so carefully... passengers put themselves in a very special sense in the hands of the driver... they trust him entirely: it is not just one person but hundreds who entrust themselves. (*Financial Times* 4/9/90: 10)

Other characteristics of offences can affect how seriously they are viewed. Offences which have taken place over a long period of time are considered more serious than 'one off', isolated incidents, a factor which also affects prosecution decisions (see Chapter 5). Sentencers may consider whether or not individuals have made a direct profit from offences, and the use to which the money or property has been put (Wheeler *et al.* 1988; Levi 1989a, 1989b). These considerations are linked closely to judgements of dishonesty and intent, which are crucial in assessing offenders' blameworthiness (Wheeler *et al.* 1988).

Blameworthiness

It was seen in Chapter 6 that defence strategies attempt to conceal information which might reveal evidence of dishonesty or intent. That these strategies may be effective is indicated by the significance which sentencers appear to attach to such information. Wheeler *et al.* (1988: 94) found that judges frequently referred to degrees of 'scheming', planning and calculation in their assessments of culpability. Similarly Levi (1989a: 424) comments that sentencers distinguish between cases of deliberate 'pre-planned' fraud and 'slippery slope' cases where 'business people – rightly or wrongly – are perceived to have started honestly, but to have traded recklessly later'.

Both Wheeler's and Levi's studies cover mainly financial frauds, heard in higher courts, for which proof of intent is necessary for conviction. For regulatory offences, however, the absence of apparent 'moral fault' may in itself account for lower sentences (Leigh 1982). This is underlined by the tougher sentences attracted by regulatory offences which do involve elements of dishonesty, such as car clocking. Leading cases clearly indicate that it is elements of dishonesty and unscrupulousness which make imprisonment appropriate. In the case of *R v Hammerton's Cars* [(1976) 3 All E.R. 758], it was argued that:

> ... the Trade Descriptions Act was intended by Parliament to provide protection for the public against unscrupulous and irresponsible traders... the courts should discourage them by taking all the profit out of the transaction and a good deal more.

Similar sentiments can be seen in *R v Gupta* [(1985) Criminal Law Review 81] where it was argued that:

> This kind of fraud called for an immediate custodial sentence, together

> with a substantial fine. It was very important that the substantial profits made from this kind of behaviour should be taken from the dishonest second hand car dealer.

Where offences are closer to 'real crime', therefore, sentences may be heavier, and prison sentences were also given to the traders involved in the organized sale of unfit meat. Indeed, it was the low maximum sentences under the Food and Drugs Act, at the time £100 per offence or six months imprisonment, that led to the raising of maximum fines in 1982. Considerable lobbying by Environmental Health Officers focused on the inadequacy of sentences for what was a highly organized fraudulent activity. However, not all business regulatory offences which apparently involve organization or dishonesty attract consistently higher sentences. For example, traders selling falsely described 'Gucchi chokers' were fined a mere £200, and fines of between £5 and £50 were given to publicans selling short measure drinks (Croall 1991). In these kinds of cases, sentencers may consider that consumers should be able to judge for themselves the evident falseness of descriptions, whereas the second-hand car buyer is in a far more vulnerable position.

There are a number of indications, therefore, that some but not all white collar offences can attract strong condemnation from sentencers, particularly where the harm done is considerable, where offenders clearly intend offences, where a serious breach of trust is involved, and where offences are persistent. It is therefore significant that, as seen in Chapter 6, it is these elements which are often disguised in court. Wheeler *et al.* (1988) found that judges often complained that they had insufficient information about offences, particularly where cases were uncontested. Their effect is also likely to be reduced by the focus of individual prosecutions on selected offences which disguises their persistence. In addition, the effect of these 'sentence aggravating factors' can in practice be outweighed by a range of 'sentencing mitigating' factors (Wheeler *et al.* 1988).

Blame-free records and process as punishment

The 'paradox of leniency and severity' arises when the characteristics of individual offenders mitigate the severity of the sentence. Particularly important are the apparently 'blame-free' records of many white collar offenders (see, for example, Wheeler *et al.* 1988). Levi (1987a), for example, observes that 32 per cent of those convicted of fraud and forgery were first offenders compared with 19 per cent of burglars. This may occur because once frauds are detected and prosecuted, offenders are less likely to be in a position to commit further offences. However, especially for regulatory offences, offenders may not, of course, be as blame-free as they appear, as prosecutions often follow the long history of negotiation characteristic of law enforcement (see Chapter 5). None the less, many offenders are able to present their offences as isolated incidents in an otherwise blame-free career (see Chapter 6).

White collar offenders also claim that the process of investigation, prosecution and trial in itself constitutes punishment. A common mitigation is that offenders, and their innocent families, have been under considerable stress as a result of the proceedings, and that their conviction will inevitably lead to loss of reputation and employment. Therefore, they argue, no further punishment is needed (Mann *et al.* 1980; Levi 1987; Wheeler *et al.* 1988). Business proprietors and companies can claim that they have lost trade, and that the combined effect of publicity and prosecution have jeopardized the survival of their businesses (Croall 1987). Many convicted tax evaders are professional advisers who argue that they have been professionally ruined and will, in any event, no longer be in a position to commit further offences. Thus, the social disgrace of conviction is presented as punishment in itself (Deane 1981; Cook 1989a), and in addition those who have lost their employment status can argue that no deterrent is necessary as they cannot repeat their offences (Wheeler *et al.* 1988; Levi 1989b).

The extent to which these arguments affect sentencers appears to vary. Wheeler *et al.* (1988) found that judges experience a dilemma. While, on the one hand, many tended to agree that conviction and its consequences did constitute punishment for many offenders, and did take this into account, they also expressed concern that offenders should not be rewarded because of their high social status, and some discounted such arguments on the grounds of fairness. Similar sentiments are revealed in the comments of Mr Justice Henry on refusing leave to appeal against a £5 million fine imposed on one of the defendants in the *Guinness* case. Pointing out that both imprisonment and a fine were required to meet the 'particular gravity' of the offences he concluded that:

> punishments are after all intended to be punitive and the court must ensure that a man's wealth and power does not put him beyond punishment. (*The Guardian* 3/10/90)

Other characteristics of white collar offenders may also be associated with lighter sentences. They are often older, which underlines claims that further punishment is unnecessary as they are not likely to offend again. Others argue that their innocent families will be further penalized by the disgrace of a prison sentence. Wheeler *et al.* (1988) found that judges did take these arguments seriously, but question whether lower class defendants do not also have innocent families who might suffer? Offenders' standing in the community can also be used in mitigation, especially where they can provide evidence that they are community spirited and generous in their support of charity or other community work. That this can be effective was evident in the Guinness case. Sentencing one defendant, whose contribution to charity work and the community was considerable, the judge commented that 'giving money is easy enough if you have enough of it', but concluded that in view of the considerable time which the defendant gave to community work, the sentence should be kept low because

> I am very conscious of the good you have done in the past and the fact that the community will lose your full force for good while you are in prison. (Cited in Levi 1991b)

Companies can also use these kinds of arguments. Their possible effect is illustrated in the comments of the judge who imposed a record fine of one million pounds on Shell following the pollution of the Mersey with 157 tonnes of crude oil. Mr Justice Mars-Jones commented that the fine would have been higher had it not been for the company's good record on conservation, its generous support for the arts and its many contributions to other worthwhile causes. That the eventual fine reflected this mitigation was indicated by his subsequent comment that the company had enormous resources and could afford to pay a fine of several million pounds (*Financial Times* 24/2/90).

It is clearly impossible to quantify the effect of all these considerations, particularly as individual sentencers may have different views about their relative importance (Wheeler *et al.* 1988). Levi (1989a) argues that there are inconsistencies in the application of general guidelines, which in any case give few indications of how individual factors are to be weighted. What is clear is that white collar offenders do not *always* receive sympathetic treatment, and that leniency may be associated with the ability of white collar offenders to present themselves as undeserving of punishment. This, in turn, raises the question of whether sentencing decisions involve class bias.

Class and status

Very few researchers have been able to relate sentencing outcomes directly to social class and status, and research in the United States has found somewhat conflicting results. Wheeler *et al.* (1982), for example, suggest that contrary to what might be expected, high status offenders were more likely to receive harsher sentences. On the other hand Benson and Walker (1988) found that high status offenders stood no greater risk of being incarcerated. The somewhat unexpected finding from the first study attracted criticism on the grounds that class, not status, was the important variable. However, a subsequent analysis of the original data using the measurements of class position suggested by Hagan (1988) did not change the original findings substantially (Weisburd *et al.* 1990). Indeed, they argue that 'judges saw higher status as an indicator of blameworthiness'

(Weisburd *et al.* 1990: 237). However class or status are measured they argue that the effect of class is 'generally not consistent with a model that places the greatest disadvantage with those lowest down the ladder' (Weisburd *et al.* 1990: 239). There are no similar British studies, partly because there are so few high status offenders (Levi 1991b). In any event it could be argued that the effect of class or status on sentencing is unlikely to be clear cut when the other factors which affect sentencers are taken into account. Their significance is also called into question by the increasing evidence that many offenders are not from high status backgrounds. As Levi (1989b: 96) argues, 'few convicted fraudsters come from any elite that judges might have a supposed interest in protecting'.

There is also little evidence that sentencers empathize with defendants on the grounds of their presumed common background. For example, Mann *et al.* (1980) argue that while their interviews with judges revealed sympathy for defendants whose position in society was very much like their own, it was an open question whether empathy played an active role. In the author's research, some sympathy for defendants was evident by magistrates' sympathetic nods and comments, but this was equally as likely to be attracted by appeals to 'business values' as by the defendant's status (Croall 1991). Indeed, it could be suggested that sentencers might be unsympathetic to fellow business persons who have 'let the side down' (Levi 1989b; Croall 1991). Wheeler *et al.* (1982) also suggest that in the post-Watergate era, judges are offended by the crimes of the wealthy, and in some areas offences can be defined as against the interests of business (Croall 1991). In addition judges may, as Levi (1991b) suggests, be increasingly sensitive to possible criticism if they are seen to be 'letting off their own kind'. Class and status, therefore, may not exercise a direct influence on sentencers, but this does not mean that they are irrelevant. This will be further discussed after some other possible influences on sentencers have been explored.

Public opinion and community interests

Sentencers can also be influenced directly or indirectly by public opinion. They may feel, for example, that deterrent sentences are required where there is public concern about particular activities, which might be the case where similar cases have attracted extensive publicity or following accidents and disasters. These influences can operate at either a national or local level. While bench or community effects have been found to influence sentencing patterns for some kinds of crimes (Hood 1972), their possible influence on white collar offences has been relatively unexplored. Indeed, an absence of public concern has been assumed to lead to leniency. Sutherland (1949), for example, commented on the absence of well organized public resentment to white collar crime, and Levi (1987a) suggests that a significant factor in low fraud sentences was an absence of public hysteria about such sentences. However, events like the Watergate scandal in the United States may have affected Judicial perceptions of offences, and Wheeler *et al.* (1982) suggest that their finding that high status offenders received heavier sentences could be attributed to a 'Watergate effect'. In Britain, Levi (1989b: 89) suggests that fraud sentences may have increased in the 'fraud scandal era' of the late 1980s.

These kinds of influences are extremely difficult to pin down. In particular, any relationship between the socio-economic characteristics of local areas and sentencing patterns is difficult to uncover as inevitably, much research has been in higher courts, in large metropolitan conurbations where more financial frauds are likely to be processed. In Britain research has focused on Appeal Court rulings (Thomas 1978; Levi 1989a) and on offenders sentenced in London (Levi 1987a). In the United States, much research has focused on New York (Mann 1985) and federal district courts in large metropolitan conurbations (Benson and Walker 1988; Wheeler *et al.* 1988). There has, therefore, been little exploration of the potential significance of local and regional variations.

Nonetheless, some studies do indicate their possible effect. Benson and Walker (1988), for example, suggest that in large metropolitan areas, where there are more large scale white collar crimes, frequent exposure of serious business offences may appear to threaten the stability of the economic order and the legitimacy of the legal order. In these areas judges are regularly confronted with what they perceive to be challenges to the ideology of equal treatment and may, therefore, sentence the occasional big time offender harshly. In smaller federal districts, where offences are less frequent they may appear to pose less of a threat to the legal order. Therefore, they suggest, structural and contextual factors, rather than post-Watergate morality account for the contradictory findings on the effects of status.

However, these effects appear to be inconsistent. An alternative argument could be that in smaller areas, where white collar crimes are less frequent, they may appear more serious and may attract heavier, rather than lighter sentences. Levi (1987a), for example, found that sentences for some kinds of frauds were higher at Manchester Crown Court than at the London Central Criminal Court. The social and economic characteristics of some areas may also mean that some offences are seen as particularly threatening, a factor which could also affect enforcement policies (Chapter 5). Tentative indications of this can be seen in some consumer protection cases. In one case, a large catering company was given a relatively high fine following conviction for a variety of pricing and weights and measures offences at a sporting ground which hosted international fixtures. In passing sentence, the magistrate commented on the significance of the ground to the local area and the importance of ensuring high standards in an area dependent on tourism (Croall 1987, 1991). In a food hygiene case in a tourist resort, a magistrate is quoted as commenting:

> the Bench takes an extremely serious view of cases such as this especially in a town like . . . which derives its livelihood from restaurants and the hotel trade. We cannot really afford to have dirty restaurants or any premises which create these problems. (*British Food Journal* Mar/Apr 1988)

Enforcement departments themselves may influence these kinds of attitudes, and one department studied by the author attempted to influence magistrates' setencing policies both privately and publicly. Thus, magistrates were publicly criticized for imposing low fines which, they argued, inhibited their efforts (Croall 1987, 1991). Therefore, the policies and practices of enforcement departments may also be significant, although their effects may be inconsistent. Braithwaite and Vale (1985), for example, report that high prosecution rates were associated with lower penalties as active prosecution departments bring less serious cases to court. It is likely, none the less, that local considerations can influence sentencing patterns and should, therefore, be the subject of future research (Benson and Walker 1988).

Summary and discussion

It can be seen, therefore, that sentencers take into account both the seriousness of the offence and the individual characteristics of the offender very much as they do for conventional offences and offenders, producing the 'paradox of leniency and severity' found by Wheeler and his colleagues (Wheeler *et al.* 1988). Sentencers can and do view some offences seriously, and are aware of the problems of sentencing high status offenders who can present strong arguments in mitigation. Simple accusations of leniency and bias are, therefore, over simplistic and the taken for granted association between sentencing and the social class or status of offenders has to be closely examined.

While it is impossible to assess objectively whether sentences are lenient, especially in comparison with other groups, it has been argued that they can be so interpreted. Many groups criticize sentences on the grounds that they are insufficiently deterrent – especially when the resources of offenders are taken into account. In addition, the low rates of imprisonment and the levels of fines given to fraudsters can be favourably compared with the treatment of burglars or thieves who constitute perhaps the closest comparative group – particularly bearing in mind the larger sums involved. When equivalent offences like social security fraud and tax evasion are compared, it is also evident that tax evaders are dealt with far less severely (Cook 1989a, 1989b).

Allegations of class bias, however, are difficult to sustain, and there is little evidence to suggest that high status defendants receive any more favourable treatment – indeed, there have been suggestions that the reverse might be true (Wheeler *et al.* 1988; Weisburd *et al.* 1990). On the whole, sentences are milder because the offences themselves are seen as less serious than many conventional crimes, particularly crimes of violence, and because offenders can present themselves as fundamentally honest and respectable citizens whose isolated offences are unlikely to be repeated and who, therefore, deserve no further punishment. White collar offenders are rarely seen as dangerous criminals who need to be locked away to protect the public.

However, this reinforces the structural advantages seen earlier in the criminal justice process. The highly selective prosecution process, coupled with the use of defence strategies, means that precisely those factors – persistence, dishonesty and intent – which sentencers see as important, are likely to be concealed. The legitimacy of arguments that the 'process is punishment' is a further illustration of the operation of structural bias. Levi (1989a; 427) refers to the probably unconscious methods of

> smuggling in social prejudices as legitimate sentencing objectives through the assumption that only members of the elite can 'fall from grace' and thus have their sentences mitigated by this.

Similarly Cook (1989a: 161), comparing the treatment of tax evaders to social security offenders, argues that

> the fact that . . . (social security offenders) . . . are almost by definition poor appears effectively to preclude the 'loss of status' plea in mitigation.

The resources of white collar offenders are also crucial. They can, for example, pay substantial fines – fines of thousands and millions of pounds could not be imposed on the vast majority of offenders. Thus, for example, tax offenders can afford to pay large fines whereas social security offenders cannot (Cook 1989a). Even their often mentioned contributions to charity are, as the judge in the Guinness case commented, made easier because of their superior resources (Levi 1991b). Wider social inequalities are also reflected in the apparently legitimate consideration that white collar offenders may lose their jobs – this, as Levi (1989a: 432) observes, 'unintentionally discriminates against the unemployed'. As is the case for women, ethnic groups or the unemployed, structural inequalities are, therefore, reflected and reinforced in court (see, for example, Carlen 1989).

These advantages are strongly related to the ambiguous criminal status of offences. It was seen in Chapter 6 that defence strategies appeal to business values and to an assumed consensus that many offenders are 'not really criminal'. While it is impossible to determine empirically whether or not these defence strategies 'work', Rothman and Gandossy (1982: 465) argue that they do affect sentences, as they 'accord with the preferences of sentencing authorities', which is underlined by the comments of the judges interviewed by Wheeler (Wheeler *et al.* 1988). In some cases seen in court magistrates' questioning and comments indicated sympathy towards defendants who pleaded that their offences had resulted from the pressures of competition and who successfully maintained the image of responsible business persons (Croall 1989, 1991). The 'cultural homogeneity' which Sutherland (1949) refers to may, therefore, derive from a shared set of business values, rather than from shared status or background.

On the other hand, these arguments may not always have the desired effect. Broadly speaking, offences which display more characteristics associated with 'real crime', like fraud or employee theft can and do receive harsher sentences, and the broad distinction between 'anti' and 'pro' capitalist offences appears to have some empirical basis. However, this is by no means a clear cut distinction, as some regulatory offences can involve dishonesty and have considerable physical as well as economic impact, both of which can lead to heavier sentences. In addition, sentencers can define some regulatory offences as 'anti-capitalist' in that they may damage the credibility of business and, thus, threaten business interests as a whole. Therefore, attempts to link sentencing to the 'interests of capitalism' are over simplistic. In respect of commercial fraud for example, Levi (1989b: 101) argues that:

> a more class *interest* based analysis of sentencing would look not only at the class of the fraudsters but also at the business interests they affected. Looked at in this way, it is possible to view heavy punishment of high status violators as rational and expected, since they have both 'let the side down' and risked harming the general level of trading.

Similar themes and issues are therefore raised throughout the criminal justice system. There is little evidence to support allegations of agency bias, as neither law enforcers, court personnel nor sentencers appear to treat offenders differently on the grounds of their class or status. However, some offenders can use their considerable resources to avoid prosecution, to secure out of court settlements, or to present more credible defence strategies and to pay substantial fines. Many, though not all, are able to present themselves credibly as honest, reputable business persons who are willing to comply with regulations, and who do not require punishment. They are further assisted by the perception, shared by law enforcers and sentencers, that many white collar offences are less serious, dangerous or criminal than many conventional ones. This gives white collar offenders a clear structural advantage which enables them to avoid prosecution, conviction or severe sentences.

III

WHITE COLLAR CRIME, LAW AND REGULATION

8

WHITE COLLAR CRIME AND THE LAW

Many aspects of white collar criminal justice are strongly related to the law itself. It has been seen, for example, that the compliance strategies of enforcers derive from their legal role. The ambiguities of the law create space for defendants to minimize their culpability, and sentences are constrained partly by the maximum sentences which the law allows. The law itself, therefore, reinforces the common distinction between many white collar offences and 'real crimes', a distinction which for many offences mirrors a real legal distinction. Any shortcomings in the treatment of white collar offenders, therefore, may be attributable to limitations in the law itself, rather than to the activities of those who enforce that law.

Many of these limitations have already been outlined. Some laws are insufficiently precise, containing ambiguities and loopholes, and to the extent that the ambiguous criminal status of offences also restricts the impact of law, then it also constitutes a limitation. To many, of course, this is unsurprising, as it provides yet a further example of the inevitable association between law and capitalist interests. On the other hand, others argue that law is inevitably constrained by the complexities of the offences involved and the difficulties of law enforcement. In order to explore these questions the nature, development and scope of the law has to be examined, along with the many debates over the role of the criminal law as a means of regulating undesirable business activities – a phrase which in itself distinguishes the laws regulating business crime from those which aim to control 'real' crime.

This chapter will explore many of these issues. First, the justifications for the use of criminal law will be outlined, along with an exploration of the development of many of the crucial features of business regulatory laws. Some of the major limitations of the criminal law will then be explored. The various ways in which business groups seek to influence law making will be described along with an exploration of the extent to which the legal framework reflects the interests of capitalism, however these may be defined. As was the case with other chapters, the approach is inevitably selective, focusing on major themes which emerge from the literature, as it would be an impossible task to examine in detail the development of even a small number of the laws in question, far less to analyse fully the complex issues of state intervention in industry.

Protecting the public – the criminal law and business regulation

The distinction between many white collar and 'real' crimes is immediately evident in the language and rhetoric of the law itself. In pollution laws, for example, the 'language of the criminal law is studiously avoided' (Richardson *et al.* 1982: 56), and the classic text on Weights and Measures law comments that:

> sanctions are . . . designed not in the main to curb the vicious will but to impose curbs on the inefficient and careless and make the master control servants. (O'Keefe 1966: 67)

Judges also frequently distinguish between 'real crime' and other offences. Often quoted is the case of *Sherras v De Rutzen* [(1895) 1 QB 918], in which it was argued that the kinds of offences covered by strict liability were 'not criminal in any real sense'. These sentiments were echoed in *Smedley's Ltd v Breed* [(1974) A.C. 839], in which Lord Hailsham argued that the offence was an absolute one, of a sort 'not criminal in any real sense, but which in the public interest . . . are prohibited under a penalty'. This indicates the stress, particularly in business regulatory law, on public protection which was seen to have such an effect on enforcement policies. This can be further illustrated in the many debates surrounding the use of the criminal law and in the development of many laws in the business regulatory area.

The development of these laws was heavily influenced by the underlying tension between free market and *laissez faire* principles and the interests of public protection, public health and welfare. Both nineteenth century and contemporary advocates of free market principles argue that public protection can best be achieved by market forces, and that state and legal intervention should be minimal. The 'invisible hand' of the market itself, according to Adam Smith, should be sufficient to secure high standards of production (Harvey 1982). Advocates of *laissez faire* also supported the legal principle of *caveat emptor* under which it is the buyer's responsibility to judge the quality or quantity of goods. This implies that if consumers are careful, they will buy only high quality goods and, therefore, shoddy goods will disappear from the market or be sold at prices which reflect their inferior quality (Borrie and Diamond 1977; Atiyah 1985). These views are echoed in contemporary 'economist' arguments that sufficient regulation can be achieved by the operation of the market. Competition itself is said to ensure high quality, as consumers 'demand' high quality products. Aggrieved consumers can also seek redress through civil law, which further encourages producers and sellers to maintain the highest possible standards (Cranston 1977, 1984; Swann 1979; Braithwaite 1984b).

Against this, proponents of the use of public rather than private law, and in particular the use of criminal law, argue that legal intervention is necessary in the many situations where the public cannot judge for themselves the nature, quality, and in particular the safety of goods. Cranston (1977: 108), for example, makes the telling observation that:

> the Thalidomide children and their parents would have difficulty appreciating an argument against government regulation of drug quality premised on the assumption that consumers can acquire information from repeated purchases.

In addition, few possess either the knowledge or resources to resort to civil law (Cranston 1977, 1984), which makes the use of public law necessary to protect all members of the public.

This tension also underlies the principle that legal intervention should be kept to a minimum, and should seek to secure a fair balance between the interests of business and commerce and those of the public. While more commonly associated with business regulatory statutes, these arguments also apply to offences whose criminal and moral status is less ambiguous. Laws against fraud, for example, are formulated not just to deal with fraud but 'to provide a regulatory framework within which commerce can function' (Levi 1987a: 85), and Clarke (1986, 1987) comments that the control of financial matters must always balance the interests of the free market with the establishment and maintenance of standards. Discussing corruption, Doig (1984: 344) points out that legislation is directed not against bribery and corruption, but at the establishment of the 'highest standards of integrity and propriety in public life'. Similarly, discussions of taxation are dominated by concerns that the intolerable inquisition of taxation should not stifle free enterprise and initiative (Cook 1989a; Clarke 1990).

These issues dominated the development of business regulatory laws, many of which originated in the nineteenth century, often hailed as the golden age of *laissez faire*, and legal abstentionism (Sugarman 1983). Most were justified on the grounds of public interest. Public health legislation for example emerged out of a growing recognition that 'the public health' was equitable with the 'public wealth' and that national economic prosperity would be endangered by the spread of disease, crime and disorder associated with poor environmental and health conditions (Richardson *et al.* 1982: 30). Early factory acts were also supported by some, though by no means all, factory owners who recognized that a healthy workforce was more productive than an overworked and undernourished one (Carson 1974).

Other developments were based on a recognition that the principles of *caveat emptor* were increasingly inappropriate. *Caveat emptor* assumes, for example, that buyers and sellers have equal power in commercial transactions. This became untenable as it became evident that buyers could not readily establish the quality of goods themselves. As Borrie and Diamond (1977: 17) point out, the origins of *caveat emptor* lay in the middle ages where most trading took place in markets where goods could be examined, their quality judged and 'only a fool would rely on the word of a stranger'. However, this was no longer the case by the nineteenth century, and even ardent proponents of *laissez faire* such as J.S. Mill accepted the need for some public protection (Atiyah 1979). The widespread existence of food adulteration, for example, created a situation in which the impossibility of judging the quality of food not only made a nonsense of *caveat emptor*, but also threatened the public health (Burnett 1966; Paulus 1974; Atiyah 1979). Other legislation was further justified on the grounds of protecting traders from the unfair competition of unscrupulous rivals (see, for example, Borrie and Diamond 1977; Atiyah 1979).

The now distinctive characteristics of business regulatory legislation emerged out of a long history of negotiation, accommodation and conflict between reformers, often called *moral entrepreneurs*, governments and industrial groups, well illustrated in studies of the Factory Acts (see for example, Carson 1974, 1979, 1980) and the Food and Drugs Acts (Paulus 1974). Paulus (1974) traces a continuity in what she describes as 'public welfare legislation' in which specific campaigns around specific problems led to the development of a similar set of legal principles which were applied to many spheres of regulation. Thus, the basic pattern of strict liability and compliance strategies of law enforcement were applied to the different problems of pollution, health and safety or consumer protection. In the first instance successive campaigns by moral entrepreneurs against numerous undesirable activities led to the criminalization of what were defined at the time as 'normal' trading or manufacturing practices. Many early laws had a very limited impact as they failed to provide arrangements for law enforcement and required proof of *mens rea*. Enforcement bodies themselves, like the Factory Inspectorate and Public Analysts, then became vocal advocates of subsequent reforms.

Gradually, an accommodation between industry and enforcers was reached. Carson (1979, 1980) describes the many problems faced by factory inspectors in their attempts to enforce the law against large and influential manufacturers, who were initially hostile and unco-operative. Prosecutions were often unsuccessful as magistrates were unwilling to convict where *mens rea* was required, and penalties were small. Inspectors came to accept that they could more readily persuade businesses to comply by limiting the use of prosecution. Gradually, therefore, they drew a distinction between acceptable violations and others. Industrialists then found that the law posed less of a threat than they had feared, leading to their acceptance of strict liability which enforcers argued was necessary to obtain any convictions. Many industrialists also came to accept that regulation could operate in their own interests. Larger manufacturers, for example, found that regulation could price smaller competitors out of the market, as they were less able to afford to comply with regulations (Carson 1974, 1979). Food manufacturers also found that regulation could work to their advantage as it prevented the use of cheap substitutes by competitors. Gradually food adulteration itself was defined as unacceptable and the need for regulation was accepted (Paulus 1974).

Throughout the twentieth century, rapid technological and socio-economic change made revisions of these laws and the development of new ones necessary. Existing consumer protection legislation, for example, was ill-adapted to meet the post-war consumer society. The development of mass produced goods and the 'affluent society' in which consumers expected washing machines, cars and televisions, led to a situation in which both buyers and sellers were incapable of judging the quality of goods, and were both dependent on manufacturers. By the 1950s it was recognized that, as goods were becoming 'technological mysteries', consumers were vulnerable to considerable exploitation. The Molony Report published in 1962 found that large sums of money were increasingly being spent on expensive and complicated items whose 'precise workings' were unknown to consumers. Modern manufacturing practices and the use of man made fibres had led to the proliferation of misleading descriptions of goods like 'linen look', and more aggressive marketing had led to a host of misleading bargain offers. There was much concern, for example, about claims like 'X washes whiter', or '6d off', with no indication of what the 6d was actually deducted from (Molony 1962; Borrie and Diamond 1977; Croall 1987). Accordingly, they recommended the introduction of the Trade Descriptions Act to control many undesirable practices.

These proposals were met with a mixed response from trade and industry. Some welcomed the prospect of greater regulation, arguing that it was in the best interests of retailing to regulate unscrupulous sales practices which could threaten the credibility of retailing as a whole. On the other hand, many feared that proposed controls over oral descriptions of goods could lead to 'innocent shopgirls' being sent to prison, and one Member of Parliament went so far as to argue that these provisions were liable:

> to bring to a silent, if not grinding, halt the service provided by the retail trade, particularly the small retailer, in giving advice and answering questions. (*Hansard* cited in Croall 1987: 97)

Ensuing debates illustrated that strict liability and compliance strategies were virtually taken for granted, and revealed the now familiar discourse of regulatory legislation. In answer to fears about shopgirls being imprisoned, the Minister of State of the Board of Trade replied that the Bill was 'not expected to lead to a great number of prosecutions' as 'officers can be relied upon to exercise the maximum discretion' (*Hansard* cited in Croall 1987: 99). Speakers also stressed the need to maintain a balance between traders and consumers and that only the unscrupulous minority of traders were likely to be prosecuted. In a speech which illustrates the discourse typical of regulatory legislation, Sir Keith Joseph stated that

> the fundamental problem for legislation of this kind is one of balance, to do justice to the consumer without so over-whelming and over-burdening the manufacturer, trader and provider of services that the purpose of the effort is defeated . . . we must – I warn the house again – be very careful that, in seeking to protect the consumer, we do not damage the services given to him to such an extent that we defeat our own purposes. (*Hansard* cited in Croall 1987: 100)

The precise nature of this balance is, however, a matter of considerable debate. By the 1980s, the free market philosophy of the Conservative Government had affected legislation and enforcement, leading to a stress on self rather than state regulation. Arguments that industry was *over* regulated and complaints of too much intervention dominated the agenda for legislative reform. Cook (1989a) also argues that the issue of *over* taxation has dominated the political agenda since the 1970s. In relation to consumer protection, much legislation of the 1960s and 70s was seen as consumerist. The Trade Descriptions Act was described as a 'consumer's charter', and the Office of Fair Trading was established in 1973 (Borrie and Diamond 1977; Cranston 1984). By 1980, however, industry was complaining about the high costs of compliance (Economist Intelligence Unit 1979) and calls for more legislation were criticized in 1980 by Sally Oppenheim, then Consumer Affairs Minister, in a speech to the National Consumer Congress which aptly illustrates the rhetoric of the 1980s. Too much protection she argued, involved the concept of a 'handholding, lecturing intervening "nanny knows best" state maternalism'. This is an insult to the consumer, who should 'stand on his or her own feet' and should be 'well informed, and, where necessary, adequately warned . . . but essentially be prepared to fight their own battles' (3/3/80, cited in Croall 1987: 298).

These kinds of attitudes have had several effects. In respect of consumer legislation, they have led to an emphasis on information rather than quality standards, which lays the onus for protection on consumers themselves (Cranston 1984). Enforcement agencies have increasingly complained of a shortage of resources as the emphasis has moved away from state to self-regulation. Tombs (1990), for example, argues that Government reports concerning the Health and Safety at Work Act, and the Factory Inspectorate are based on an underlying assumption that business is hampered by regulations. Deregulation is rarely overtly discussed or advocated, but the declining resources allocated to the Inspectorates coupled with the 'strident hegemony' of free enterprise culture amounts, he argues, to *ad hoc* deregulation (see also Box 1987). This arguably limits the effectiveness of regulation.

The limits of the criminal law

Several other features of the criminal law have been said to limit its effectiveness. In the first place, reducing the extremely complex activities involved to criminal offences may be very difficult and difficulties also arise in defining with sufficient precision the borderline between legal and illegal activities. In addition, technological advance renders many laws obsolete necessitating continual revision. The consequent ambiguities and loopholes can lead to the proliferation of practices which are perfectly legal, but which clearly violate the spirit of the law, and in some instances involve deliberate law evasion, some of which has already been described (Chapter 4).

Defining offences

Many ambiguities arise from the difficulties of specifying which activities are legal or illegal. This is less difficult with offences which involve clear elements of theft or fraud, as the essence of these offences is well established (Hadden 1983). It was seen in Chapter 2, for example, that much computer crime is readily reducible to theft by an employee (Wasik 1989; Lloyd 1990), and many other clearly dishonest transactions can similarly be encompassed within the ambit of existing laws (Hadden 1983). Difficulties arise where the activities to be criminalized are less easy to define. For some offences the distinction between legitimate and illegitimate activities is one of degree rather than substance. For example, demanding or receiving payment for what are considered to be reasonable expenses or services rendered differs only in degree from what can amount to bribery or corruption (Hadden 1983). Normal marketing, advertising and selling strategies can involve omitting and selecting information in such a way that it borders on deception. Indeed, Hadden comments that:

> it may even be argued that a degree of deception is of the essence of the market system, in that profitable dealing in many spheres depends on the exploitation of information which is not generally available. (Hadden 1983: 501)

Similarly, Leigh (1982) comments that since the purpose of the seller is to persuade the buyer that goods are worth buying, it is difficult to define where acceptable persuasion ends and deception begins. These kinds of problems allow defendants to argue that their activities fall on the legal side of a very thin line.

Organizational offences create further problems, many of which have already been outlined. It has already been seen, for example, that the 'ideology of individualism' (Braithwaite and Condon 1978) of the criminal law, in which notions of individual intent and responsibility are crucial, creates difficulties where responsibility is diffuse and the many problems of corporate criminal liability are also well documented (see, for example, Leigh 1982). Therefore, some argue that the criminal law is severely hampered in its ability to respond to corporate crime, particularly in respect of corporate manslaughter (Wells 1988, 1989; Bergman 1990b). While, as will be seen in Chapter 9, these difficulties are not insurmountable, they enable the kind of defence strategies seen in Chapter 6, in which corporate defendants can readily claim that they are not to 'blame'.

More problems arise when laws drafted to proscribe specific activities are followed by the development of new ones which do not fall within the specific terms of the legislation (Hadden 1983; Clarke 1987). For example, while much computer crime can be incorporated within existing theft acts, legal problems have been encountered in England and Wales, when it is not money which is stolen, but information, lists of clients or data bases. These are intangible and, therefore, not covered by theft acts (Lloyd 1990), which has necessitated new legislation. Other laws are directed against specific practices and cannot be used when essentially similar practices are developed which quite clearly breach the spirit of the law, but evade its specific provisions. This is the case, for example, with tax laws, where the prohibition of specific avoidance schemes are followed by new ones – leading to a game of 'legal leapfrogging' (McBarnet 1988).

The alternative to drafting specific laws is to introduce general prohibitions, which are inclusive but often ambiguous (McBarnet 1987). This is the case in many business regulatory statutes. For example, the Food Acts prohibit the sale of food 'not of the nature, quality or substance demanded by the consumer' (Cranston 1984). However, in practice, this leaves considerable scope for interpretation. Similar problems are found in specifying precisely what amounts to 'noxious emissions' (Richardson *et al.* 1982), or 'misleading descriptions' (Croall 1987). Broad prohibitions are supported by an enormous number of specific standards which may apply to specific foods, products or production processes (Cranston 1984). Many standards regulate the quality and contents of different products, and the information which producers or sellers must provide on labels, known as information standards. However, the sheer impossibility of devising specific standards to cover every situation leads to what some have described as legislative 'lag' and to the existence of many gaps and loopholes. Therefore, standards may apply to cheese, but not to toothpaste, to meat products, but not to fish products (Cranston 1984).

The spirit and the letter of the law – legal loopholes

These gaps and loopholes can be exploited in a number of ways, either through planned and deliberate law evasion, or by the development of new practices which fall outside the scope of the law. Space prohibits an examination of all but a few examples of these problems, which are well illustrated in the case of food laws. It has already been seen, for example, that modern food processing techniques have led to the 'legalized adulteration' of food (Cannon and Walker 1985). This includes the addition of water to food, one of the oldest forms of adulteration. Legally, water may be added to meat products without being indicated on the label if it does not exceed ten per cent of the product. However, in the preparation of meat, solutions containing water may be added, which can increase the 'legal' amount of water to 15 per cent (Cannon and Walker 1985). Meat itself may have water added to it – for example, chickens are often injected with water to give 'weight gain'. The London Food Commission list many other ways in which water can be added to food products including soaking foods prior to cooking, ice-glazing, the use of chemical additives, tumbling and massaging, reforming, reshaping and restructuring meats (London Food Commission 1988). This produces a situation in which water may be sold at the price of meat and consumers are essentially paying for water which is not declared on the label. For example, Cannon and Walker (1985) estimate that consumers can pay around 63 pence per pack for iced water in sea food products, which, they argue, amounts to fraud.

The legal definition of meat is extremely complex – well illustrated in descriptions of the contents of sausages, described by Cannon and Walker (1985: 131) as the 'dustbin of the meat industry'. The contents of a typical sausage have been described as 'head meat, back fat, mulled gristle, emulsified ground rind, rusk, seasonings, soya flour and ice' (Roberts 1985). Legally, a sausage must contain 65 per cent meat. But what is meat? Bone is not meat, but it is not non-meat. Fat is included in the definition of meat – as is skin, rind, gristle and sinew. Legally, therefore, a pork sausage could consist of 29 per cent lean meat, 36 per cent pork fat, extra poultry or other meat fat, rusk and water, together with a dose of chemical cocktail (Cannon and Walker 1985). All this, of course, is not indicated on the label, leading one commentator to observe that

> if the requirement of the law was that the recipe should be given and amounts used stated . . . what chance the continued production of that particular product given full consumer choice? (Roberts 1985: 1358)

Other forms of 'legalized adulteration' can include the use of meat substitutes, along with the use of many kinds of additives, flavourings and colourings which can deceive the consumer about the quality and contents of food products, some of which contain so little 'real food' that they can be described more accurately as 'additive cocktails' (London Food Commission 1988). Many additives have been linked with risks to health, and their use can be inherently deceptive in that they are used to make food look more natural and appealing, and to disguise poor quality food, and substitute 'real food' with an assortment of chemicals. While labelling laws are becoming more comprehensive, the issue of additives illustrates some of the problems of the current preference for information, rather than quality standards. Labelling regulations do not cover all food products or drinks – many alcoholic drinks, for example, are exempt – and not all additives need be declared. In addition, probably very few consumers can fully understand labels or appreciate the finer points of legal descriptions – how many readers, for example, know the difference between an 'orange drink', 'orange juice', an 'orange flavoured drink' and an 'orange flavour drink'? Each contain different amounts of orange, with the latter containing nothing which resembles an orange! In short, consumers can still be misled by many food descriptions, and the London Food Commission (1988: 74) argue that it would be far better to encourage high food standards than to rely on labelling – as 'consumers have better things to do with their time than scrutinise the small print on labels in supermarkets'.

This indicates the associated problem of defining exactly what constitutes a misleading description. It was seen in Chapter 2, for example, that the borderline between fraud, misleading descriptions and normal marketing strategies is a very narrow one, and that regulations controlling weights and measures leave many loopholes. Similar problems occur in defining a 'bargain'. While some price comparisons are prohibited, consumers can still be misled into thinking that prices have been reduced by the use of ambiguous phrases like 'after sale price' or 'normal' price, which are mainly inventions and take advantage of the many loopholes in the law (French 1981). The use of these practices is justified on the grounds of competition, but even a Woolworth's marketing director accepted that many are deceptive (*Sunday Times* 9/1/86). These examples amply illustrate the many difficulties of devising laws sufficiently specific to cover the complexities of production processes, and retailing and commercial practices, and the ample opportunities which this provides for the proliferation of practices lying on the borders of legality and illegality.

The international nature of trade and commerce also provides considerable scope for law evasion. Controls in one country may not be present in other, especially underdeveloped, countries, and even where there are controls, law enforcement may be weak. Thus, Braithwaite (1979), discussing the problem of transnational corruption, points to the considerable opportunities provided in third world countries where legal controls and standards are very different, a point also made by Box (1987). Reference has already been made to the problem of dumping unsafe goods and drugs into countries with weaker controls and the study of cross border frauds has revealed the possibility of 'jurisdiction shopping' (Van Duyne 1991). Gaps in the laws can also assist many frauds on the European Economic community, where some aspects of legislation and control have been described as 'fraudster friendly' (Leigh and Smith 1991). Clarke (1987: 272) also points to the rapid rise of maritime frauds involving 'rust bucket scuttling' and illegal cargo deviation and sales. These are facilitated by the absence of any provisions for an adequately financed and staffed international police force to investigate or prosecute offences. The international nature of financial transactions and use of sophisticated computer technology to pass large sums of money around the globe has also led to the creation of 'computer crime havens' (Lloyd 1990: 168).

The list of gaps and loopholes could be endless and they provide many opportunities for planned and deliberate law evasion (see Chapter 4). In relation to tax laws, for example, Cook (1989a) comments that the blurred line separating avoidance and evasion may lead to the creation of an ideological and practical 'space' within which tax fiddles can be committed without attracting the full weight of the criminal law. Many of these strategies form part of what McBarnet (1988) describes as a sophisticated tax avoidance 'industry' which specializes in the creation and marketing of many legal methods of minimizing and avoiding tax. These have included devices like 'bed and breakfasting' in which artificial losses are created and offset against gains, and the use of off-shore roll-up funds in which interest subject to taxation is invested in off-shore funds and then re-imported as capital. These and many other devices show considerable ingenuity and skill.

Business interests and the law

The many limitations of the laws regulating business offences are often cited in support of arguments of Marxist and radical criminologists that the criminal law is fundamentally class-based in that it fails to criminalize the anti-social activities of business to the same extent as those of the lower classes. Originally, it was argued that this resulted from business influence on the law-making process. However, this was difficult to substantiate and was also challenged by the very existence of the many laws which do prohibit and criminalize business and commercial practices. On the other hand, the practical weaknesses of these laws could be taken to indicate that they are merely symbolic and, therefore, reflect capitalist or business interests. The very discourse in which regulatory law and compliance strategies are justified in itself can be interpreted as reflecting what Pearce and Tombs (1990) describe as the 'hegemony of corporate ideology'. McBarnet (1984: 231) gives an eloquent summary of these arguments:

Law was made by the state: the state was run by the ruling class; and

> law was obviously in the interests of the class which made it. Law which at first sight did not quite fit with the model, such as health and safety regulation or pollution control could be readily dismissed as merely ideology, ineffective in practice, or in the 'real' interests of the capitalist class – if not in the short term, in the long term, if not in their financial interests, in their ideological interests, if not in the interests of individuals nonetheless in the overriding interests of the survival of the class.

One problem is that it is not always easy to discern the 'interests of capitalism', particularly in relation to specific laws. Indeed, there may be a distinction between the interests of 'capitalism' in general and the sectional interests of individual groups of capitalists (Levi 1987a). None the less, business influence is evident at all stages of the law-making process. Relevant groups are generally consulted in advance of legislative reform and particular industries are indirectly represented in Parliament through sponsorship of individual members, many of whom also have industrial links through investments and company directorships. As Box (1987) argues – industrial interests have 'clout'. The most obvious example of this 'clout' is the considerable lobbying which accompanies major law reforms. Levi (1987a, 1987b), for example, notes that special interest lobbying was the keynote of the long run up to the passage of the Financial Services Act, through which business groups expressed concern that the volume of trade and flexibility of the city should not be prejudiced by unnecessarily protective rules. Indeed, almost all laws in regulatory areas have at some point been criticized for giving in too much to the business lobby.

This influence does not end when laws are passed. Laws must be implemented and enforced, and standards are continually reviewed. These standards are set by relevant Government departments, normally on the advice of a host of advisory committees. The majority of these standard setting committees, while technically impartial and expert, receive representations from industry which may strongly affect their decisions. In relation to consumer protection, for example, committees have been found to be reluctant to interfere with industry and trade representatives appear to be able to veto many regulations (Cranston 1984).

The development of food standards well illustrates the pervasive influence of industrial interests. Food regulations are the responsibility of the Departments of Agriculture and Health, and are set following the advice of a large number of committees including the Food Advisory Committee, the Food Standards Committee, and the Food Additives and Contaminants Committee (Cranston 1984; Cannon and Walker 1985). Despite an official rhetoric of 'neutrality' industrial interests tend to predominate. For example, a representative of the Consumer's Association on the Food Advisory Committee has argued that the influence of the producer lobby is so strong that the consumer interest often takes second place (Yeomans 1985). The membership of committees further indicates this predominance. Miller (1985), for example, found that four members of the Food Advisory Committee were employed by food companies and that others were strongly linked to the food industry. Out of a total of fourteen members, only one represented the Consumer's Association, in a 'personal capacity', and only one Trading Standards Officer was a member. Thus, she argues, it is not surprising that their decisions tend to favour the interests of food manufacturers.

Committees involved in setting standards have to review enormous amounts of technical and scientific information, much of which is provided directly or indirectly by industry. While members of Committees may be independent researchers, very often research institutes are funded by industry and research grants are frequently dominated by industrial interests (Miller 1985; Cannon and Walker 1985). This can mean that industry have a virtual monopoly of relevant scientific knowledge and information, as consumer, worker or other interest groups rarely have the resources to engage in the kinds of research which could provide countervailing evidence and argument (Otake 1982). This is facilitated by the secrecy surrounding the work of many Committees, whose members may be obliged to sign the Official Secrets Act. Industrial arguments that many industrial processes, such as food processing, are commercial secrets are accepted, which further inhibits consultation and independent scientific evaluation (Millstone 1985). Therefore, industrial influence extends from direct influence over law-making to control over much of the information on which standards are based.

Given the scope and pervasiveness of business and industrial influence, it is tempting to conclude that it does, indeed, amount to a conspiracy. On the other hand, there are many arguments that the range of influences on legislation cannot simply be reduced to class or conspiracy theories. In the first place, capitalists frequently disagree among themselves over what direction legislation should take, and over what threat is posed by particular laws (Levi 1987a). Specific laws may benefit some groups at the expense of others. It was seen, for example, that some industrialists accepted that early regulatory laws could be advantageous to their interests and adversely affect their competitors. In addition, many laws have a different impact on different industrial groups, encouraging sectional as opposed to collective representation. In the development of consumer protection legislation, considerable lobbying and behind the scenes bargaining involved such diverse groups as coal merchants, bakers and biscuit manufacturers who sought to limit controls on their specific practices and argued special cases. Biscuit manufacturers were particularly influential in preventing moves towards unit pricing and controls over deceptive packaging, and retailers in preventing the general prohibition of price comparisons (Croall 1987).

Similarly, there are many competing interest groups in the financial world, evident in the special interest lobbying preceding the Financial Services Act, and the interests of finance capital may take precedence over those of industrial capital (Levi 1987a).

Governmental priorities may not be the same as business priorities and governments can also find themselves mediating between sectional interests, or facing opposition to regulation which they favour. On occasion government and industrial interests may coincide, but are not identical. Carson (1981), in his study of the regulation of Health and Safety in the North Sea, found that the government's interests were to develop the oil fields as quickly as possible in order to benefit from the extra revenue. For this, they needed the co-operation of oil companies, who had an obvious interest in securing a favourable regulatory environment. The 'safety second' policy which emerged suited the *different* interests of government and industry. Governments can also be more sensitive to the 'public interest', particularly where public confidence in institutions or commercial life are seen to be important. Levi (1987a) suggests that government concerns about city scandals and the possible effect of the 'big bang' resulted in greater powers being given to DTI inspectors. In addition, the Conservative government's privatization programme and the ideology of wider share ownership required the involvement of small investors. This meant that regulation had to be credible, and may have led to the retention of the interventionist Office of Fair Trading (Clarke 1986; Levi 1987a). Conflict between governments of whatever political persuasion and industry may also be inevitable where taxation is concerned.

Enforcement agencies also play a part in law making, often campaigning for stricter controls and greater powers. Public analysts and Inspectorates were part of the campaigns in the nineteenth century for tougher regulations (Paulus 1974; Carson 1979, 1980) and many continue to be active campaigners. Both Trading Standards and Environmental Health Institutes have been active lobbyists in relation to law reform, and lobbying by Environmental Health Departments was instrumental in raising the maximum sentences under Food and Drugs legislation (Croall 1987).

Finally, while the effectiveness of laws regulating business and commercial life can be criticized, they do have some effect in controlling the worst abuses. Thus, Hutter (1988) argues that the power of business is not monolithic as there have been improvements in the environment which might not have been possible if enforcement was as weak and business interests as strong as a ruling class model suggests. This is not to deny that business influence and power does affect law making and regulation. Levi (1987a: 105), for example, concludes that while there are significant conflicts of interest both between and among business, government and professional representatives, the significance of 'class fractions' cannot be understated. Concluding that the relationship between business interests and the law is better described in terms of a 'coherence without conspiracy', Nelken (1983) argues,

> if it is proper to resist the assumption that legislation inevitably serves to reinforce the existing distribution of power in society it is also wise to note that most legislative intervention does have this effect – even if the route which it follows to this end is uneven and not necessarily consciously designed.

Summary and discussion

Many aspects of law underline the distinctive characteristics of the regulation of white collar offences in comparison with conventional crime. Their development has been dominated by the conflict between principles of *laissez faire* and public health and welfare, which led to the emphasis, throughout debates, on the need to maintain a fair balance between the competing needs of industry and public protection, and to minimize legal intervention. The *moral* unacceptability of deceptive or dangerous business practices is, thus, underplayed as evidenced in the view that criminal law should only be used sparingly against activities which are defined as 'not really criminal'. The repeated use of the phrase 'business regulation' in itself distinguishes these aspects of the criminal law from 'crime control'.

This, combined with the many ambiguities and loopholes which limit the effectiveness of these laws, is often taken to reflect the operation of what McBarnet (1984: 232) aptly describes as the 'unholy trinity' of law, state and capitalist interests. Business groups have been seen to exert a considerable influence on particular laws and the balance between business interests and public protection has often been criticized as heavily weighted towards the former. Indeed, the very extent to which businesses are consulted about the laws regulating their own activities distinguishes this area of criminal law making from many others – thieves and burglars, for example, are rarely consulted about the laws directed against their activities and do not regularly play a part in law reviews. However, it has also been seen that it is difficult to discern any coherent strategy on the part of capital*ists* to secure favourable legislation (see, for example, Nelken 1983; Levi 1987). The proliferation of activities which exploit legal loopholes and the many instances of 'legal leapfrogging' further suggest that the relationship between business power and law is more complex than class models suggest (McBarnet 1988).

It could also be argued that the limitations of the law reflect the inherent difficulties of using the criminal law against the complex activities to be regulated. Indeed, as will be seen in Chapter 9, some argue that the criminal law is a particularly ineffective weapon. However, this kind of approach in itself underlines the ideological distinction between business crimes and 'real crime', as arguments which focus on the effectiveness of the criminal sanction inevitably underplay the moral element inherent in the use of criminal law. It could be argued, for example, that the criminal law is not a very effective weapon in preventing rape or robbery, and thereby protecting the public, but few would dispute that it ought to be used on moral grounds. These different interpretations of the use of the criminal sanction are not only relevant to the academic analysis of the development of business regulatory law, but form the basis of different approaches to the question of how present arrangements can be improved.

9

WHAT IS TO BE DONE ABOUT WHITE COLLAR CRIME?

The limited impact of criminal law on white collar crime has been illustrated in many previous chapters. Indeed, the prevalence of offences in occupations and organizations where they are widely tolerated in itself demonstrates this limited effect. Enforcement problems, the small number of prosecutions, and the leniency of sanctions further constrain the preventive and deterrent value of law – which many see as its primary justification. This is exacerbated by the many ambiguities and loopholes in specific laws illustrated in Chapter 8. Few disagree that the law has a limited impact, but there are conflicting analyses of why this is the case and what should be done about it.

Broadly speaking three distinct approaches to these questions can be discerned. Following the logic of what might be called a 'regulatory' approach, some argue that the criminal law should be used sparingly given the cost and ineffectiveness of prosecution. The nature of the activities to be regulated in any event create problems for law and its enforcement and, therefore, greater emphasis should be placed on self-regulation and administrative sanctions, which are cheaper and more effective, and thus better protect the public. A very different agenda is advocated by those who argue that the laws are weakened by their failure to treat the crimes of wealthy and powerful offenders with the same vigour applied to conventional offenders. White collar crime, they argue *is* crime and *ought* to be dealt with as severely as other crimes. Accordingly, the criminal law should be strengthened, more offenders should be prosecuted and sanctions should be tougher. This view is often associated with Marxist and radical criminology (see, for example, Pearce and Tombs 1990).

These views represent somewhat extreme positions, and elements of both can be combined. It can be accepted that self-regulation and administrative sanctions may well be more effective in preventing and even deterring offences, but also that they may not be sufficient. It can also be accepted that public prosecution and punishment are necessary on the grounds of morality and justice, as the offences *are* offences and offenders *do* enjoy advantages. Sentencing policies should therefore aim at prevention and deterrence *along with* justice and equity. Braithwaite (1989), for example, in his theory of 're-integrative shaming' suggests a mixture of policies combining self-regulation and state punishment, which would shame offenders without stigmatizing them, and provide for stiffer punishments to underline the moral unacceptability of offences.

This chapter will explore many of these issues. It will start by outlining some of the current debates about the aims of the criminal sanction and their application to white collar crime. Following this, some specific suggestions for improving the regulation and control of business offences will be outlined – ranging from arguments for decriminalization and an increasing emphasis on self-regulation on the one hand, to arguments for strengthening enforcement policies and sanctions on the other.

White collar crime and punishment

The inability of criminal law to substantially reduce crime is not restricted to white collar crime. It is now widely accepted that what are generally known as reductive sentencing policies, which aim to either deter or rehabilitate offenders, are relatively ineffective in preventing recidivism, and have little effect on the volume of crime as only a small minority of conventional offenders are ever caught and subjected to punishment (see, for example, Ashworth 1989). Deterrent policies have other limitations. It has often been argued, for example, that the majority of the population do not commit crimes because they feel they are morally wrong, and tend to be more worried about the reactions of friends and family than about particular forms of punishment (see, for example, Braithwaite 1989). These kinds of arguments can be used in support of a 'just deserts' model which justifies punishment on the grounds that offenders have done wrong and, therefore, 'deserve' punishment. Sentences should be based on considerations of culpability and should be in proportion to the gravity or seriousness of the crime, thus ensuring equity and justice. In theory, this should eliminate the inequities and disparities often attributed to individualized sentencing based on rehabilitative considerations (see, for example, Hudson 1987; Ashworth 1989).

Recent proposals to reform sentencing policy indicate a shift away from rehabilitation and deterrence in favour of principles of just deserts, and in addition stress the importance of incapacitation, which may be necessary for public protection (Home Office 1990). These kinds of proposals reflect a general consensus that prison should be used less, and should be reserved for the most serious, persistent, violent and dangerous offenders, however these might be defined. Current proposals also suggest that more emphasis should be placed on 'punishment' in the community (Home Office 1990; Vass 1990). Crime reduction, on the other hand, is better achieved by strategies aimed at preventing crime, where more responsibility is placed on individual citizens to protect themselves. Extensions of private policing, neighbourhood watch and the plethora of crime prevention strategies such as 'target removal', 'target hardening' and environmental design are all aimed at reducing the opportunities for crime (Heal and Laycock 1986).

These arguments have also affected analyses of white collar crime, although the application of specific policies and proposals may be somewhat different. Many conventional crimes are unambiguously regarded as criminal and, therefore, few would dispute that burglars *should* be prosecuted or punished, however ineffective this may be in reducing the total amount of burglary. The many differences between white collar offences and offenders, and their conventional criminal counterparts also means that the application of principles of deterrence, retribution, incapacitation and rehabilitation may be very different (Braithwaite and Geis 1982), especially in relation to organizational crime.

It is often assumed that a major aim of sentencing white collar offenders is deterrence. This reflects a general view that offenders are more deterrable than others, as offences are assumed to be economically motivated and involve calculated risks by rational actors (Braithwaite and Geis 1982). Defendants' arguments that the 'process is punishment' also reflect the potential deterrent value of the law as many individual offenders do risk losing their employment and reputation, high incomes and comfortable life styles. Corporations are often assumed to be future orientated, concerned about their reputation and 'quintessentially rational' (Braithwaite and Geis 1982). Unfavourable publicity and the harrowing experience of investigation, prosecution and trial, therefore, can and do act as deterrents (Levi 1987a).

None the less, this deterrent potential can be undermined by the low rates of detection and prosecution, and the limited impact of sentences. The view that offences arise from rational and conscious decision making can also be questioned, particularly in relation to organizational crime where individuals may not intend to commit offences. The criminogenic elements of organizations may also remain whatever punishment follows conviction, thus effectively neutralizing any deterrent effect (Moore 1987). In addition, Levi (1987a) argues that the 'fall from grace' effect may be exaggerated. Some offenders may lose their occupational status, but may be able to pursue alternative careers and may even benefit indirectly from their offences. For example, many of the Watergate conspirators profited greatly from their memoirs! In other cases, offences may be a consequence of the failure or poor performance of a business; therefore, offenders have already lost everything anyway.

Whether or not deterrence works in practice, it can also be argued that it is not and should not be the only principle underlying the use of the criminal law or the sole aim of punishment. Proponents of a 'just desert' approach, for example, argue that offenders should be publicly prosecuted and punished for their offences, and many object to the implicit inequity of treating one group of offenders differently from any other group. However, the 'just deserts' approach also creates several problems, particularly in relation to white collar crime (Braithwaite 1982; Braithwaite and Pettit 1990). Just deserts models rely on notions of guilt, blame and culpability, which could lead to less 'justice' for white collar offenders, given their ability to minimize elements of intent and culpability. In addition, to prosecute all white collar offences, let alone all conventional offenders, would be prohibitively costly. Principles of just deserts further stress that punishment should reflect the harm done. However, it was seen in Chapter 7 that offences are often considered to be less serious and, therefore, any equation of punishment to harm done might have little effect. A general problem with the implementation of just deserts models lies in the difficulties of determining which crimes are more serious than others, and whose definitions of seriousness are adopted. Application of just deserts models could well perpetuate class based and ideological definitions of the seriousness of crime (Hudson 1987), thus confirming the distinction between white collar crimes and 'real crimes'.

There has been less discussion of the application of other principles of sentencing to white collar and especially corporate crime. After all, corporations cannot be sent to prison or subjected to psychiatric treatment. High status white collar offenders are rarely seen as being in need of help, advice or counselling as they are assumed to have made rational choices. Therefore, rehabilitative policies have rarely been considered. As will be seen, however, there are many arguments that rehabilitation can be if anything more appropriate for corporate than for individual offenders (Braithwaite and Geis 1982). Similarly, incapacitation has rarely been considered. Offenders are not likely to be defined as 'dangerous', and they may have been effectively incapacitated by losing their jobs before conviction. They may not, therefore, have the opportunity to become persistent offenders, although many corporations amass a fairly high number of convictions. However, as is the case for rehabilitation, it can be argued that incapacitation *can* be a useful approach for both corporate and individual offenders (Braithwaite and Geis 1982). Individual offenders can be disbarred or disqualified, and corporations can be effectively incapacitated by closures or nationalization.

Whatever sentencing policies are adopted, their effect in reducing crime and thereby protecting the public may be limited. Thus, as is increasingly the case for conventional crimes, much emphasis is placed on public protection and prevention, emphases which underlie the use of preventive and compliance strategies. Braithwaite (1984a), for example, points out that if pharmaceutical companies are selling an unsafe drug the public is best protected by its immediate removal from the market. This can be done more speedily with the co-operation of companies, who may refuse to co-operate if enforcers are seen as adversaries interested only in prosecution. The role of self-regulation is also of great signficance, as ultimately more crime can be prevented within organizations themselves. Effective regulation may, therefore, require *both* preventive policies and a range of different sentencing policies.

Such a combination is suggested by Braithwaite (1989) in an attempt to develop an approach which can be applied to both conventional and white collar crime. Accepting that traditional sentencing policies and strategies of crime control have failed, he argues that the most effective social control exists where offenders experience shame for their actions and where there is strong moral disapproval of wrongdoing. This is the case in families, and in what he describes as 'communitarian societies'. A 'family model of punishment' suggests that firm discipline coupled with advice and support provides the most effective means of social control. However, discipline in the family must be backed up by state punishment. This suggests an approach based on re-integrative shaming which can be applied to juvenile delinquency and white collar crime alike. Tough formal punishment should underline the moral unacceptability of offences and policies should encourage shaming. None the less, punishment should not be too severe, as this can create 'outcasts' and 'organized subcultures of resistance'. Policies should, therefore, aim at support and re-integration rather than stigmatization.

For most kinds of white collar crime, he argues,

> the moral educative functions of the law are sorely neglected by insufficient levels of formal punishment coupled with state shaming. (Braithwaite 1989: 132)

Punishment for organizational crime should, therefore, maximize the sense of shame which

> communicates the message that white collar crime is as abhorrent to the community as crime in the streets. (Braithwaite 1989: 143)

Policies should, therefore, underline the moral unacceptability of white collar crime, by encouraging widespread publicity which would shame offenders along with firmer punishments where necessary. The closest approximation to the 'family model of punishment' for white collar crime is self-regulation within organizations, which should encourage moral disapproval of non-compliance. This, however, must be backed up by state punishment. Therefore, neither prosecution nor persuasive models best fit the requirements of reintegrative shaming – adversarial approaches threaten to make outcasts of otherwise compliant businesses and compliance strategies underplay the moral educative function of the criminal law. Effective business regulators he argues, are those who are flexible enough to persuade offenders who are willing to comply and at the same time use punishment against the recalcitrant.

Many strategies are suggested by these arguments. Some focus almost exclusively on prevention and protection of the public, leading to suggestions for increased self-regulation and even decriminalization. Others wish to see the criminal law tightened and penalties made more severe, and yet others argue that new strategies should be developed which may be more appropriate to the specific problems posed by white collar offences and offenders. Many strategies can be used in conjunction with others, leading to the kind of combination suggested by Braithwaite. Some of these suggestions and proposals will be outlined in the following sections.

Decriminalization

It has already been seen that the use of the criminal law and, in particular, the use of strict liability is unpopular among both lawyers and business groups. Hardly surprisingly, therefore, there have been calls for decriminalization. An influential *Justice* report in 1980 (cited in Levi 1984) advocated a drastic reduction in strict liability offences and argued that the criminal law should be restricted to offences which are clearly *mala in se*. Arguing that the use and proliferation of strict liability offences decreases respect for the criminal law, it recommended the creation of a category of 'contraventions' subject to civil penalties. Decriminalization was also an option favoured by the Royal Commission on Criminal Procedure of 1981 and in the Law Society's recommendations to the Keith Committee on Revenue Law which observed that:

> Routine regulatory mechanisms should not, in the tax field, be fenced with criminal sanctions. Automatic civil surcharges and penalties are more appropriate, and more reliable in their application. (Cited in Levi 1984: 251)

Decriminalization has also been proposed by David Tench, legal Adviser to the Consumer's Association, who suggests that consumer and other regulatory offences should be dealt with in a new 'middle system of law', which would be neither civil nor criminal. This would remove the sense of grievance expressed by offenders and could lead to higher penalties:

> under the new system the court may well feel much more at ease in awarding a civil penalty that really hurts, once the obloquy of a

criminal conviction is removed from the transgression. (Tench 1981: 21)

For 'crooks' and 'real fraud', Parliament should determine that some acts are to be considered as 'wicked and forbidden', while others should be considered to be 'not wicked', but in need of regulation. Public funds would be saved as many cases would not go to court. This system should be clearly distinguished from criminal law by using a different language – words like penalty, liability, contravention, transgression and violation would all be suitable unlike crime, offence, guilty or fine, imprisonment, prosecute and charge (Tench 1981). Hardly surprisingly, perhaps, these proposals were supported by business associations such as the Retail Trading Standards Association (Croall 1987).

There are many problems with these kinds of proposals. Deterrence could be further undermined by the absence of public prosecutions (Borrie 1980). In addition, while strict liability does enable defendants to minimize their blameworthiness and may lead to lower penalties, the difficulties of proving intent might lead to very few prosecutions of the really 'wicked', who would all presumably deny dishonesty or intent (Borrie 1984; Croall 1987). Despite the many protests about the injustice of convicting morally innocent business persons, selective prosecution policies and low penalties in themselves make such injustices unlikely (Levi 1984). Finally, many object to the ideological assumption underlying decriminalization proposals that these 'contraventions' or violations are essentially different from crimes and offences.

Self-regulation

Much of the responsibility for preventing and detecting white collar offences lies with industry itself, either through the internal arrangements of individual companies and businesses, or through trade associations and self-regulatory organizations, like those which exist in the City of London. Many offences are, indeed, more likely to be discovered within organizations than by outsiders, and many are dealt with by private policing and private justice (Clarke 1990). Some self-regulatory organizations can also disqualify offenders or apply other sanctions, and industrial and trade associations also monitor compliance with standards (Braithwaite and Fisse 1987). The scope and significance of self-regulation is, therefore, enormous. Accordingly, many argue that far greater emphasis should be placed on improving and strengthening arrangements for self-regulation, which can be more effective and less costly, as many of the costs of enforcement are borne by industries or trade associations themselves.

Braithwaite and Fisse (1987), on the basis of their research in the pharmaceutical and other industries, summarize the many benefits of self-regulation. Inspections carried out by company inspectors, they argue, can be more exhaustive compared to the often ineffective coverage of government inspectors. Corporate inspectors tend to be better trained, have a more specialized knowledge of the company's operations, and are in a better position to detect cover-ups and set up traps for suspected wrongdoers. To be effective, however, self-regulatory arrangements must have informal clout and management backing. Ideally, there should be provisions for accountability for compliance through line management accompanied by effective monitoring. In addition, problems must be effectively communicated to those capable of taking action and those involved should be adequately trained and supervised.

While few dispute that self-regulation *can* be more effective than public regulation, many doubt whether its potential can be realized, as many industries and especially trade associations have shown a marked reluctance to institute systems with sufficient clout. As Braithwaite and Fisse (1987) point out, industries often need to be threatened by increased state regulation before they are prepared to institute sufficiently rigorous controls. Furthermore, much self-regulation has been criticized for prioritizing industrial interests, and giving less weight to the interests of workers, consumers or the public at large (Cranston 1984). The practical effects of self-regulation can, therefore, be limited. A further objection to an over-emphasis on self-regulation is that it is not publicly accountable and offenders are not publicly prosecuted (Clarke 1987).

On the other hand, state and self-regulation can and do operate side by side, and as Braithwaite (1989) argues, to be effective self-regulation should be backed up by stiffer penalties, a combination central to his proposed theory of re-integrative shaming. Self-regulation should, he argues, attempt to foster corporate cultures in which an absence of compliance is seen as morally wrong, and should be based on trust and co-operation, involving all employees. He therefore rejects the kinds of self-regulatory systems which increase levels of monitoring and surveillance, and create more and more 'auditors' and 'monitors' which, he argues, merely exacerbate the diffusion of responsibility, and in which organizational complexity is used to 'protect people from their own consciences' (Braithwaite 1989: 147). To encourage the development of such a culture, organizations should encourage 'whistle blowing' and going direct to the top where non-compliance is found. Trust is essential in such a system, where everyone is a guardian and no-one is the ultimate guardian.

Administrative sanctions

The many powers and sanctions available to both self-regulatory organizations and public regulators, which can involve the closure of businesses, have already been outlined (Chapter 5). Businesses can be closed down if, for example, they pose a direct threat to the public health or if their operations are clearly fraudulent and the proprietors are bankrupt (Levi 1987a). Under Part III of the Fair Trading Act, the Office of Fair Trading can order firms to 'cease and desist' unfair trading practices (Cranston 1984). These powers have many advantages. They are deterrent, as they threaten the very survival of a business, they protect the public and prevent further offences. Accordingly, there are many suggestions that they should be extended and used more often.

However, in practice these various powers are rarely used. Commenting on their use in cases of insolvency, for example, Levi (1987a: 348) argues that there appears to be an attitude that trading at the risk of others is a 'right to be curtailed only under the most rigorous conditions'. Borrie (1982) argues that it is extremely costly to use the powers under Part III of the Fair Trading Act against large concerns as the proceedings are complex and there is a risk of putting innocent employees out of work. In addition, adds Levi (1987a), there are considerable difficulties involved in enforcing such orders. None the less, powers to close businesses are important, and they form a crucial part of the 'big stick' of law enforcers.

In certain circumstances, offenders can be disqualified. Such incapacitation can be achieved, argue Braithwaite and Geis (1982: 307) 'swiftly and without barbarism'. In Britain, individuals can be prohibited from running insurance and financial service businesses, and from professional practice in accountancy if they are deemed to be not a 'fit and proper person' (Levi 1987a, 1989b). Such a judgement is not necessarily related to offences, as convictions are neither a necessary nor sufficient condition for being banned, and they can be made where a lack of commercial probity, gross negligence or total incompetence is present (Levi 1987a, 1989b). Theoretically, these powers are deterrent and punitive, and also incapacitative. However, there are some practical problems. Where individuals have not been convicted, it may be difficult to obtain sufficient evidence to demonstrate whether or not someone is a 'fit and proper person' and, of course, many at one time considered to be 'fit and proper', none the less, commit offences (Levi 1987a: 348). Levi also points out that disqualified persons can readily set up new companies under a front person who has not been disqualified. The effect of disqualifications is further limited by what Braithwaite and Geis (1982) describe as substitution problems – one person within a business or corporation may be removed, but subsequently replaced by another person who may be prepared to commit the same offences. Finally, of course, they are only applicable where qualifications are required.

The power to grant or withdraw licences also has considerable potential, in that it is preventive and threatens profitability and survival. Indeed, these powers can shift the balance of power in favour of regulators (Pearce and Tombs 1990). Environmental Health officers, for example, are strongly in favour of introducing requirements that food businesses should be licensed, and criticize new requirements that food premises should register with Local Authorities as insufficient (Croall 1987; *Daily Telegraph* 25/6/90). While it is often objected that extension of the principle of licensing would be prohibitively costly, it could form part of a more punitive policing strategy (Pearce and Tombs 1990).

Many self-regulatory organizations and public enforcement agencies can also impose financial penalties, powers which many argue should be increased, which is implicit in proposals for decriminalization. They also have a considerable deterrent value and amount to punishment while avoiding costly and risky prosecutions. Other strategies can also provide financial disincentives to offend. Some economists, for example, advocate the introduction of pollution taxes, which could be levied on companies exceeding effluent emission standards (Braithwaite 1989), but these can be criticized as effectively condoning a certain level of pollution, and essentially giving industry the 'right' to pollute. In addition, they have been said to reduce the control of the environment to an economic rather than a moral issue (Braithwaite 1989; *The Times* 1/1/91). Of course, all these alternatives to prosecution, whatever their benefits, fall short of the public prosecution and punishment which many see as imperative, not only on the grounds of deterrence, but also of justice.

Criminal law and enforcement

However effective many of these administrative measures may be, most accept that the criminal law must be used as an ultimate sanction, if only for the most recalcitrant or 'wicked' offenders. Others argue further that the criminal sanction is also necessary to underline moral disapproval of activities which *are* criminal offences. Furthermore, private justice is not publicly accountable and leads to a situation in which a different set of rules is applied to different groups of offenders, a situation which would be exacerbated by a greater emphasis on alternatives to prosecution. Accordingly, therefore, there have been many suggestions for strengthening the criminal law, and making both enforcement and sentencing policies more punitive.

Against the view that the criminal law is inevitably limited, it could be argued that many of its gaps and loopholes could be plugged. It is impossible to examine here the many proposals for strengthening different laws, which include proposals for the criminalization of many more dangerous and fraudulent practices. In addition, the problems of corporate liability are not, many argue, irresolvable, even in relation to the vexed problem of corporate manslaughter. The law could, for example, clarify the duties and responsibilities of company directors, and the circumstances in which they could be judged to have neglected these duties. In relation to corporate manslaughter, for example, a new crime could be created

> whereby a director faced large fines and possible imprisonment if his failure to abide by his duties caused a person to die. (Bergman 1990b: 1501)

Pearce and Tombs (1990) further suggest that business enterprises should only be allowed to operate if they take all practicable means to operate safely. Like motoring offences which assume that motorists have a duty to avoid endangering others on the road, offences of 'careless employing' and more appropriately 'reckless employing' could be developed.

The creation of laws is undoubtedly important, but when created they have to be enforced, and there are many ways in which enforcement could be strengthened. Previous chapters have shown how resource constraints can lead to a lower rate of detection and prosecution which, in turn, reduces the deterrent and preventive value of the law. Accordingly, there have been many calls, not least from enforcement agencies themselves, for increased resources. It could, of course, be argued that the allocation of extra resources to the police force has not so far affected the upward trend in the crime rates. However, Levi (1987a) provides several arguments in support of increasing the resources for the policing of commercial fraud. In the first place he points out that while the contribution of detective work to the clear up rates for many conventional crimes is negligible, allocating more resources to the fraud squad *would* increase the amount of fraud detected. The investigation of serious frauds is often cost driven and more resources would enable the follow-up of more serious cases. This could increase the credibility and effectiveness of the police, which might in turn lead to victims reporting more offences. Finally, there may be some political benefits in increasing detection rates, as law and order is not well served by fraudsters appearing to get away with large profits. While increasing resources would not necessarily be cost effective, 'no policing is' (Levi 1987a: 281).

While these arguments relate to fraud, they have general applicability. More resources for Inland Revenue departments would not only lead to the detection of more offences, but would also maximize the amounts of money recovered (Cook 1989a). More resources for regulatory enforcement agencies would enable them to carry out more inspections and testing, which would increase their chances of detecting offences and, thereby, improve public protection. Allocating more resources to enforcement might, in turn, result in a greater number of prosecutions, which can be justified on the grounds of both deterrence and justice. It could be argued, for example, that for some, particularly high status offenders, public prosecution in itself is an important deterrent, and public awareness of offences might be enhanced by more prosecutions. A higher rate of prosecutions would also reduce the inequities produced by the present situation in which business and white collar offenders are more likely to be subject to private justice and less to public justice than conventional offenders (see Chapter 5).

Making offenders pay

While more prosecutions might constitute a deterrent, this could well be undermined by insignificant fines. Raising the level of fines is, therefore, seen by many commentators as imperative. This can be done by increasing maximum fines and encouraging the use of higher fines within the permitted range. Many argue, for example, that fines should better reflect the illegal profits made from offences (Braithwaite 1984a) and, in respect of car clocking, Borrie (1984) has called for more 'robust' fining. Fines could also be more closely related to the offender's ability to pay. There have been many arguments for the adoption of a 'unit fine' system in which fines are calculated on the basis of units which are then related to the offender's means. These have now been introduced and their effect on fines for white collar offenders could be substantial. Levi (1989a) argues not only that very large fines should be imposed where appropriate, but that the media should be encouraged to take a more sophisticated attitude when reporting sentences by relating fines to offenders' means. Many of these points have been implicitly accepted by the introduction of unit fines and the raising of fines for many regulatory offences. For example, the new Environmental Protection Act of 1990 increases the maximum fines for Pollution offences from £2000 to £20,000 (*The Times* 1/1/91). It remains to be seen, however, whether these changes will result in higher average fines.

It could be objected that fining companies too severely could penalize innocent parties like shareholders whose dividends might be cut or consumers who might suffer if the cost of fines were passed on by way of higher prices. However, both Braithwaite (1984a) and Leigh (1977) argue that shareholders accept an element of risk by investing and also that companies may not be able to raise prices in competitive markets. Punitive fines could also make shareholders ask more questions about the responsibilities of senior executives (Geis 1978). One problem which could arise in relating fines to offenders' ability to pay is how this ability can be ascertained. As Levi (1987a) points out, the self-reported income and debt statements of the accused are not the most valid method of data gathering in professional fraud or organized crime cases!

In addition to fines, offenders can also be made to pay through the imposition of compensation orders or the confiscation of assets. For example, courts may order confiscation of assets in cases of serious frauds, involving sums of over £10,000. However, Levi (1987a) points out that these powers may be limited in practice, as assets may be in foreign bank accounts which are difficult to access. Compensation orders can also add to the total financial penalty, and can be used where fines are low to increase the total sum (Croall 1987). There are, therefore, many ways in which offenders can be made to pay for their crimes. However, financial penalties for the very rich can still be of limited value as they may have to be very high to be sufficiently deterrent and they may not have an equitable effect – they can, for example, perpetuate the situation in which the rich can pay for their crimes whereas the poor are less able to do so (Cook 1989b).

Tougher sanctions?

Imprisonment

While many argue that sentences should be more punitive, it is not easy to determine how this can be done. An obvious suggestion is that more white collar offenders should be sent to prison for longer periods of time on the grounds that the threat of imprisonment is deterrent, and that it is widely regarded as the most severe sanction under the criminal law (Levi 1987a). Geis (1978) also argues that more use of imprisonment would be retributive, and would encourage moral outrage and media attention. On the other hand, arguing for *more* prison sentences contradicts the general consensus that prison serves little useful purpose and that its use ought to be reduced (Braithwaite 1984a). It could also be seen as somewhat ironic to suggest that rich and wealthy offenders should be maintained at the state's expense. Finally, arguing that one group of offenders ought to be imprisoned more, while arguing that other groups should be imprisoned less, contradicts principles of equity (Leigh 1977).

Even when imprisoned, white collar offenders continue to enjoy favourable treatment, more often being sent to open prisons on the assumption that they present a smaller security risk. They are more likely to be paroled, and less likely to be seen as being in need of rehabilitation (Levi 1987a, Doig 1984). Some of the *Guinness* defendants were sent to Ford open prison, which used to be known as 'the gentleman's prison' in which there is reputed to be a more relaxed regime, and where offenders could issue business instructions, freely use the phone and write letters (*The Times* 29/9/90). White collar offenders' experience of prison may, therefore, involve fewer pains than that of conventional criminals.

There are other ways of devising more draconian sentences for white collar offenders, although few have followed up the suggestion of the previous President of Pakistan, who, denouncing tax evasion, argued that if, under the Islamic code, a hand could be chopped off for theft, the whole arm might be cut off for tax evasion (Levi and Suddle 1989). This might be retributive but it would scarcely be preventive. It is also difficult to contemplate what draconian punishment for corporations could consist of, bearing in mind the need to prevent penalizing innocent workers. There are, none the less, many suggestions for incapacitation.

Incapacitation

Despite the apparent difficulties of incapacitating white collar offenders, Braithwaite and Geis (1982: 307) argue that:

> although incapacitation is not apt to be very effective or acceptable for controlling traditional crime in a humane society, it can be a highly successful strategy in the control of corporate crime. Indeed, it can be more workable with corporate crimes because their kind of criminal activity is dependent on their being able to maintain legitimacy in formalized roles in the economy.

Disqualifications are, of course, in themselves a form of incapacitation – as Braithwaite and Geis (1982: 307) further comment,

> we do not need to cut off the hands of surgeons who increase their income by having patients undergo unnecessary surgery . . . all we need do is deregister them.

Corporations can be incapacited by revoking their charter, placing them in the hands of a receiver or nationalizing them. This amounts in essence to 'corporate capital punishment' and it could, of course, be objected that it could adversely affect both investors and employees. However, nationalization would have no such effect and, argues Moore (1987), corporate assets could also be sold or transferred to new parent companies.

While these strategies may be both deterrent and preventive, their potential use and effect is likely to be somewhat limited. Box (1983: 72) comments, for example, that they might well be seen as 'draconian and ideologically repugnant'. In addition, as Levi (1987a) points out, the individuals involved could set up new operations under assumed names or in countries less stringently regulated.

Rehabilitating offenders

It has already been indicated that rehabilitative policies can be appropriate for white collar offenders, including organizations (Braithwaite and Geis 1982; Box 1983; Braithwaite 1984a). Indeed, Braithwaite (1984a) argues that corporations can be rehabilitated more easily than conventional criminals as standard operating procedures and organization charts are easier to change than individual psyches. As was shown in Chapter 4, many attribute organizational offences to organizational defects, and it therefore seems logical that 'treatment' be directed at the criminogenic features of organizations (Moore 1987).

Probation orders

Following these arguments, 'corporate probation orders' could be devised.

Box (1983), for example, argues that new probation officers, paid for by companies, could be appointed to monitor operating procedures and Braithwaite (1984a) suggests a system of probation orders under auditors. Sentences could be deferred until companies devise new operating systems, bearing the cost themselves. In a sense, this is similar to what already happens in persuasion strategies and such orders could strengthen the educative role of enforcers. They could be particularly appropriate for small business offenders, who might be more adversely affected by any increase in fines and whose offences are often attributed to ignorance of the law or poor financial management. Thus, they could readily be seen as being more in need of 'help' than punishment, like the conventional offenders for whom rehabilitative policies were originally designed. Probation orders would also be preventive. While they might be seen as too 'soft', they could, where appropriate, be used in conjunction with other sentences (Braithwaite 1984a).

Community service

A mixture of retributive and rehabilitative arguments underlies the use of community service orders, rarely used for white collar offenders and generally assumed to be inapplicable to corporate offenders. None the less, their potential value is enormous, and they have been used in the United States, in conjunction with prison sentences, for notorious white collar criminals such as Ivan Boesky (*The Times* 29/8/90). The skills of individual offenders could well be useful to the voluntary organizations often involved in the administration of community service, provided, of course, that they are adequately supervised. Levi (1989a: 434), in characteristic style, supports their use, but only for those who will not flee abroad, commenting that:

> even if the unsupervised running of Black Enterprise schemes on Broadwater Farm were considered too great a risk, decorating in Tower Hamlets or helping with The Embankment Soup Run while one's former colleagues are weekending the Antibes might be a suitable piece of moral symbolism which might also change some elite offenders' views of the world.

In the United States, community service programmes have been developed for corporate offenders. Braithwaite (1984a) cites the example of Allied Chemicals who were required to fund an environmental protection programme following a major pollution disaster. He also suggests that a suitable Community Service Order for pharmaceutical companies could be the development of 'service drugs' for victims of rare diseases which are not profitable because demand is so small. Variations of these ideas could apply across a wide range of offences. Dirty restaurants, once they have been cleaned and duly inspected by enforcers, could be required to give free meals to deprived groups, and traders and large manufacturers could be required to donate goods to children's homes, especially importers and manufacturers of dangerous toys (see, for example, Box 1983). Following Braithwaite's suggestion for pharmaceutical companies, food manufacturers could be required to provide special 'additive free' products for allergy sufferers. Large and small businesses alike could, therefore, be required to make various kinds of contributions to the community where their skills and resources could be of enormous value. Further advantages of the community service model are that sentences can be retributive, reintegrative, and can also heighten community consciousness. Enforcers, who may not prosecute because penalties are so low, might be more encouraged to do so if they felt that sentences could support their goals or help the community.

Shaming offenders

Publicizing offences can be a major deterrent and can also, argues Box (1983), act as a catalyst by raising public consciousness. Publicity is also central to the shaming strategies outlined by Braithwaite (1989) who points out that as white collar offenders have a more profound stake in conformity they are more deterrable by publicity.

There is considerable evidence that white collar offenders do fear adverse publicity. Benson (1985) found that offenders whose cases had been reported felt embarrassed or embittered, whereas offenders whose cases had not been reported felt relieved. Although the financial loss incurred through adverse publicity may not be as great as feared, it has a considerable impact on staff morale and companies do feel that their reputation has been damaged (Hopkins 1980; Fisse and Braithwaite 1983). Hutter (1988) also found that court appearances and publicity were a source of worry to offenders. She cites the case of the Cafe Royal, who, following press reports about impending food hygiene prosecutions took out a half page advertisement in the national press, inviting consumers to inspect the premises and see their cleanliness for themselves. Leigh (1977) further argues that publicity is likely to be particularly effective in cases involving consumer law as the public are likely to pay attention to publicity surrounding the safety or quality of a product they are likely to buy. An illustration of this was observed by the author, where several members of the public, waiting for other cases in court, examined the court list for the day. A local bakery was appearing on several summons involving the presence of foreign bodies, in this case a pen and sticking plaster, in its bread. 'Oooh, look at that', commented one lady, 'I won't go there again!!' The power of publicity is also clearly recognized by enforcement officers as evidenced by attempts to increase the attention cases receive in the media (Chapter 5).

None the less, despite the considerable publicity surrounding major cases, publicity does not inevitably follow conviction, especially for regulatory offences, which are often heard in lower courts, and only irregularly covered by the media (Croall 1987). Therefore, many argue that courts should have powers to order some kind of publicity. However, determining the form that court ordered publicity might take creates difficulties. There have been some experiments with 'corporate atonement' policies in the United States, where companies are required to pay for advertisements correcting misleading ones, but companies often used specialist journals, rather than the consumer journals used for the original advertisements (Box 1983). Some have argued that the public might simply get bored with long lists of advertisements reporting convictions. Publicity could, however, be targeted, with companies being required to pay for advertisements in suitable media such as, for example, women's magazines, consumer journals and special interest publications (Box 1983; Braithwaite 1984a). Levi (1987a) also argues that courts could require offending firms to take out an advertisement in either the local or national press to publish details of their violations. Fisse and Braithwaite (1983) recommend a variety of schemes including adverse publicity orders as a formal sanction, calling press conferences immediately after corporate convictions, and encouraging consumer activism and investigative journalism by rationalizing defamation laws.

Summary and discussion

Many of the suggestions reviewed above are relatively uncontroversial. The potential benefits of more effective self-regulation are rarely disputed and a tougher use of the administrative powers of agencies similarly attracts widespread support. Stiffer fines are almost universally advocated, and may result from current legislation. While the use of probation or community service orders, specially designed to be appropriate to white collar offenders has been less widely discussed, few disagree that they could be useful additions to the present range of sentences. What is more contentious is the relative emphasis to be placed on public prosecution and punishment as opposed to administrative and private justice. These discussions reflect fundamentally different approaches to the analysis of white collar crime itself and how it can best be dealt with (see, for example, Pearce and Tombs 1990; Hawkins 1990).

To those adopting what was described at the beginning of this chapter as a regulatory approach the main issue is how compliance and, thereby, public protection can best be achieved. Thus, decriminalization, self-regulation and the greater use of administrative sanctions tend to be preferred options, on the grounds that they are more effective and less costly. Criminal law may be seen as more or less necessary, depending on intepretations of its deterrent value. While many disagree about the relative merits of specific proposals, what distinguishes discussions within such an approach is their focus on pragmatic considerations of cost effectiveness rather than on issues of equity, justice or morality. These are rendered unproblematic by the distinction between the 'violations' of the majority who need not be publicly sanctioned and the 'offences' of the minority for whom the limited use of criminal law should be reserved.

To proponents of a more radical approach the discourse and assumptions of the 'regulatory' approach reflect and perpetuate the 'ideological hegemony' of corporate capital (see, for example, Pearce and Tombs 1990). Legal and economic constraints on enforcers arise from political decisions, which reflect the low priority assigned to the control of corporate crime. Compliance strategies and lenient sentences further perpetuate the fundamentally inequitable treatment of business offenders. Issues of criminalization, law enforcement and sentencing are, therefore, political and ideological issues. Accordingly, political agendas can and should be changed, and tougher laws and enforcement can and should be placed on these agendas. While the desirability and, indeed, the possibility of specific strategies may be disputed, the main thrust of these arguments is that white collar crime should be dealt with as crime and that more prosecution and public punishment is necessary, both to provide a greater deterrent and to satisfy the interests of justice and equity. Arguing for a range of proposals including the reform of company law, and the further development of licensing arrangements and severe punishments, Pearce and Tombs (1990: 440) argue that 'a punitive policing policy is necessary, desirable and practicable'.

As indicated at the start of this Chapter however, elements of both of these approaches can be combined to produce a range of strategies which satisfy the interests of both public protection and justice. It can, for example, be accepted that in certain circumstances compliance strategies can more effectively prevent offences and protect the public without at the same time implying that white collar crimes are any more morally acceptable than conventional ones (Hawkins 1990). It can also be recognized that a different range of policies may be appropriate for white collar crime without at the same time treating them any less severely. Tougher and more effective self-regulation along with the more stringent use of administrative powers can, therefore, be supported along with proposals to strengthen the criminal law, give more resources to enforcers, and develop tougher and more appropriate sentencing policies. Such a combination is suggested in Braithwaite's analysis, discussed at length above, in which he argues that self-regulation is ultimately the most effective means of securing and maintaining high standards, provided that it aims at the development of compliance cultures within organizations. At the same time this must be backed up by tough formal state punishment. Thus, publicity and severe punishment, like for example, 'corporate capital punishment' should be used to underline the moral unacceptability of offences and to shame offenders, and rehabilitative policies and community service to 're-integrate' them. Such a range of policies would also satisfy those who argue for greater equity and justice along with those who wish to see the public better protected.

10

CRIMINOLOGY AND THE PROBLEM OF WHITE COLLAR CRIME

Throughout this book many diverse views about white collar crime have been examined. Its definition is disputed and the concept itself is controversial. It is claimed to be more prevalent and serious than so-called conventional crime, yet its existence is hidden and victims are unaware of its actual or potential threat. It is generally associated with the rich and powerful yet convicted offenders tend to be the not so rich or powerful. Prosecution is rare and punishments are light, yet there is little evidence of class bias. Laws are said to reflect the interests of offenders, yet public protection is their stated aim. Suggestions for improving regulations range from decriminalization, on the one hand, to tougher punishment, on the other. Underlying these many conflicting views is the debate over whether white collar crime is 'really crime'.

It is no easy task to categorize or label these many divergent approaches. Pearce and Tombs (1990: 423), for example, have recently attacked what they describe as 'compliance theories' on the grounds that they accept that 'the illegal conduct of corporations necessarily calls for different forms of regulation than do other kinds of law-breaking'. Hawkins (1990: 445), on the other hand, argues that these criticisms amount to a 'straw man or Aunt Sally school of academic critique', by setting up an artificial theoretical position in order to criticize it. Pearce and Tombs, he argues, falsely assume that studies which attempt to describe and understand the reality of regulatory law enforcement also accept the assumptions on which it is based.

It is also difficult to associate approaches to white collar crime with current criminological approaches such as 'left idealism', left realism, or 'establishment' or administrative criminology (see, for example, Young 1986). Indeed, these categorizations themselves, especially that of left idealism, have also been attacked as creating 'straw men' (Sim *et al.* 1987). The significance of white collar crime or the crimes of the powerful to these approaches is, indeed, unclear. Young, for example, has criticized radical criminology and left idealism for its over concentration on the crimes of the powerful, which, he argues, underplays the 'real' problem of street crime, and Lea and Young (1984) call for a double thrust against both white collar and street crime. On the other hand, criminology as a whole, particularly in Britain, has been criticized for its neglect of these crimes. Much of the work often associated with radical criminology of either the left realist or left idealist variety has, with some exceptions, been concerned with the policing of lower class crime and on issues of police accountability, race and gender, rather than on corporate or white collar crime, about which much is often inferred and assumed rather than being subject to research or analysis.

Accordingly, no attempt will be made to attribute labels such as left idealism, left realism, or administrative criminology to the various approaches to white collar crime which have been outlined in previous chapters, although some clear parallels are evident. Nor is it the intention, in comparing and contrasting different approaches to create yet more 'straw men' (or even women!). However, as argued in Chapter 9 distinct approaches can be discerned which derive from very different assumptions about the nature and legal regulation of white collar crime and therefore focus on a different set of questions. Comparing these approaches can make some sense of the many divergent strands of discussion and debate.

From Sutherland's early work to the development of radical criminology, the so-called white collar crime 'debate' has hinged around its identification with high class offenders and the crimes of the powerful. This has imbued the concept with ideological connotations, and its existence became part of the critique of criminological theories which focused on the crimes of the powerless. The main underlying question is why the law and its associated agencies fail to treat white collar crime in the same way as conventional crime. Analyses focused, therefore, on the policies and practices of law enforcers, and on the law itself, both of which were seen to treat white collar crime with insufficient severity – thus perpetuating the fundamentally ideological distinction between white collar and real crime. Thus, the street and property crimes of the powerless are both legally and publicly defined as 'real crime' whereas the equally if not more anti-social activities of the powerful are not. This, in turn, was often attributed to the ability of the powerful to secure advantageous laws.

To others, often lawyers or enforcers, the main problems raised by white collar crime are the more practical ones of how it can best be regulated. Thus, what was earlier described as a 'regulatory' approach has some parallels with the concerns of what Young (1986, 1988) describes as administrative or establishment criminology. These approaches discuss the use of the criminal law and enforcement policies in the morally neutral language of cost effectiveness. The limitations of the law are seen as technical rather than ideological problems and policies of law enforcement as a response to the real enforcement difficulties posed by the offences themselves. Class bias is denied, the white collar crime debate is seen as a political one, and issues of equity and justice rendered irrelevant to those who tend to accept that the majority of white collar offences and offenders are not really criminal.

An increasing number of writers accept that both sets of questions are important. A focus on offences rather than offenders directs attention to the real difficulties of detection and prosecution to which the much maligned compliance strategies are a response. At the same time, however, the distinction implicit in both legislation and enforcement between white collar crimes and others is essentially an ideological one, and white collar offenders do enjoy many advantages in the criminal justice process. Therefore, issues of both equity and justice are important, as the failure, for whatever reason, to treat white collar crimes severely can in itself encourage their proliferation. The contrasts between these different approaches have dominated discussion of the crucial issues in the white collar crime debate – how it is to be defined; whether it is 'really criminal'; whether it constitutes a crime problem; how it is treated in the criminal justice system; and how it should best be controlled.

What is white collar crime?

It was argued in Chapter 1 that despite its many problems, the concept of white collar crime is still useful and that the phrase is worth retaining if only on the grounds that it is widely recognized by academics, practitioners and the general public. It was also argued that its definition should be dissociated from the class, status or respectability of offenders. Subsequent analyses confirm the merits of such an approach. The automatic equation of white collar crime with high status offenders has been challenged by repeated findings that offenders come from all levels of the occupational hierarchy. By focusing on offences irrespective of the status of offenders, the concept is considerably strengthened or 'liberated' (Shapiro 1990) as it highlights the distinctive characteristics of crime committed in the course of legitimate occupational roles. The complexity and invisibility of offences which, along with the diffusion of responsibility, lead to the many difficulties of measuring, detecting and prosecuting offences are thus revealed as crucial characteristics which distinguish this kind of crime from others. Such a definition also directs attention to the 'illegitimate opportunity structures' and criminogenic characteristics of occupations and organizations which not only assists an understanding of the offences themselves but also has profound significance for their prevention.

It could be argued that such an approach denies the significance of class status and power. However, this need not be the case, and their significance has been revealed throughout analyses of offences, legislation and criminal justice. Shapiro's analysis of the social organization of trust, for example, points to the greater opportunities for abusing trust higher up the occupational ladder. It also reveals the power of those who enjoy trusted positions. Professional occupations, for example, identified as particularly 'fiddle prone' (Mars 1982; Chapter 4), may be able to control both the service which they provide and appropriate levels of remuneration (Johnson 1972). Ignorant consumers and employers are, therefore, particularly vulnerable to exploitation by the knowledgeable specialist, whether professional or not. As Hagan argues, a focus on the status of offenders

> glosses over what is potentially most salient in Sutherland's attention to differential social organization; the differential power that derives from structural location in the social organization of work. (Hagan 1988: 20)

It has also been seen that the many structural advantages enjoyed by offenders in the criminal justice process derive from both their occupational status and economic resources.

Is white collar crime really crime?

These advantages are also affected by the perception that many offences are not really crime and this ambiguous criminal status permeates analysis of all aspects of white collar crime. It is reflected in the discourse of enforcers, legislators, sentencers and defendants, which implicitly or explicitly distinguishes many offences from 'real crime'. Thus, they are more often described as infringements or violations than as crimes or offences. They are said to be caused by mistakes or oversights rather than being the result of wickedness or scheming. They require penalties or sanctions rather than punishment. It has been seen that the whole language of regulation or compliance is very different to that of crime control and punishment. It is not only in the legal arena that such distinctions are made as the taken for granted distinctions between fiddles, perks, cons and rip-offs, and theft and fraud illustrate. These also reveal the gap between social and legal definitions of 'crime', and the extremely blurred lines between acceptable, legal, illegal and criminal activities.

But is white collar crime any 'less criminal' than other offences? Many so-called conventional crimes enjoy a similarly ambiguous status – some drug offences and motoring offences, for example, can also be seen as not really criminal. In addition, there are many arguments that white collar offences do possess the basic elements regularly associated with the definition of crime. They involve many forms of lying, cheating and stealing (Shapiro 1990), and force and fraud (Hirschi and Gottfredson 1987). Furthermore,

> as with common crime, the white collar offender clearly seeks personal benefit. This benefit may come directly to the offender or indirectly to the offender through the group or organization to which he or she belongs (Hirschi and Gottfredson 1987: 953).

Nonetheless, the ambiguous criminal status of offences has been a central feature of the white collar crime 'debate' with many allegations and counter allegations of ideological and political bias. Those who assert the essential criminality of white collar offences and the need to treat them as crimes are accused of political bias by those who argue that the criminal law is used primarily as an expedient against activities which are only technically criminal, an argument which in turn is attacked as ideological. To many this confirms that the very definition of crime itself is a political one.

Whatever its basis, the ambiguous criminal status of offences has enormous significance for their analysis and treatment. It gives many offenders a moral justification for law breaking and arguably, therefore, makes that law breaking more likely. It also provides the space for offenders to minimize their 'guilt' in court. To the extent that law enforcers and sentencers share a perception that the offences are not really crime, it underlies compliance strategies and sentencing decisions. Finally, it gives credibility to those who argue that business is *over* regulated, and that decriminalization and an emphasis on administrative measures rather than prosecution and tougher penalties are desirable.

Is white collar crime a problem?

Partly as a result of its ambiguous criminal status, white collar crime rarely features in public discussions of the 'crime problem'. Few questions about white collar crimes are asked in victim surveys or in Home Office studies of public estimations of crime seriousness. A recent survey of judgements of crime seriousness, for example, listed fourteen offences, of which only one, tax evasion, was a white collar offence (Pease 1988), and this was seen as one of the least serious offences. Of course, many argue that white collar crime is more widespread and has a more serious impact than conventional crime (Chapter 2). While the well-known problems of measuring the 'real' incidence of either white collar or conventional crime make it impossible to substantiate this claim, it was seen in Chapter 2 that its amount and impact are enormous.

However, it has been argued that however prevalent offences may be, they are not as serious as conventional crime. Their impact on victims is often trivial, they rarely involve violence, and they feature little in the public's fear of crime. Thus, Wilson (1975) has argued that conventional crime is more serious as people do not bar and nail shut their windows, avoid going out at night or harbour deep suspicions of strangers because of unsafe working conditions or massive consumer fraud. In addition Young (1986) has criticized so-called left idealists for their over concentration on elite crime which underplays the 'real' problems of street crime. None the less it can be argued that while the public may well be less likely to fear white collar crime or to define it as crime, this does not make it any the less serious.

Despite this, it could be argued that street and property crime disproportionately victimize the poor and powerless, whereas white collar crime has a diffuse effect and some offences primarily victimize those who have more to lose. Offences like insider dealing and fraud, for example, are more often directed against businesses and investors, and it was seen that institutional victims are perceived by sentencers as less victimized (Chapter 8). However, the vulnerability of the poor to street crime is compounded by the rippling and often unrecognized effects of white collar crime (Lea and Young 1984). What makes affluent citizens less vulnerable to street crime is their ability to protect themselves by avoiding victimization by, for example, not walking on the streets in high crime areas, moving home and installing burglar alarms (Lea and Young 1984). In much the same way they can also move home to avoid pollution from the local factory and can afford to avoid buying cheap bargain goods, mass produced convenience foods or cheap second hand cars.

It has also been argued that white collar crime involves the power of the expert over the ignorant, the producer over the consumer, or the employer over the employee - even the employee over the employer. However, middle class citizens are more likely to be knowledgeable, aware of their rights and even if ignorant can seek advice. They are more likely to be readers of consumer journals and more aware of the hazards of pollution, unsafe goods or foods. This knowledge is likely to steer them away from unsafe investments, ill advised purchases and the inferior services provided by either blue or white collar 'cowboys'. They are also more able to take action to secure compensation should they be victimized. Finally, they are better able to shoulder the burden of higher prices and higher taxes which may be the result of tax evasion and employee offences. The poor and powerless, therefore, are more vulnerable to exploitation and victimization from white collar, corporate and conventional crime.

Some groups, by virtue of their structural location may be specially vulnerable to particular offences. Women are arguably more vulnerable as consumers. In addition to being the main shoppers, they are more likely to buy cosmetics, perfumes or designer outfits - all of which are subject to counterfeit frauds in addition to being among those products inadequately regulated (Croall 1987). They are the main consumers of slimming aids, many of which are subsequently revealed to be dangerous and inadequately tested. They are generally assumed to be ignorant of financial and technical matters, making them particular targets for bogus investment schemes and car repair frauds. The present author has, on several occasions, been told that expensive repairs are required to her not very expensive car. It has been assumed, correctly, that she cannot judge for herself whether brake pads are worn or the suspension is faulty! Subsequent examination by a more reliable garage has found that these repairs are not required. While many male academic colleagues confess to similar ignorance, they are less vulnerable as they are assumed to be more knowledgeable. Women are also likely to be particularly vulnerable to the marketing of unsafe contraceptives and drugs as the Dalkon Shield and Thalidomide cases demonstrate (Braithwaite 1984a; Perry and Dawson 1987). Children are victimized as consumers of sweets and junk foods loaded with unsafe additives, or by cheap, attractive, but unsafe toys. Schools and hospitals have also been major purchasers of unfit meat (Croall 1987).

The apparent triviality of many white collar offences and the absence of a fear of white collar crime do not mean therefore that they are 'really' less serious. Indeed, their very invisibility underlines the vulnerability of victims. The power exercised by offenders is less naked and less violent than in many conventional offences, but preys rather on the ignorance of the victim. In addition, public indifference cannot be taken for granted. When questions about white collar offences are included in surveys of public estimations of crime seriousness, some, particularly those which result in physical injury, are rated as more serious than many conventional crimes (Levi and Jones 1985; Grabosky *et al.* 1987). This indicates that the public could take white collar crime more seriously were they to be sensitized to its dangers – an assumption underlying many of the suggestions for greater publicity (Box 1983). It can, therefore, be argued that white collar crime is a 'real' crime problem.

White collar crime and criminal justice

These arguments indicate why the treatment of offenders in the criminal justice system has been such a major source of contention. Given the serious impact of white collar crime, it seems eminently reasonable to ask why so few offenders are prosecuted and severely punished. The many debates surrounding this issue were reviewed at length in Chapters 5, 6 and 7 and, therefore, need little re-iteration here. The major source of contention is, of course, the extent to which white collar crime can be said to be dealt with leniently and if so, whether or not this results from class bias.

It cannot be disputed that white collar crime is subject to different regulatory arrangements and that these can be interpreted as lenient – if only on the grounds that fewer are prosecuted and subjected to public as opposed to private justice. In relation to prosecution this arises largely because regulatory enforcers are more likely to take the view that they are not dealing with 'crimes' and are less concerned with issues of 'just deserts'. As Braithwaite and Pettit (1990: 191) argue:

> In every country where empirical work on business regulatory enforcement has been done, a similar picture of more benign enforcement by the regulatory agencies than by the police has emerged. One of the authors has done research on dozens of business regulatory agencies on four continents without discovering one agency for which just deserts was a significant priority or even a subsidiary goal. The day the literature reports a business regulatory agency driven by desert, it will be akin to a zoologist announcing the discovery of a new species.

In addition, sentences can be described as equally benign particularly when the seriousness of offences and resources of offenders are taken into account.

Explaining this, therefore, becomes the major issue. Taking the criminal justice process as a whole, it was seen that the more extreme positions of competing approaches are largely unjustified. There is little evidence of agency bias, either on the part of 'captured' or sympathetic law enforcers, or sentencers unwilling to punish high status or elite offenders. In any event white collar offenders do not form a homogenous group. Indeed, some white collar offenders would appear to be relatively disadvantaged compared with others in respect of their relative vulnerability to prosecution and punishment. Offenders do not always receive the sympathy to which they often appeal and some can be seen as 'letting the side down'.

On the other hand, claims that current policies are justified on the grounds of efficiency, and are necessitated by the exigencies of law enforcement are equally questionable. Claims that compliance strategies are uniquely more efficient can be disputed on their own terms as it could well be argued that *more* prosecutions are necessary on the grounds of deterrence. Enforcers themselves complain about insufficiently deterrent sentences, especially in view of their highly selective prosecution policies. They further complain about the lack of resources which constrains their efforts and further limits prevention and deterrence.

It has been argued that the explanation for leniency lies in the many structural advantages enjoyed by many white collar offenders, either in comparison with other white collar or some conventional offenders. In the first place their superior resources can be used variously to avoid breaking the law, to avoid detection, to avoid prosecution and to avoid severe punishment. They can buy themselves out of prosecution by negotiating out of court settlements and out of prison by paying enormous fines. Many offenders can exploit the ambiguous criminal status of offences by providing credible arguments that they are honest, reputable business persons whose offences are isolated mistakes and who, therefore, don't deserve severe punishment, particularly as they have suffered enough already. The law itself further compounds these advantages as it encourages the use of compliance strategies and the minimal use of prosecution, provides for out of court settlements, and contains the many loopholes and ambiguities which allow defendants to minimize their culpability. It also creates categories of offences which are legitimately defined as 'not really criminal' giving yet more offenders the opportunity to deny intent, to conceal the persistence and seriousness of their offences and thus attract lighter sentences which are themselves constrained by legal maxima.

Thus, the more favourable treatment of white collar offenders cannot be attributed either to class bias or to the nature of offences alone. While the logic of compliance strategies may be justifiable to enforcers, and while sentences may appear 'fair' to sentencers, the outcome is inequitable compared to the treatment of many lower class conventional offenders. Burglars, for example, are more likely to be prosecuted and persistent burglars are likely to be incarcerated for considerably longer periods of time than persistent fraudsters, whose offences involve larger sums of money. Therefore, the outcome of the decisions of law enforcers and sentencers reinforce and reflect wider structural inequalities.

Can white collar crime be better controlled?

Criticisms of the criminal justice process are inextricably linked to criticisms of the law itself, whose many limitations were outlined in Chapters 8 and 9. The law is limited in scope, has many loopholes, and insufficient resources constrain enforcers. To some adherents of a regulatory approach this is less of a problem than to others, as criminal law should in any event only be used as a last resort, and better self-regulatory arrangements, coupled with market forces can be equally effective. Decreasing the use of the criminal law and the role of public enforcement, therefore, shifts the burden of preventing offences to industry and the public themselves. To Marxist and other radical theorists this, of course, is yet a further illustration of the law failing to act against the crimes of the powerful.

Increasingly, however, it is being acknowledged that the issues are more complex than suggested by *either* approach. Law represents a combination of influences, negotiations, compromises and accommodations between the conflicting interests of capitalists, individual groups of capitalists and governments, and reflects the changing priorities of these groups in response to specific political and economic pressures. None the less, its impact on white collar offending is limited, and these limitations do appear to favour business interests over those of the public, particularly in an economic and political environment in which over regulation and the high costs of compliance and enforcement dominate the political and economic agenda. However, this has not necessarily led to the deregulation which some have feared. Indeed, Braithwaite and Ayres (1991) argue that the situation is more one of regulatory 'flux', and that assertions that deregulation is on the agenda overstate the position. In addition, Pearce and Tombs (1990), from a Marxist perspective, argue that political agendas can be changed. Therefore, white collar crime need not inevitably be treated more favourably than other crimes.

Changing the present arrangements, therefore, appears possible leaving the question of what range of strategies and policies are desirable and on what grounds they are to be advocated. Clearly, they should be effective, and most accept the prioritization of public protection. Greater controversy surrounds the vexed issue of whether the interests of 'justice' require that white collar offences should be treated in the same way as conventional crimes. While accusations of direct class bias are largely unfounded, it has nonetheless been argued that offenders do enjoy a structural advantage. Any range of policies, therefore, should attempt to redress this balance, and if white collar crime is crime it ought to be treated as crime. However, this need not necessarily mean that white collar offenders should be subjected to the same kinds of punishment as conventional offenders, as conventional offenders could also be treated differently. As Braithwaite and Pettit (1990), advocating a 'republican' theory of justice argue, full implementation of just deserts for *either* white collar *or* conventional crimes is impracticable and would be prohibitively costly. Protecting the public and justice, they argue, can better be achieved by a minimal use of prosecution and punishment for *both* white collar and conventional crimes. It might be more appropriate to argue for less punitive strategies towards many conventional crimes, than more punitive strategies towards many white collar crimes.

In practice a combination of more effective self-regulation and compliance strategies and tougher laws, policing and punishment would appear to be desirable. It was seen in Chapter 9 that such a combination can satisfy demands for both equity and cost-effectiveness. Increasing the resources of enforcers could improve their ability to protect the public and could also be deterrent. Tougher and more appropriate penalties could support these policies, and at the same time redress the balance between white collar and conventional offences. They could also underline the moral basis of the law, and if combined with publicity, would have the added advantage of sensitizing the public to the nature of offences and the possibilities of remedial action. The evidence that the public can take white collar crimes seriously, along with increasing public concern over the accountability of financial institutions, the environment, and food and health issues further indicate that efforts to increase public awareness of white collar and corporate crime could have a real effect on public tolerance.

Arguing for tougher policies need not, however, involve more white collar offenders being imprisoned, given larger and larger fines or forcefully subjected to hounding by the press. Levi (1991b), for example, points to the dangers of excessive 'shaming' and the degradations which could follow such policies. Braithwaite's analysis stresses that shaming should be re-integrative and, therefore, while punitive policies are desirable they should also be constructive. This makes suggestions for the development of white collar equivalents to probation or community service particularly appealing as they can be retributive and re-integrative.

In conclusion, therefore, it can be argued that white collar crime is a real 'crime problem'. A greater understanding of its origins and effects is, therefore, imperative, not simply to expose the crimes of the powerful and the victimization of the powerless, but to assist the development of effective policies for its control. In order for this to be done both academics and the public need to be more sensitive to the real problems involved, about which there are many misconceptions and misleading assumptions. More research needs to be carried out in order to assist an appreciation of the nature of different forms of white collar crime, their effect on victims, and the many ways in which they are culturally and subculturally tolerated. In addition, a greater understanding of how offences are structurally generated within occupational roles and organizations, and by external pressures can be of considerable value to enforcers, criminologists, and public and private organizations. Finally, it can be argued that like any other crime, it should be subject to both informal social control, and such public prosecution and punishment as is necessary to both protect the public from victimization, and underline the moral unacceptability of serious white collar offences.

REFERENCES

Aldrich, H. *et al.* (1981) 'Business development and self-segregation: Asian enterprise in three British cities', in C. Peach, V. Robinson and S. Smith (eds) *Ethnic Segregation in Cities*. London, Croom Helm.

Ashworth, A. (1989) 'Criminal justice and deserved sentences', *Criminal Law Review*, 340–55.

Atiyah, P.S. (1979) *The Rise and Fall of Freedom of Contract*. Oxford, Oxford University Press.

Aubert, V. (1977) 'White collar crime and social structure', in G. Geis and R.F. Maier (eds) *White Collar Crime: Offences in Business, Politics and the Professions – Classic and Contemporary Views*, revised edn. New York, Free Press, Collier and Macmillan.

Benson, M.L. (1985) 'Denying the guilty mind: accounting for involvement in a white collar crime', *Criminology*, **23** (4) 583 604.

Benson, M.L. and Walker, E. (1988) 'Sentencing the white collar offender', *American Sociological Review*, **53**, April 294–302.

Bergman, D. (1990a) 'Manslaughter in the tunnel?', *New Law Journal*, August 3 1108–29.

Bergman, D. (1990b) 'Recklessness in the boardroom', *New Law Journal*, October 26 1496–501.

Beynon, H. (1973) *Working for Ford*. Harmondsworth, Penguin.

Borrie, G., Sir (1980) 'Laws and codes for consumers', *Monthly Review*, **88** (12).

Borrie, G., Sir (1982) 'The roles of the Office of Fair Trading and Trading Standards Departments', address to Trading Standards Officers reprinted in *Monthly Review*, **90** (4).

Borrie, G., Sir (1984) *The Development of Consumer Law and Policy—Bold Spirits and Timorous Souls*. London, Stevens.

Borrie, G., Sir and Diamond, A.L. (1981) *The Consumer, Society and the Law*, 4th edn. Harmondsworth, Penguin.

Bottomley, A.K. and Pease, K. (1986) *Crime and Punishment: Interpreting the Data*. Milton Keynes, Open University Press.

Bottoms, A.E. and McLean, J.D. (1976) *Defendants in the Legal Process*. London, Routledge & Kegan Paul.

Box, S. (1983) *Power, Crime and Mystification*. London, Tavistock.

Box, S. (1987) *Recession, Crime and Punishment*. London, Macmillan.

Braithwaite, J. (1978) 'An exploratory study of used car fraud', in J. Braithwaite and P. Wilson (eds) *Two Faces of Deviance: Crimes of the Powerless and the Powerful*. Brisbane, University of Queensland Press.

Braithwaite, J. (1979) 'Transnational corporations and corruption: towards some international solutions', *International Journal of the Sociology of Law*, **7** 143–67.

Braithwaite, J. (1982) 'Challenging just deserts: punishing white collar criminals', *Journal of Criminal Law and Criminology*, **73** (2) 723–63.

Braithwaite, J. (1984a) *Corporate Crime in the Pharmaceutical Industry*. London, Routledge & Kegan Paul.

Braithwaite, J. (1984b) 'Limits of economism in controlling harmful corporate conduct', in A.I. Ogus and C.G. Veljanowski (eds) *Readings in the Economics of Law and Regulation*. Oxford, Oxford University Press.

Braithwaite, J. (1985) 'White collar crime', *Annual Review of Sociology*, **11** 1–25.

Braithwaite, J. (1989) *Crime, Shame and Re-Integration*. Cambridge, Cambridge University Press.

Braithwaite, J. and Ayres, I. (1991) 'Transcending the regulation versus deregulation debate', unpublished paper to Second Liverpool Conference on Fraud, Corruption and Business Crime, University of Liverpool 17–19 April 1991.

Braithwaite, J. and Condon, B. (1978) 'On the class basis of criminal violence', in J. Braithwaite and P. Wilson (eds) *Two Faces of Deviance: Crimes of the Powerless and the Powerful*. Brisbane, University of Queensland Press.

Braithwaite, J. and Fisse, B. (1987) 'Self regulation and the control of corporate crime', in C. Shearing and P. Stenning (eds) *Private Policing*. London, Sage.

Braithwaite, J. and Geis, G. (1982) 'On theory and action for corporate crime control', *Crime and Delinquency*, April, 292–314.

Braithwaite, J. and Pettit, P. (1990) *Not Just Deserts: A Republican Theory of Justice*. Oxford, Clarendon Press.

Braithwaite, J. and Vale, S. (1985) 'Law enforcement by Australian Consumer Affairs Agencies', *Australian and New Zealand Journal of Criminology*, **18**, September 147–63.

Brogden, M. *et al.* (1988) *Introducing Police Work*. London, Unwin Hyman.

Burnett, J. (1966) *Plenty and Want: Social History of Diet in England from 1815 to the Present Day*. London, Pelican.

Cannon, G. and Walker, C. (1985) *The Food Scandal*. London, Century Publishing Company.

Carlen, P. (1976) *Magistrates' Justice*. London, Martin Robertson.

Carlen, P. (1989) 'Crime, inequality and sentencing', in P. Carlen and D. Cook (eds) *Paying for Crime*. Milton Keynes, Open University Press.

Carson, W.G. (1971) 'White collar crime and the enforcement of factory legislation', in W.G. Carson and P. Wiles (eds) *Crime and Delinquency in Britain*. London, Martin Robertson.

Carson, W.G. (1974) 'Symbolic and instrumental dimensions of early factory legislation: a case study in the social origins of criminal law', in R. Hood (ed.) *Crime, Criminology and Public Policy*. London, Heinemann Educational Books.

Carson, W.G. (1979) 'The conventionalisation of early factory crime', *International Journal of the Sociology of Law*, **7** (1) 37–60.

Carson, W.G. (1980) 'The institutionalisation of ambiguity: early British Factory Acts', in G. Geis and E. Stotland (eds) *White Collar Crime: Theory and Research*. London, Sage.

Carson, W.G. (1981) *The Other Price of British Oil*. London, Martin Robertson.

Chibnall, S. (1977) *Law and Order News*. London, Tavistock.

Clarke, M. (1986) *Regulating the City: Competition, Scandal and Reform*. Milton Keynes, Open University Press.

Clarke, M. (1987) 'Prosecutorial and administrative strategies in the control of business crime: private and public roles', in C. Shearing and P. Stenning (eds) *Private Policing*. London, Sage.

Clarke, M. (1989) 'Insurance fraud', *British Journal of Criminology*, **29** (1) 1–20.

Clarke, M. (1990) *Business Crime: Its Nature and Control*. Cambridge, Polity Press.

Clinard, M.B. (1983) *Corporate Ethics and Crime*. Beverly Hills, Sage.

Clinard, M.B. and Yeager, P.C. (1980) *Corporate Crime*. New York, Free Press.

Cohen, S. and Young, J. (eds) (1973) *The Manufacture of News*. London, Routledge & Kegan Paul.

Conklin, J.E. (1977) *Illegal but not Criminal*. New Jersey, Spectrum.

Cook, D. (1989a) *Rich Law, Poor Law: Different Responses to Tax and Supplementary Benefit Fraud*. Milton Keynes, Open University Press.

Cook, D. (1989b) 'Fiddling tax and benefits: inculpating the poor, exculpating the rich', in P. Carlen and D. Cook (eds) *Paying for Crime*. Milton Keynes, Open University Press.

Cranston, R. (1977) 'Creeping economism: some thoughts on law and economics', *British Journal of Law and Society*, **4** (1) 103–15.

Cranston, R. (1979) *Regulating Business*. London, Macmillan.

Cranston, R. (1984) *Consumers and the Law*, 2nd edn. London, Weidenfeld & Nicolson.

Cressey, D. (1986) 'Why managers commit fraud', *Australian and New Zealand Journal of Criminology*, **19** 195–209.

Criminal Statistics for England and Wales 1977 and 1987. London, HMSO.

Croall, H. (1987) *Crimes against the Consumer: An Analysis of the Nature, Extent, Regulation and Sanctioning of 'Trading Offences'*. Unpublished PhD thesis, University of London.

Croall, H. (1988) 'Mistakes, accidents and someone else's fault: the trading offender in court', *Journal of Law and Society*, **15** (3) 293–315.

Croall, H. (1989) 'Who is the white collar criminal?', *British Journal of Criminology*, **29** (2) 157–74.

Croall, H. (1991) 'Sentencing the business offender', *Howard Journal of Criminal Justice*, **30** (4) 280–92.

Deane, K. (1981) 'Tax evasion, criminality and sentencing the tax offender', *British Journal of Criminology*, **21** (1) 47–57.

Denzin, N.K. (1977) 'Notes on the criminogenic hypothesis: a case study of the American liquor industry', *American Sociological Review*, **42** 905–20.

Dickens, B.M. (1970) 'Discretion in Local Authority prosecutions', *Criminal Law Review*, 618–33.

Director General of Fair Trading. *Annual Reports* 1982, 1983, 1987, 1988. London, HMSO.

Ditton, J. (1972) 'Absent at work: or how to manage monotony', *New Society*, 21 December.

Ditton, J. (1976) *Dual Morality in the Control of 'the Fiddle'*. London Outer Circle Policy Unit.

Ditton, J. (1977) *Part Time Crime: an Ethnography of Fiddling and Pilferage*. London, Macmillan.

Doig, A. (1984) *Corruption and Misconduct in Contemporary British Politics*. Harmondsworth, Penguin.

Economist Intelligence Unit (1979) Pilot Study of the Additional Costs to The British Consumer of Compliance by Industry with Consumer Legislation Summary Volume Nov. 1979. London, Economist Intelligence Unit.

Ermann, R. and Lundman, R. (1987) *Corporate and Governmental Deviance: Problems of Organizational Behaviour in Contemporary Society*, 3rd edn. New York, Oxford University Press.

Evans, S. and Lundman, R. (1987) 'Newspaper coverage of corporate crime', in R. Ermann and R. Lundman (eds) *Corporate and Governmental Deviance: Problems of Organizational Behaviour in Contemporary Society*, 3rd edn. New York, Oxford University Press.

Fisse, B. and Braithwaite, J. (1983) *The Impact of Publicity on Corporate Offenders*. Albany, State University of New York Press.

French, T.R. (1981) 'More than was bargained for!', *Monthly Review*, **89** (5).

Garfinkel, H. (1956) 'Conditions of successful degradation ceremonies', *American Journal of Sociology*, **61** 420–4.

Geis, G. (1978) 'Deterring corporate crime', in R. Ermann and R. Lundman (eds) *Corporate and Governmental Deviance*. New York, Oxford University Press.

Geis, G. and Edelhertz, H. (1973) 'Criminal law and consumer fraud: a socio-legal view', *American Criminal Law Review*, **2** 989–1010.

Geis, G. and Maier, R.F. (eds) (1977) *White Collar Crime: Offences in Business, Politics and the Professions—Classic and Contemporary Views*, revised edn. New York, Free Press, Collier and Macmillan.

Goldthorpe, J., Lockwood, D., Bechhofer, F. and Platt, J. (1969) *The Affluent Worker: Industrial Attitudes and Behaviour*. Cambridge, Cambridge University Press.

Grabosky, P.N., Braithwaite, J. and Wilson, P.R. (1987) 'The myth of community tolerance toward white collar crime', *Australian and New Zealand Journal of Criminology*, **20** 33–44.

Gross, E. (1978) 'Organizations as criminal actors', in J. Braithwaite and P. Wilson (eds) *Two Faces of Deviance: Crimes of the Powerless and the Powerful*. Brisbane, University of Queensland Press.

Hadden, T. (1970) 'Strict liability and the enforcement of factory legislation', *Criminal Law Review*, 496–504.

Hadden, T. (1983) 'Fraud in the city: the role of the criminal law', *Criminal Law Review*, 500–11.

Hagan, J. (1988) *Structural Criminology*. Oxford, Polity Press.

Hagan, J., Nagel, I. and Albonetti, C. (1980) 'The differential sentencing of white collar offenders in ten federal district courts', *American Sociological Review*, **45** October, 802–20.

Harvey, B.W. (1975) 'Consumer Law - Ancient and Modern', *Local Government Chronicle*, 24 October.

Harvey, B.W. (1982) *Law of Consumer Protection and Fair Trading*, 2nd edn. London, Butterworths.

Hawkins, K. (1983) 'Bargain and bluff – compliance strategy and deterrence in the enforcement of regulation', *Law and Policy Quarterly*, **5** (1).

Hawkins, K. (1984) *Environment and Enforcement: Regulation and the Social Definition of Pollution*. Oxford Socio-Legal Studies, Clarendon Press.

Hawkins, K. (1990) 'Compliance strategy, prosecution policy and Aunt Sally – a comment on Pearce and Tombs', *British Journal of Criminology*, **30** (4) 444–67.

Heal, K. and Laycock, G. (eds) (1986) *Situational Crime Prevention*. London, HMSO.

Health and Safety Executive (1988) *Annual Report 1987/8*. London, HMSO.

Hogarth, J. (1971) *Sentencing as a Human Process*. Toronto, University of Toronto Press.

Home Office (1990) *Crime, Justice and Protecting the Public: The Government's Proposals for Legislation*. London, HMSO.

Hood, R. (1972) *Sentencing the Motoring Offender*. London, Heinemann.

Hood, R. and Sparks, R. (1970) *Key Issues in Criminology*. London, Weidenfeld & Nicolson.

Hopkins, A. (1980) 'Controlling corporate deviance', *Criminology*, **18** (2) 198–214.

Hirschi, T. and Gottfredson, M. (1987) 'Causes of white collar crime', *Criminology*, **25** (4) 949–74.

Hudson, B. (1987) *Justice Through Punishment*. Basingstoke and London, Macmillan.

Hutter, B. (1986) 'An Inspector Calls', *British Journal of Criminology*, **26** (2) 114–28.

Hutter, B. (1988) *The Reasonable Arm of the Law?* Oxford, Clarendon Press.

Hutter, B. and Lloyd Bostock, S. (1990) 'The power of accidents: the social and psychological impact of accidents and the enforcement of safety regulations', *British Journal of Criminology*, **30** (4) 409–22.

Hyman, R. (1977) *Strikes*. Glasgow, Fontana.

Institute of Environmental Health (1981) *Briefing Note on the Food and Drugs Amendment Bill*.

Johnson, T. (1972) *Professions and Power*. London, Macmillan.

Lea, J. and Young, J. (1984) *What is to be done about Law and Order?* Harmondsworth, Penguin.

Leigh, L.H. (1977) 'Policy and punitive measures in respect of economic offences', in L. Leigh (ed.) *Criminological Aspects of Economic Crime*. Council of Europe Collected Studies in Criminological Research, Vol XV, Strasbourg.

Leigh, L.H. (ed.) (1980) *Economic Crime in Europe*. London, Macmillan.

Leigh, L.H. (1982) *The Control of Commercial Fraud*. London, Heinemann.

Leigh, L.H. and Smith, A. (1991) 'European fraud laws and their reform with reference to the EEC', unpublished paper presented to the Second Liverpool Conference on Fraud, Corruption and Business Crime, University of Liverpool, April 1991.

Leigh, L.H. and Smith, A. (forthcoming) *Fraud in Europe: Towards 1992*. London, Blackstone Press.

Leonard, W.N. and Weber, M.G. (1977) 'Auto-makers and dealers: a study of criminogenic market forces', in G. Geis and R.F. Maier (eds) *White Collar Crime: Offences in Business, Politics and the Professions—Classic and Contemporary Views*. New York, Free Press, Collier and Macmillan.

Levi, M. (1983) 'Blaming the jury: frauds on trial', *Journal of Law and Society*, **10** (2) 257–69.

Levi, M. (1984) 'Business regulatory offences and the criminal law', *Company Lawyer*, **5** (6) 252–8.

Levi, M. (1987a) *Regulating Fraud: White Collar Crime and the Criminal Process*. London, Tavistock.

Levi, M. (1987b) 'Crisis? What Crisis? Reactions to commercial fraud in the UK', *Contemporary Crises*, **11** 207–21.

Levi, M. (1988) *The Prevention of Fraud*, Crime Prevention Unit, Paper 17. London, HMSO.

Levi, M. (1989a) 'Suite justice: sentencing for fraud', *Criminal Law Review*, 420–34.

Levi, M. (1989b) 'Fraudulent justice? Sentencing the business criminal', in P. Carlen and D. Cook (eds) *Paying for Crime*. Milton Keynes, Open University Press.

Levi, M. (1991a) 'The victims of fraud', unpublished paper given at the 2nd Liverpool Conference on Fraud, Corruption and Business Crime, Liverpool University, April 1991.

Levi, M. (1991b) 'Sentencing white collar crime in the dark?: Reflections on the Guinness four', *Howard Journal*, November 1991 (forthcoming).

Levi, M. (1991c) 'Developments in business crime in Europe', in F. Heidensohn and M. Farrel (eds) *Crime in Europe*. London, Routledge.

Levi, M. and Jones, S. (1985) 'Public and police perceptions of crime seriousness', *British Journal of Criminology*, **25** 234–50.

Levi, M. and Pithouse, A. (1989) 'The victims of fraud', unpublished paper presented at the British Criminology Conference, Bristol Polytechnic, July 1989.

Levi, M. and Suddle, S. (1989) 'White collar crime, shamelessness and disintegration: the control of tax evasion in Pakistan', *Journal of Law and Society*, **16** (4) 489–505.

Lloyd, I. (1990) 'Computer crime', in C. Reed (ed.) *Computer Law*. London, Blackstone.

London Food Commission (1988) *Food Adulteration and How to Beat It*. London, Unwin Paperbacks.

McBarnet, D. (1984) 'Law and capital: the role of legal form and legal actors', *International Journal of the Sociology of Law*, **12** 231–8.

McBarnet, D. (1987) 'Limits of criminal law', unpublished paper presented to Criminal Law Reform Conference, 27–30 July, Inns of Court, London.

McBarnet, D. (1988) 'Law, policy and legal avoidance: can law effectively implement egalitarian policies?', *Journal of Law and Society*, **15** (1).

McIntosh, M. (1974) *The Organization of Crime*. London, Macmillan.

Mann, K. (1985) *Defending White Collar Crime*. New Haven and London, Yale University Press.

Mann, K., Wheeler, S. and Sarat, A. (1980) 'Sentencing the white collar offender', *American Criminal Law Review*, **17** 479–500.

Mars, G. (1973) 'Hotel pilferage: a case study in occupational theft', in M. Warner (ed.) *Sociology of the Workplace*. London, George Allen & Unwin.

Mars, G. (1982) *Cheats at Work, an Anthropology of Workplace Crime*. London, George Allen & Unwin.

Mars, G. and Nicod, M. (1984) *World of Waiters*. London, George Allen & Unwin.

Miller, M. (1985) *Danger! Additives at Work*. London Food Commission.

Mills, C.W. (1956) *The Power Elite*. Oxford, Oxford University Press.

Millstone, E. (1985) 'Food additive regulation in the United Kingdom', *Food Policy*, August 237–52.

Moloney Report (1962) *Final Report of the Committee on Consumer Protection*, Cmnd 1781. London, HMSO.

Moore, C.A. (1987) 'Taming the giant corporation? Some cautionary remarks on the deterrability of corporate crime', *Crime and Delinquency*, **33** 379–402.

Morris, T. (1976) *Deviance and Control: The Secular Heresy*. London, Hutchinson University Library.

Naylor, J.M. (1990) 'The use of criminal sanctions by UK and US authorities for insider trading: how can the two systems learn from each other?', *Company Lawyer*, **11** (3) 53–61; (5) 83–91.

Nelken, D. (1983) *Limits of the Legal Process*. London, Academic Press.

Nelken, D. and Passas, N. (1991) 'The legal response to agricultural fraud in the EC', unpublished paper presented at the 2nd Liverpool Conference on Fraud, Corruption and Business Crime, April 1991.

O'Keefe, J. (1966) *Law of Weights and Measures*. London, Butterworths.

O'Keefe, J. (1968) *The Law Relating to Trade Descriptions*. London, Butterworths.

Otake, H. (1982) 'Corporate power in social conflict: vehicle safety and Japanese motor manufacturers', *International Journal of Sociology of Law*, **10** (99) 75–103.

Passas, N. (1990) 'Anomie and Corporate Deviance', *Contemporary Crises*, **14** 157–78.

Paulus, I. (1974) *The Search for Pure Food: A Sociology of Legislation in Britain*. London, Martin Robertson.

Pearce, F. (1976) *Crimes of the Powerful*. London, Pluto Press.

Pearce, F. and Tombs, S. (1990) 'Ideology, hegemony and empiricism: compliance theories and regulation', *British Journal of Criminology*, **30** (4) 423–43.

Pease, K. (1988) *Judgements of Crime Seriousness: Evidence from the 1984 British Crime Survey*, Home Office Research and Planning Unit, Paper 44. London, HMSO.

Perry, S. and Dawson, J. (1985) *Nightmare: Women and the Dalkon Shield*. New York, Macmillan.

Perry, S. and Dawson, J. (1987) 'Nightmare: women and the Dalkon Shield', in R. Ermann and R. Lundman (eds) *Corporate and Governmental Deviance: Problems of Organizational Behaviour in Contemporary Society*, 3rd edn. New York, Oxford University Press.

Quinney, R. (1963) 'Occupational structure and criminal behaviour: prescription violation by retail pharmacists', *Social Problems*, **11** 179–85.

Quinney, R. (1977) 'The study of white collar crime: toward a re-orientation in theory and practice', in G. Geis and R.G. Maier (eds) *White Collar Crime: Offences in Business, Politics and the Professions – Classic and Contemporary Views*. Free Press, Collier and Macmillan.

Reiner, R. (1985) *The Politics of the Police*. Brighton, Wheatsheaf Books.

Richardson, G. with Ogus, A. and Burrows, P. (1982) *Policing Pollution: A Study of Regulation and Enforcement*. Oxford, Clarendon Press.

Richardson, G. (1987) 'Strict liability for regulatory crime: the empirical research', *Criminal Law Review*, 295–306.

Roberts, D. (1985) 'When is a sausage not what it seems?', *Municipal Journal*, 16 August 1358.

Rothman, M. and Gandossy, R. (1982) 'Sad tales: the accounts of white collar defendants and the decision to sanction', *Pacific Sociological Review*, **25** (4) 449–73.

Rothschild, D. and Throne, B. (1976) 'Criminal consumer fraud – victim oriented analysis', *Michigan Law Review*, March 661–707.

Sanders, A. (1985) 'Class bias in prosecutions', *Howard Journal* **24** (3) 176–99.
Schraeger, L.S. and Short, J.F. (1977) 'Towards a sociology of organisational crime, *Social Problems*, **25** 407–19.
Scraton, P. and South, N. (1984) 'The ideological construction of the hidden economy', *Contemporary Crises*, (8).
Shapiro, S. (1990) 'Collaring the crime, not the criminal: re-considering the concept of white collar crime', *American Sociological Review*, **55** June 346–65.
Shearing, C. and Stenning, P. (eds) (1987) *Private Policing*. London, Sage.
Sim, J., Scraton, P. and Gordon, P. (1987) 'Crime, the state and critical analysis', in P. Scraton (ed.) *Law, Order and the Authoritarian State*. Milton Keynes, Open University Press.
Smith, D. and Gray, J. (1985) *Police and People in London*. Aldershot, Gower.
Smith, G. (1982) *The Consumer Interest*. London, John Martin.
Social Trends (1989) London, HMSO.
Stone, C.D. (1978) 'Social control of corporate behaviour', in R. Ermann and R. Lundman (eds) *Corporate and Governmental Deviance*. New York, Oxford University Press.
Sugarman, D. (1983) 'Law, economy and the state in England 1750–1914', in Sugarman, D. (ed.) *Legality, Ideology and the State*. London, Academic Press.
Sutherland, E.H. (1949) *White Collar Crime*. New York, Holt, Rinehart & Winston.
Sutton, A. and Wild, R. (1985) 'Small business: white collar villains or victims?', *International Journal of the Sociology of Law*, **13** 247–59.
Swann, M. (1979) *Competition and Consumer Protection*. Harmondsworth, Penguin.
Sykes, G. and Matza, D. (1957) 'Techniques of neutralization', *American Sociological Review*, **22**.
Tappan, P. (1977) 'Who is the criminal?', in G. Geis and R.F. Maier (eds) *White Collar Crime: Offences in Business, Politics and the Professions – Classic and Contemporary Views*. Free Press, Collier and Macmillan.
Tarling, R. (1979) *Sentencing Practice in Magistrates' Courts?* Home Office Research Study No 56. London, HMSO.
Taylor, I., Walton, P. and Young, J. (1973) *The New Criminology*. London, Routledge & Kegan Paul.
Taylor, L. and Walton, P. (1971) 'Industrial sabotage: motives and meanings', in S. Cohen (ed.) *Images of Deviance*. Harmondsworth, Penguin.
Tench, D. (1981) *Towards a Middle System of Law*. London, Consumer's Association.
Thomas, D.A. (1978) *Principles of Sentencing*, 2nd edn. London, Heinemann.
Tombs, S. (1990) 'Industrial injuries in British manufacturing industry', *Sociological Review*, 324–43.
Tutt, N. (1989) *Europe on the Fiddle*. London, Christopher Helm.
Uglow, S. (1984) 'Defending the public purse: prosecuting in social security, revenue and excise cases', *Criminal Law Review*, 128–41.
Van Duyne, P. (1991) 'Large scale fraud and organised crime', unpublished paper presented to the Second Liverpool Conference on Fraud, Corruption and Business Crime, University of Liverpool, April 1991.
Van Duyne, P. and Levi, M. (1991) 'Enterprise crime in the Netherlands and the UK', unpublished paper presented at the British Criminology Conference, York University, July 1991.
Vass, A. (1990) *Alternatives to Prison: Punishment, Custody and the Community*. London, Sage.

Walklate, S. (1989) *Victimology: The Victim and the Criminal Justice Process.* London, Unwin Hyman.

Wasik, M. (1989) 'Law reform proposals on computer misuse', *Criminal Law Review,* 257–70.

Weisburd, D., Waring, E. and Wheeler, S. (1990) 'Class, status and the punishment of white collar crime', *Law and Social Enquiry,* **15** (2) 223–43.

Wells, C. (1988) 'The decline and rise of English murder: corporate crime and individual responsibility', *Criminal Law Review,* 789–801.

Wells, C. (1989) 'Manslaughter and corporate crime', *New Law Journal,* July 7 931–4.

Wheeler, S., Weisburd, D. and Bode, N. (1982) 'Sentencing the white collar offender: rhetoric and reality', *American Sociological Review,* **47** 641–59.

Wheeler, S., Mann, K. and Sarat, A. (1988) *Sitting in Judgement: The Sentencing of White Collar Criminals.* New Haven and London, Yale University Press.

Wilson, J.Q. (1976) *Thinking about Crime.* New York, Basic Books.

Yeomans, L. (1985) 'A consumer view of food policy issues', University of Reading Conference on Food Policy issues and the Food Industries, Paper No. 3.

Young, J. (1986) 'The failure of criminology: the need for a radical realism', in R. Matthews and J. Young (eds) *Confronting Crime.* London, Sage.

Young, J. (1988) 'Radical criminology in Britain: the emergence of a competing paradigm', in P. Rock (ed.) *A History of British Criminology.* Oxford, Oxford University Press.

INDEX